HOMER LEA,
SUN YAT-SEN,
AND
THE CHINESE REVOLUTION

HOMER LEA,
SUN YAT-SEN,
AND
THE CHINESE REVOLUTION

Eugene Anschel

PRAEGER SPECIAL STUDIES • PRAEGER SCIENTIFIC

New York • Philadelphia • Eastbourne, UK
Toronto • Hong Kong • Tokyo • Sydney

Library of Congress Cataloging in Publication Data

Anschel, Eugene.
　　Homer Lea, Sun Yat-sen, and the Chinese revolution.

　　Bibliography: p.
　　Includes index.
　　1. Lea, Homer, 1876–1912.　2. Sun Yat-sen,
1866–1925.　3. United States—Foreign relations—
China.　4. China—Foreign relations—United States.
5. China—History—1862–1899.　6. China—History—
1900–1949.　7. Diplomats—United States—Biography.
8. Soldiers—United States—Biography.　9. Generals—
China—Biography.　I. Title.
E748.L39A67　1984　　327.73051　　84-15999
ISBN 0-03-000063-7 (alk. paper)

Published in 1984 by Praeger Publishers
CBS Educational and Professional Publishing,
a Division of CBS Inc.
521 Fifth Avenue, New York, NY 10175 USA

456789 052 987654321

Printed in the United States of America
on acid-free paper

Acknowledgments

I am indebted to a number of individuals and institutions for their help in writing this book. Joshua B. Powers, stepson of Homer Lea, graciously gave of his time to tell me of his mother and his boyhood memories of Lea and opened his family papers to my scrutiny. The late Professor Jung-pang Lo, grandson of K'ang Yu-wei, although severely ill, eagerly responded to my various queries. Clare Boothe Luce, Dr. Eve Ma, Professor Harold Z. Schiffrin, and Dr. Robert L. Worden also took the time to answer my questions, as did my friend Professor Hellmut Wilhelm who, in addition, translated a few of the Chinese references for me. Tu Nien-Chung undertook the translations of others. Brenda J. Butler discovered some letters and documents at the Bancroft Library in Berkeley, California, that I had overlooked, and Gary M. Miller, Archivist at the Federal Archives and Records Center in Laguna Niguel, California, found for me the records of the criminal case against Ansel O'Banion. Dr. Arthur Waldron read the first rough-hewn draft of my manuscript and encouraged me to go on. Eva Chou applied her editorial competence to a part of the manuscript and made suggestions that helped me to give focus and shape to the work. The Hoover Institution on War, Revolution and Peace gave me access to its archives, and Ronald Bulatoff, its Archival Specialist, was most helpful. I found ready assistance also at the Archives of the Stanford University Libraries, the Manuscript Divisions of the Bancroft Library and the Library of Congress, the National Archives, the National Army Museum (London), the Public Record Office of Great Britain, the Special Collections of the University of Iowa Library, the Connecticut State Library, the Library of the U.S. Military Academy at West Point, the Harvard University Archives, and the Library of the California State University at Hayward. The Los Angeles Public Library provided me with copies of newspaper reports, while the Inter-Library Loan Division of the New York Public Library procured numerous microfilms of articles and documents for me. The staff of the East Asian Library at Columbia University willingly located for me publications in both English and Chinese.

Last, but not least, my thanks go to Eva Anschel. She helped me with the tedious job of proofreading after I had forced her to live with *Homer Lea* far longer and much more intimately than could decently be expected. This book is dedicated to her.

v

Contents

Illustrations

Prologue

A short, boyish-looking, hunchbacked American dressed in the uniform of a Chinese republican general stood by Sun Yat-sen's side at the moment when the success of the revolution suddenly focused world attention on Sun as its leader. That puzzling figure was Homer Lea. He was, it had been reported, to be chief of staff when Sun assumed the post of President of the Republic of China. He discussed the future of the new China with American and other officials and gave eloquent and seemingly authoritative interviews on the subject. Half a dozen years before, Homer Lea had paraded through the streets of American cities in the uniform of the Chinese constitutionalist monarchists. President Theodore Roosevelt had received him together with the head of that worldwide movement. U.S. politicians like Senator Elihu Root saw him and corresponded with him, as did foreign statesmen and military officers, including Count Okuma of Japan and Field Marshal Lord Roberts of Great Britain. Long after his death, men as diverse as Lenin, the German General von Seeckt, and General Douglas MacArthur praised his concepts of military and political strategy. Even today books on U.S. policies in the Far East and publications on militarist thought mention his theories.

Who was Homer Lea? What do we know of his background and life story? What had made him notorious and what had brought him to join the Chinese revolutionary movement and, in particular, how had he arrived at his prominent position with Sun Yat-sen? Answers were readily supplied, not the least by Homer Lea himself, but the trouble was that there were too many answers and they were all grand, but if pursued far enough, most of them vanished into uncertainty. The urgency of the questions soon lessened, however, for shortly after his arrival with Sun in Shanghai and Sun's election in Nanking as Provisional President of the new Chinese Republic, Lea suffered a stroke. Convalescence was slow, during which he returned to California. He never fully recovered and half a year later, in November 1912, he had a relapse and died in Santa Monica, at the age of only 36.

Homer Lea himself bore a good deal of responsibility for the uncertainties that surround his life and activities and for the contradictory, confusing, and incomplete pictures drawn by his contemporaries as well as succeeding generations. For most of a dozen years, he had struggled to make a role for himself, first in China's reform movement, and then among the Chinese revolutionaries who eventually toppled the reigning Manchu dynasty. To do so, he was not averse to inventing all kinds of stories about himself. Nor was he hampered by any scruples to leave uncorrected the even more colorful tales concocted by others. Moreover, for reasons of his own, he clothed at times his actions in secretiveness while, at others, he boasted of or exaggerated his doings. Many documents that could either correct or confirm his and others' statements have been lost. After Lea's death, his widow had to move out of their rented bungalow in Santa Monica and look for employment. Homer Lea had accumulated a large quantity of correspondence, documents, and notes, which in her situation were a burden. She also feared, as did some of his former friends and associates, that these papers might fall into the wrong hands. Several years before, Lea's home had been broken into several times by people who apparently searched not for loot but for information. With the Chinese Revolution still unfolding, some papers that referred to conspiracies in which Lea had been involved might be used to discredit the cause he had championed and to compromise some of his associates. Several of them had their own reasons for keeping certain documents out of the hands of strangers. One of them had engaged, perhaps with Lea's knowledge, in some undertakings of a questionable nature. Another, a lawyer who later became a judge, had an interest in the disappearance of papers that might connect him with activities that were possibly illegal. And so the decision was made to burn the papers. Bundle after bundle went up in smoke.

Another reason why the story of Homer Lea's life has been difficult to piece together accurately and with a sufficient degree of authenticity has been his ambiguous posthumous reputation. He had published two books on military strategy and political philosophy, one dealing with the situation in the Pacific area and the evolving conflict between the United States and Japan, and the other concerning the danger to and the possible decline of the British Empire. During the dark days of World War II, writers and military officers recalled his thesis that confrontation with Japan was unavoidable. During the Cold War and in more recent years, his statements on Russian aggressiveness were acclaimed by some who hailed him as a genius and seer. Still others pointed to the extreme militaristic theories he had propounded in his books. Stimulated by this renewed interest in Lea, friends and acquaintances from his school and college years rivaled each other in publishing reminiscences of his early days. As they searched their memories, they added facts of a questionable and sometimes legendary nature to whatever they remembered. One of them entrusted his remembrances to a popular writer who produced two books with what he called "fictionalized" accounts of Lea's life and exploits. In 1950 a Harvard undergraduate ferreted out for the first time a number of documents and a quantity of contemporary reports. The story, however, as presented in his short thesis is woefully incomplete and inadequate. The student relied to a large extent on untrustworthy accounts by Lea's friends and associates. But the documents he discovered included some that Lea's widow had saved, including most, but not all, of Sun Yat-sen's surviving letters to Lea.

These papers and others were later deposited by Joshua B. Powers, Mrs. Lea's son from a previous marriage, at the Hoover Institution on War, Revolution and Peace at Stanford University. Laurence Boothe, the son of an associate of Lea, also gave the Institution a collection of documents and letters exchanged between his father, Sun, Lea, and others. Several scholars in modern Chinese history have used documents from these two collections in their work, together with material gleaned from other archives. More extensive searches have yielded additional documents and facts so that, at last, an assessment of Homer Lea's short life and his participation in Chinese political affairs appeared possible.

There remain, however, many gaps in the story that cannot be filled and many uncertainties that cannot be dispelled. Some of the gaps extend over several years of Lea's life. Undependable accounts that appeared in print and tried to fill in the lacunae have added to the obscurity that shrouds these episodes. All the same, the high points of Lea's story are amply documented: his association with the political movement of K'ang Yu-wei, the great Chinese reformer and scholar, and with K'ang personally; and even more so the years of Lea's attempts to foment a revolution in China on his own and his subsequent cooperation with Sun Yat-sen. An important part of that record, Sun Yat-sen's letters to Homer Lea and to Lea's associate, Charles B. Boothe, is presented at the end of our narrative (see Appendices I and II) for the first time in the United

States. In short, when the story of Homer Lea's life is shorn of embroideries, embellishments, and outright falsehoods and is recounted on the basis of contemporary reports and the substantial quantity of documentary evidence now available, Lea still emerges as an interesting and colorful figure; his work for the Chinese Revolution forms a surprising and singular chapter of history, and his writings are a unique and idiosyncratic contribution to U.S. political and military thinking.

HOMER LEA,
SUN YAT-SEN,
AND
THE CHINESE REVOLUTION

—1—

Personal Background

The obscurity that veils periods of Lea's life begins at the very beginning, with his ancestry. When his name first appeared before the public, it was of paramount importance to Lea to be known as a military expert. It would help him greatly, for example, if he could point to a soldierly lineage. At that time he had been trying to have the leaders of the San Francisco Chinese community send him to China to help in the overthrow of the Empress Dowager and her court clique. To that end he had to convince them that his presumed military knowledge was the outcome of a long family tradition. Apparently he succeeded. Their letter of introduction to the leaders of the Chinese reform movement described him as "a white man . . . well up in war ways. . . . He is about to travel and talks well. His people are all great warriors, many of them having figured in the war of North and South in America."[1] Before his departure, he gave an interview in which he claimed "a military ancestry through all American wars."[2] And, in an interview after his return, a newspaper reporter called him "a descendant of a collateral branch of the Lee family which gave the South its great general."[3] As a result, numerous accounts published in later years spoke of him as a Virginian or a man of Virginian stock.[4] A popular writer found that "a member of Homer Lea's family on the paternal side distinguished himself as a general in the Civil War."[5] Chinese newspapers even referred to him as General Robert E. Lee of the Civil War.[6]

The truth, however, is far from the legend. Homer Lea's family came from Tennessee, founded by a James Lea, one of three brothers who had arrived from England in 1740.[7] The Leas of Tennessee were not related to the Lees of Virginia, who were descendants of Richard Lee who, also born in England, had died in America in 1664, almost 100 years

before the landing of James Lea. Homer Lea took advantage of the ho-
mophone of the two names and, as far as is known, never attempted to
correct statements that called him a Virginian or a member of the Lee
family of Virginia.

Homer Lea's father, Alfred Erskine Lea, had been born in or near
Cleveland, Tennessee, one of nine children of Dr. Pleasant John Graves
Lea. In 1859 Dr. Lea took his second wife and the children from his first
marriage to a large farm home in Jackson County, Missouri, which had
belonged to his first wife. That section of the country was soon affected
by the Kansas-Missouri Border War. Dr. Lea seems to have been a peaceful man, although popular writers trying to relate Homer's militaristic
leanings to his family background called the Leas mettlesome and a family of soldiers.[8] At any rate, Dr. Lea decided at the end of 1861 to remove
his family from the ravages of war. He sent his four daughters and the
youngest son to relatives behind the Confederate lines in Tennessee. Another son drove his pregnant stepmother and her sister in a covered
wagon to Sedalia, Missouri, from where they were to take the railroad to
Cleveland, Ohio. On August 6, 1862, Dr. Lea put his son, Alfred
Erskine, then 14 years old, on a wagon train owned by a friend, Dr. Par-
mer of Independence, Missouri. That wagon train eventually reached
Denver, Colorado. A month after saying goodbye to Alfred Erskine, Dr.
Lea was murdered near his home in Jackson County, Missouri, by a gang
of raiders in the Border War.

Alfred Erskine established himself in Denver, a town that had been
settled only four years before his arrival. In time he set up a business
abstracting titles. He was the first in the county to compile a set of ab-
stract books.[9] Alfred married Hersa Coberly from Indiana. They had
three children, two girls and the youngest child a son, Homer, born November 17, 1876. The mother died when Homer was still a small child,
and he as well as his sisters were sent to live with their maternal grand-
mother in Indiana. The children returned to the household in Denver
after their father took a second wife, Emma Wilson, whom he had
known in Missouri when a young boy.

It had been noticed as soon as Homer began to walk that he stooped
to one side. Later, when he climbed stairs, he started to wheeze and had
to rest frequently. His father had hoped that the return to the better air in
Denver might cure what seemed to be asthma, but the little boy's condition showed no improvement. Eventually, it was discovered that he suffered from a curvature of the spine, and he was sent to the National Sur-
gical Institute in Indianapolis,[10] but the treatment was not successful.
Gradually, he developed a hump that was to stay with him all his life.
According to one account, his infirmities were caused by having been
dropped as an infant, but from other sources they appear to have been
congenital.[11]

When Homer was about 15, his stepmother insisted he rejoin the family in Denver. Apparently she was concerned about his missing school for such long periods of time. Emma, a teacher, taught him for about a year at home. In September 1892, two months before his sixteenth birthday, he entered East Denver High School. A teacher at that school remembered him as small, quiet, and serious, and sometimes an almost melancholy boy. His physical condition made it hard for him to take part in the activities of other boys, and this left him bitter and "a bit satirical at times." His stepmother's tutoring seemed to have been effective, however, for he did well in math and was rated excellent in English.[12]

About this time Alfred Erskine acquired an interest in mining properties, which appears to have provided him with a modest but steady income for the rest of his life. This was fortunate because he suffered from a back ailment that soon forced him to spend most of the day lying down.[13] Hoping to benefit from the milder climate, he moved the family to Los Angeles soon after Homer had completed a year at high school. Homer spent his second high school year at the University of the Pacific and the last two at Los Angeles High School.

While at Los Angeles High, Homer suffered occasionally from violent headaches, which forced him to stay in a darkened room while they lasted.[14] But at that school he seems to have overcome his shyness and aloofness. He made a number of friends, some of whom remained close to him to the end of his life. Disregarding his physical impairments, he took part in the social life of the school and made it a point to accompany his friends on strenuous excursions. He did not permit anyone to make allowances for his weaknesses, but joined in hunting and fishing trips and even took up fencing. He was active in school politics, acted as election manager for a classmate, and showed himself adept in situations that required sharp observation and rapid decision. He played a particularly active role in the local group of a national organization known as the Lyceum League of America. Under the sponsorship of Theodore Roosevelt, the League endeavored to introduce young people to civic affairs and acquaint them with parliamentary rules and political issues. His budding interest in political affairs and his oratorical abilities gained Homer Lea the presidency of the local chapter. "His dramatic way of speaking, his piercing eyes, the intonation of his voice, and his characteristic gesture of raising his hand with his long forefinger extended, brought home the point generated by his keen mind," a school friend, Marshall Stimson, recalled.[15]

His interest in military science and in Chinese matters seems to have awakened already in his high school years. In the backyard of his father's house, he laid out the formations and constellations of the famous battles of Caesar, Napoleon, and Robert Lee to study their strategies.[16] Reports from boyhood friends (there are several such accounts going back to the early years) are sometimes the product of hindsight. Perhaps more plausible are memories of the visits Lea and his high school friends made to Chinatown, which was close to their school. The boys were fascinated by the strange environment and the people in their native garb, the men still wearing pigtails. Fighting among Chinese gangs, the war of the tongs, was not uncommon and excited the interest of the boys, who attended some of the resulting court trials.[17] These excursions may have also awakened Lea's sympathies toward the Chinese, which showed up later when the anti-Chinese sentiment that prevailed in California did not deter him from associating with the Chinese community. In dealing with the Chinese, he showed no sign of a racist attitude. This is a sharp contrast to his stand against Japanese immigration, which he adopted in later years, and against the increase of other foreign-born populations in the United States at the expense of the Anglo-Saxon element, which he bewailed in his writings.

Lea graduated from high school in June 1896 and took his freshman year at Occidental College in Los Angeles. He planned at the end of the year to transfer to Harvard where he intended to study law.[18] For that reason he selected a college curriculum equivalent to that given to Harvard freshmen, which included Latin, Greek, French, English, and Math. He also took the examinations given in San Francisco to prospective Harvard students, passing in most subjects required for admission. He left the examinations in geometry, algebra, and physics for September but never took them because his hopes came to naught. "Unexpected financial difficulties" intervened, as he wrote to David Starr Jordan, president of Stanford University, when he applied for admission to that school.[19] His letter was written on stationery of the Lyceum League. By thus calling attention to his work in that organization, Homer Lea revealed a trait he was to show all his life: never to miss an opportunity for self-promotion. He added to his application a letter of recommendation by the vice-president of Occidental College, who called him an unusually bright student.[20] When Lea entered Stanford in 1897, he still harbored hopes that eventually he would take law at Harvard.[21]

One of the friends he made at Stanford, Will Irwin, later a reporter, remembered him as "pathetically hunchbacked, his torso [seeming] only a bulb fastened on to his legs and his face [having the] appearance of a wise child common among people with his affliction. For all that, he carried himself with a defiant dignity. He seemed to repel most advances toward intimacy, probably because he felt that pity prompted them."[22] Another friend, Robert Sullivan, also later a reporter, recalled how "his abnormally cramped stature emphasized the length of his arms and when he shot out a forefinger to make a point, the finger seemed to stab the opponent."[23] Homer's sister, Ermal, protested later against statements that made her brother appear like a dwarf. She said he was five feet three inches tall, his arms were not at all "monstrously long," as somebody had claimed, and his weight was 100 pounds.[24] A reporter who met Lea when he was 28 put his height at scarcely above five feet and his weight at no more than 120 pounds. "His complexion is dark and his face smooth shaven. He has dark brown hair and it is parted in the middle and is carefully brushed. His eyes are dark grey, and they look earnestly through gold rimmed spectacles. . . . His voice is soft and low, and remarkably musical. He is earnest in his utterances, and when he talks his grey eyes light up with enthusiasm."[25] At any rate, one may refer to the description in the passport he obtained on June 22, 1911, for his appearance: "Age 34 years. Stature 5 Feet - Inches Eng. Forehead high. Eyes blue. Nose medium. Mouth regular. Chin pointed. Hair brown. Complexion medium. Face oblong."[26]

Lea continued an active social life at Stanford and also maintained his interest in military problems. To cultivate his gift of speech, he joined a debating society.[27] Dr. David Starr Jordan remembered that among the students Lea "was known as a 'cub' reporter, a remarkable poker player in a small way, and an inveterate student of Napoleon's campaigns and of the military philosophy of England and Germany."[28] He also recalled this "hunchback dwarf" as "a youth of extraordinary parts—ready memory, very vivid imagination, imperturbable coolness, and an obsession for militarism and war." Lea's friend Irwin noticed the bent toward military interests when playing chess with him: "He was always drawing the analogy between chess and war. A clever move with his castle and, 'See, I've brought my heavy artillery into action,' he would say. I found then that war was his hobby."[29]

He had a strong competitive drive. His stepson Joshua recalled that about ten years later, when Homer had acquired an automobile, he would provoke other drivers to race him. Then, at some point, he would suddenly cross the path of the other car, barely avoiding a collision and forcing the other man to bring his vehicle to a veering, screeching halt.[30]

Lea was still at Stanford when the Spanish-American War broke out. The wave of patriotism that engulfed campuses all over the United States also inundated Stanford. Military drilling became the daily routine of many students. Notwithstanding his size and condition, Lea joined a cavalry unit. When some of his friends left for the Philippines with the California National Guard, he must have seen them leave with a bitter feeling. But he made it a point to keep in touch with them and he put these contacts to good use when, a few years later, he looked for men with military experience.

Meanwhile, Lea's health grew steadily worse. His severe headaches became more frequent, and during these bouts his weak eyes developed a sensitivity to light that forced him to remain for days in a darkened room. In a letter of May 18, 1898, a physician who had been treating Lea for several months attested to his poor health, probably to excuse Lea's frequent absences from classes: "His eyes are in such a condition that he could not use them but for a few minutes at a time."[31] The letter also mentioned several nasal operations and confinement to a room for several days on various occasions to relieve his weak eyes. In that first year, Lea had already been away from the campus for a prolonged period. Earlier, in January, the university newspaper carried a notice that a few days ago "Homer Lea, '99, who left the University last semester on account of sickness, returned." Later that year, in September, the paper again noted his return, this time after he had been "reported as having entered Harvard."[32] The reference to Harvard may indicate that, in his desire for publicity, Lea was responsible for the paper's reporting his goings and comings. Finally, in May 1899 Lea asked for a leave of absence until September, based upon the statement of another physician who considered it necessary for him "to discontinue his work at once on account of ill health."[33] The leave was granted. This time Lea did not return and so, after two fitful years, his academic studies came to an end. His sickly condition persisted, however, which, together with weak eyesight, plagued him throughout his remaining years.

For a year after he left Stanford, no information on Homer Lea's activities is available. The silence about him was suddenly and dramatically interrupted in April 1900 when a long article in a prominent San Francisco newspaper reported on his preparations to set sail for China in order to take part in the country's regeneration.[34] From that article and a statement by Ng Poon Chew made a dozen years later,[35] a picture can be pieced together of Lea's plans and the actions he took to realize them. In particular, it becomes clear how he proceeded to create a role for himself that combined the two main concerns of his life, his obsession with military matters and his preoccupation with China and the Chinese.

Lea's first step in this direction was made with the help of Ng Poon Chew, a friend of his parents. Ng was the pastor of a Chinese Presbyterian church in San Francisco and a political activist. As such he was a prominent member of a reform group known as the Pao Huang Hui or Protect the Emperor Society. In the United States the branches of the Pao Huang Hui were associated in, and often known as, the Chinese Empire Reform Association. That group worked for the return to power of the young Kuang-hsü Emperor, who favored political reforms including the establishment of a constitutional monarchy. In 1898 the Emperor had attempted to institute such reforms, prompted by his counsellor, K'ang Yu-wei, a neo-Confucian scholar, who was supported by his pupil, Liang Ch'i-ch'ao, also a leading Chinese intellectual. That period, which lasted about three and a half months, became known as the Hundred Days Reform Period. But in a coup d'etat, the wily Empress Dowager Tz'u-hsi, his aunt, had deprived the Emperor of his powers and held him virtually a prisoner.

The Reverend Ng was also a member of the Chinese Free Masons, known as Chih Kung T'ang,[36] who at the time were closely allied with the reform group. The Chih Kung T'ang formed part of the Triads, a secret society active in many regions of China and composed mostly of lower-class people. The Triads, apart from the social character of the society, also played a political role. They were enemies of the Ch'ing, the reigning Manchu dynasty that was of foreign origin. The Triads aimed to supplant it with the native Ming dynasty, which had been overthrown by the Ch'ing centuries before.

Reverend Ng was ideally suited for introducing Lea to the political side of Chinese life in the United States and to the political trends in China. Ng was well known among the Chinese population in California as a leader in their fight against discriminatory laws and practices. Through his membership in the Chinese Empire Reform Association and the Free Masons, he was involved in the political movements in China itself.

Lea appears to have joined both organizations.[37] He also made serious efforts to immerse himself in the Chinese culture. He tried to learn the language and studied the history of China. Among his surviving papers, there is a "Students Notebook" in which he had laboriously copied Chinese ideographs, their transliteration, and their English meaning.[38] The notebook also contains a listing of Chinese dynasties and emperors starting with the semimythical period of about 2637 B.C., along with an outline of a history of China entitled, "The Reawakening of China." According to Lea's introductory summary, in this work, "the political development of the Chinese people [was] to be viewed as the foundation of their future greatness. This requires a brief view of their ancient history up to the middle of the 19th century & then a critical examination in the apparent causes of . . . decline."[39] The title of the outline is revealing: the reawakening of China was indeed the task in which this ambitious and singleminded youth intended to play a part after the possibility of a law career had disappeared.

But in throwing in his lot with the Chinese reformers, Homer Lea was not content to serve merely as a foot soldier. He saw himself as a military expert, albeit self-taught, and as such he aspired at leadership. Two historical figures inspired his dreams of glory, the monk Chu Yüan-chang, an ancient liberator of China from foreign yoke, and Napoleon I whose campaigns he had studied assiduously. It has been said that many of his acquaintances thought he resembled Napoleon with his "clear-cut, earnest face . . . the high brow and piercing eyes, together with his small stature."[40]

Lea's Chinese idol, Chu Yüan-chang, the "Martial Monk," had overthrown the foreign rule of the Mongols and founded the Ming dynasty in 1368. In his *The Valor of Ignorance*, published in 1909, Lea called for a second Chu Yüan-chang for China: "Shall the Chinese as a nation survive . . . or shall they utter themselves . . . into such oblivion as awaits the decadent nation?" he asked. In his florid prose Lea gave the answer: "Unless there rises out of the uttermost depths of her bosom the militancy of another Martial Monk the still hour has come when this ancientest kingdom shall make its solemn salutation to mankind, indifferent in the noisy buzz of his diurnal flight."[41] According to Lea, the savior of modern China need not be Chinese. In his novel, *The Vermilion Pencil*, published in 1908, the protagonist is a foreigner, a Breton, and also a monk. This character delivers the Chinese heroine of the story from her fate and the humble Chinese masses from their bondage. He is "one of those nameless Europeans whom fate has utterly cast adrift in those mysterious currents of the Orient Seas."[42] Homer Lea was ready to be carried by these same currents. If it is correct that he had joined the Chinese Free Masons, he had entered the powerful and widespread secret society of the Triads. He had gone through an elaborate, secret ritual of initiation, which, incidentally, he described in lurid detail in his novel, and had sworn a solemn oath of brotherhood and obedience, thus completing his identification with the Chinese cause.

His other idol, Napoleon, fascinated him not only by his military strategy but also by his charisma and leadership qualities. "What is it that forced him on," he wrote a dozen years later when he drove over the Simplon Pass, "over the wonderful road built by that wonderful man—Napoleon. What is it . . . lust of war,—love of power,—desire for wealth? Who knows? The world still wonders at the brilliancy of this meteor that shot across the heavens of Europe. He was the instrument of Fate—the Man of Destiny—the Iconoclast—destined to free man from superstitions more binding than chains." Furthermore, Lea states, "The love and loyalty of his men, and now I am one, are repaid with an affectionate care that even the most humble feels. They labor on, cheerful and gay, sad and weary, because his magnetic personality so dominates them that they can do no less."[43] Like Napoleon, Lea thirsted to lead men and, in his inflated style of writing, called for the same inspiration and loyalties among the Chinese military: "To drill troops . . . to the highest degree of perfection; to supply them with the most powerful ordnance and the finest equipment would be of no avail unless those who lead, not alone the army but the nation, are inspired with militant idealism to the extent that their selfishness and transitory aspirations shrink into such small compass that a single tear submerges them and they are lost on a grain of salt, while the idealism of the race is broadened to the pillars of the Five Seas. . . . Chinese as a race do not lack valour nor endurance;

they are as capable of fortitude and heroic deeds as any other nation but the spirit of militancy . . . is not amongst them and until means are taken to supply this void . . . it is useless to arm the Chinese soldier, useless to drill him."[44] Who was to fill this void? Who was to drill and lead the Chinese soldier? Homer Lea, this slight, myopic, and sickly hunchbacked youth not only dreamed of leadership and glory but also took steps to achieve his goal.

It was probably Ng Poon Chew who introduced Lea to Tom Tsai Hin, a member of the reform movement and leader of the Los Angeles branch of the Chinese Empire Reform Association.[45] Somehow he convinced Tom that to advance the reform in China, the Association should send him to China as head of the military arm of the movement. The first news of Homer Lea after he left Stanford thus came in headlines.[46]

Young Californian is Plotting to Become Commander-in-Chief of the Rebel Forces
His Plans Are All Laid to Help the Chinese Emperor to the Throne and Make Himself Head of the Army

The text was preceded by photographs of the Kuang-hsü Emperor; of the chief leaders of the reform movement, K'ang Yu-wei and Liang Ch'i-ch'ao; of Tom Tsai Hin and another local Chinese leader; of two of Lea's friends from Stanford, L. E. Taggart and Dr. E. H. Samuels; and, of course, of "Homer Lea of Stanford University." Not only the photographs but also numerous details and dates contained in the report make it obvious that it could only have been inspired by Homer Lea himself. It betrayed the young man's eagerness to assume a military role in an uprising planned by the worldwide reform movement. Although this was not specifically explained, Lea's trip was seen by himself and by his sponsors as a part of the reform movement's plan for an uprising that would restore the Emperor to power and make its leaders, K'ang and Liang, his advisers. The article described, however, the organization of the Protect the Emperor Society with its branches in Macao, Hong Kong, Yokohama, Nagasaki, Honolulu, Victoria, B.C., Portland, Los Angeles, and San Francisco. Funds collected in these places and wherever the reformers counted on support for the uprising among Chinese abroad were reported to be $7–8 million, but the "real trump card which the society is preparing to play is the acquisition of an American citizen. Homer Lea has joined hands with the Chinese revolutionists." A man "well up in military affairs . . . Homer Lea will be rewarded if he and the revolution are successful. He will be a great man in China and there will be plums in the shape of diplomatic positions."

Tom Tsai Hin had informed K'ang and the branches of the society in Honolulu, Yokohama, Nagasaki, Hong Kong, and Macao of the valuable convert to the cause and provided Lea with a letter of introduction to them. The letter, written in Chinese and probably translated into English by Tom Tsai Hin, who may have collaborated with Lea in the publicity, spoke of Lea's military prowess and the military traditions of his family. It went on to say that "Mr. Lea feels greatly for China on account of her weakness and does not like to see things unequal. He wants to teach Chinese to become soldiers, so as to become free. He is willing to go to the interior of China to get up a school to teach 2000 soldiers. He is going to visit different parts of China, calling on Hong Kong, Macao and different cities—together with Jeong Goog Sing, who is a Yung Ping man, also living in this city and learning war methods on sea and land at a big school."

Details of the life of Jeong Goog Sing, who was to accompany Lea, are lost to history. It may be surmised that he was to act as an interpreter and that his studies of "war methods on sea and land" had been conducted at a military academy. His identification as a "Yung Ping man" may mean that he was a member of the Hung Pang, or Red Party, another name for the Triads whose members wore red headbands.

There remained the question of financing the venture. Lea was reported to have received a generous monthly allowance of $300 from his father. When informed of his son's plans, the father apparently stopped the payments, saying: "I will supply you with money to attend college, but none to start revolutionary wars."[47] In any event, the monthly stipend would not have been sufficient for Lea's ambitious plans. Money would have to be raised by the Chinese community in San Francisco, for it was more than three times as large as that of Los Angeles. The Reverend Ng Poon Chew, by then the editor of the *Chung Sai Yat Po*, a reformist newspaper in San Francisco, introduced Lea to the leading reformers in that city. Among them was Dr. Tom She Bin who, with seven others, invited Lea on March 16 "to a banquet in his honor at a swagger restaurant." At that opportunity Lea presented his plans through an interpreter: "He would start a revolutionary war at either Hong Kong or Macao; he would go up the river as far as Foochoo [Foochow] and establish three way stations, and if given entire charge of the military forces he would agree to bring them to military perfection by providing them with equipment and subsidiary officers in thorough going fashion. He promised that he would be able to cope with any armed forces."

According to the same newspaper report, Lea hoped he would be given command of 20,000 men. That army would be reinforced by 1,200 discharged U.S. soldiers who were to be organized by "Charles White, Third Artillery, commissary department of the United States army now at Manila." Charles White was a friend and fellow student from Stanford with whom Lea obviously had kept in contact. Three other "white men" were also ready to lend their assistance: Dr. E. H. Samuels, a New

Zealander, would staff a field hospital with 25 physicians; L. E. Taggart, a Stanford engineering student, would be in charge of the engineering corps; and John York, an attorney in Los Angeles and a major in the California National Guard, another friend from Stanford, would head the signal corps.[48]

Some of these figures reappeared a few years later when Lea organized military units for the reformers in the United States. Likewise, in later years, he enlisted discharged U.S. soldiers for service in China and, from time to time, proposed to send them there. In the meantime, however, there are no indications that the scheme he developed before the group of reform leaders in San Francisco had been coordinated with the military plans of the Chinese reform movement. It is also not known if K'ang or other individuals who prepared a coup ever knew of Lea's project or considered giving him a role in their planned uprising. It appears that the project Lea outlined at the banquet was the product of the imagination of this youthful military amateur whose meager information on political and military conditions in China was founded on hearsay. Moreover, it remained a question whether Lea's disclosure of his fantastic battle plans and the names of his associates was of help to his undertaking and that of the reformers. In fact, Ng Poon Chew complained 12 years later that the "big write-up about Lea and his aim . . . spoiled the plan of his trip, because the Chinese Consul here apprised the authorities in China."[49]

Indeed, the Imperial Chinese Consul General in San Francisco reacted immediately. He must have been given the newspaper report to read before its publication, for the same issue carried a letter from him complimenting the paper "upon the completeness of this exposé." "The Chinese plotters," he added, "both here and in China, have all been placed under the most watchful surveillance." As to Homer Lea and his American associates, the Consul deplored their desire for self-aggrandizement and their "grasping for riches stained with the blood of misguided rebels. . . . It is unfortunate that an American should submit to be made the tool of these insurrectionists, under the guise of reforming China."[50]

At that time, secretiveness was not yet part of Lea's ways or, perhaps, his wish for recognition overcame the discretion that is essential to the type of enterprise he proposed. In any case, he served, if not his cause, then history well by broadcasting his plans, which otherwise would have remained unknown.

—2—

Into the Fray

On June 22, 1900, Homer Lea boarded a steamer, appropriately named *China*, destined for the Orient. His style did not permit him to travel incognito, and he made sure that a San Francisco newspaper published his departure on its front page.[1]

During those days the antiforeign Boxer Rebellion, which for weeks had made headlines in U.S. newspapers, was reaching its critical phase. The foreign legations in Peking were under siege, which British Vice-Admiral Seymour, head of an international expeditionary force, was trying to relieve. On the day before Lea's sailing, the Empress Dowager had issued a declaration of war against the foreign powers. Two days earlier, the German Minister in Peking had been shot and killed by Chinese soldiers. The advance of the expeditionary force and Lea's plan to raise a regiment of U.S. soldiers and take command of the army of the reformers were linked together and presented in the newspaper report as episodes in the Boxer Rebellion. Hence, the headline over the news of Lea's trip reads "Twenty Thousand Foreign Troops Soon to Be Marching on China Soil." There also appeared a photograph of Britain's Seymour in an admiral's uniform, drawings of Western-type marines and of a Chinese soldier decapitating a kneeling Westerner, together with the photograph of a sober-looking, bespectacled youth in a business suit, identified by the paper as "Homer Lea, a Young Californian and Agent of the Chinese Reformers, Who Has Started for China to Aid the Movement against the Dowager Empress."

The story that followed referred not at all to the situation in Peking but only to Lea's plans. "It is believed that Lea has in his possession about $60,000 collected in this country by the Chinese Empire Reform Association, a branch of the Po Won Woi [Pao Huang Hui], which is to

12

be used in outfitting an army intended to support Quong Su [Kuang-hsü], the young emperor, in overthrowing the Empress Dowager." Lea's ambition was "to become a commanding general in the Chinese reformers army. The story of his life and ambition was recently published in this newspaper and attracted wide attention. Since that time he has received hundreds of letters from American and English army officers, both active and retired, asking for enlistment under his banner. Many of his fellow students at Stanford, it is stated on reliable authority, and at least one professor, have agreed to follow him to China when the call comes."

The "reliable authority" was perhaps none other but Lea himself. His plans for setting up a military organization could only be furthered by the publicity. The amount of $60,000, a paltry sum for outfitting an army though a substantial contribution to the coffers of the reformers, if it really existed, also figured in a notice about Lea in the *Stanford Alumnus*. That notice, too, was probably placed by Lea, to impress his former classmates and professors and to gain recruits for his cause. It read, "Homer Lee [*sic*], ex-'Ol, has gained a great deal of notoriety recently on account of his connection with the Pow Wong Wui [Pao Huang Hui], the Chinese reform party, which is attempting to restore the deposed emperor to power. Mr. Lea has just sailed for China with $60,000 in his possession which he is to carry to the revolutionists, who are being opposed by the Boxers."[2] Actually, the Boxers were not hostile toward the reformers. If anything, they were indifferent to them while, on their part, the reformers looked at the Boxers with hostile eyes, for they considered them allies of the Empress Dowager. But it seems to have been important to Lea to stress the political difference between the two camps in order to explain to anybody not familiar with the details of the situation in China that his enterprise had nothing to do with the antiforeign Boxer Rebellion.

The publicity about Lea's trip again aroused the attention of Chinese diplomats in the United States. The Consul General in San Francisco saw a connection between Lea's trip and Liang's who, he said, traveled to China from Honolulu on the very next steamer following the *China*. A New York paper picked up the story. "The plan of Homer Lea and his Chinese schemers," the Consul was reported as saying, "was to raise an army of forty thousand malcontents in the Southern treaty ports of the empire and march to Peking."[3] The same paper also reported that according to a "trustworthy Chinese authority," "as soon as Leung Chi Tso [Liang Ch'i-ch'ao] arrives in the Orient and the leaders of the reform movement have conferred with the allied forces one of the biggest revolutions in the history of mankind will break forth. There will be a million young Chinese who have had a taste of Western civilization allied with the Powers of Europe, America and Japan against the untutored hosts of the Dowager Empress. . . . The scheme seems to be to get an understanding with the allied Powers that the Emperor Kwang Su [Kuang-hsü] will be restored to power on the suppression of the Boxer movement. With this agreement the signal will be given, and the reformers throughout the Empire will arise as one man and march with the allies against the Boxers and the forces of the Empress Dowager."[4]

The Consul's statement betrayed the fear of the government in Peking that the reformers might succeed in enlisting the support of the foreign powers, while the second report reflected the reformers' hopes for an understanding with the foreign powers. The reformers hoped that, upon suppression of the Boxers, the powers would turn to them for establishing a new government. This was wishful thinking, for neither then nor later were the allies, especially the United States and Great Britain, prepared to work with any group opposed to the Manchu government. Thus the reformers, as well as other Chinese oppositionists, tried to gain their objectives by taking advantage of the upheaval caused by the Boxers. But it is not known whether Lea's trip was coordinated with Liang's, nor whether the two met during Lea's sojourn in the East.

In effect, there is no evidence, aside from the newspaper article inspired by him, that Lea sailed on the S.S. *China*. The ship's manifest is no longer available, and nobody has ever been reported as having seen him off or met him on board. He did, however, travel to the Orient, although this fact has been questioned.[5] Dr. David Starr Jordan, who spent the summer of 1900 in Japan, met him in Nagasaki in July. Lea was "then on his way to see Mr. Buck [Alfred E. Buck, U.S. Minister to Japan] and hoping through him to induce the powers of Europe to intervene in behalf of the lawful Emperor of China as against the Empress Dowager."[6] Whether Lea was able to see Buck is not known. He is not mentioned in Buck's dispatches to the State Department. It is of interest, however, that already at this early stage of his career Lea spoke of mediating between the Chinese opposition and the United States Government. He actually tried to play that role in 1911 after the outbreak of the revolution.

Twelve years later Lea was reported having had another meeting in Japan, one that, if it occurred, was to be of great significance to him. He was said to have met Sun Yat-sen. In an article entitled "My Reminiscences,"[7] which was published by a London magazine in March of 1912, Sun described the time and circumstances of his first meeting with Lea:

"The whole world knows the story of the Boxer troubles. During that terrible time I was speaking and writing and lecturing. . . . It was now that another important event happened to me. I was speaking to a company of my followers when my eye fell on a young man of slight physique. He was under five feet high; he was about my age; his face was pale, and he looked delicate. Afterwards he came to me and said:—

" 'I should like to throw in my lot with you. I should like to help you. I believe your propaganda will succeed.'

"His accent told me he was an American. He held out his hand. I took it and thanked him, wondering who he was. I thought he was a missionary or a student. I was right. After he had gone I said to a friend:—

" 'Who was that little hunchback?'

" 'Oh, that,' he said, 'is Colonel Homer Lea, one of the most brilliant—perhaps *the* most brilliant military genius now alive. He is a perfect master of modern warfare.'

"I almost gasped in astonishment.

" 'And he has just offered to throw in his lot with me.'

"The next morning I called on Homer Lea, now General, and the famous author of the 'Valour of Ignorance.' I told him that in case I should succeed and my countrymen gave me the power to do so, I would make him my chief military adviser.

" 'Do not wait until you are President of China,' he said. 'You may want me before then. You can neither make nor keep a Government without an army. I have the highest opinion of Chinamen as troops when they are properly trained.' "

Here the account of meeting Homer Lea ended. The article turned to other matters, and Homer Lea was not mentioned again.

Sun did not give the dates of the two days when he saw and spoke with Lea, but he placed them at the time of the Boxer trouble, that is, in the summer of 1900. We know that Lea was in Japan in July of that year. It is also known that a boat on which Sun returned from Singapore where he had tried, unsuccessfully, to see K'ang left Hong Kong for Japan on July 20. The meeting, therefore, could have taken place in the latter part of July, for before the end of that month Lea had already been in Hong Kong. Sir Henry Blake, the British Governor of Hong Kong, reported to his government that "from the United States an American named Lee [*sic*] has been delegated to cooperate with the reformers in China. . . . He, with some of Dr Sun Yat Sen's party went to Macao on the 30th July to consult with Kang Yu Wei's people as to a coalition."[8] It appears, therefore, that, if they did meet at that time, Lea left very shortly after his second talk with Sun.

Although Sun was specific in placing the meeting with Lea at the time of the Boxer troubles, its date has remained controversial. Most accounts, including Sun's official Chinese biographer, date it in 1904,[9] others in 1901, 1905, 1909, or as late as 1911, and place it in either Los Angeles or San Francisco. Because Lea's role in the reform movement was later questioned, it seems important to establish how well they knew each other before 1910 and when their acquaintanceship began.

It is certain that they met in 1910, but that was in Los Angeles and occurred under circumstances quite different from those related in "My Reminiscences." Before 1910 there were three other possible occasions of a meeting, the first and second in Japan either in July of 1900 or early in 1901 when Lea returned from China. The third chance of a meeting arose in California on the occasion of Sun's visit to the United States in 1904. But a first meeting in 1904 is quite unlikely if Sun's account of their conversation is accepted. Lea's American accent would not have been found worthy of Sun's comment had he spoken to him in the United States. Nor would he have thought of Lea as a missionary unless he encountered him at a place where foreign missionaries would stand out, as in the Orient where they constituted a large segment of the Western residents. Moreover, a 1904 meeting between the two would not have been one of chance or surprise. When Sun arrived in San Francisco that year, American immigration officials questioned the U.S. citizenship which he had claimed by falsely stating that he had been born in Hawaii. While held in quarantine, Sun chanced to see the name of Ng Poon Chew, Lea's sponsor in 1900, listed in a San Francisco Chinese newspaper as its general manager. Sun had with him an introduction to Ng from mutual friends in Canton. He was able to have a boy deliver the letter to Ng Poon Chew, who helped to have him released. Thereafter, Sun is said to have stayed at Ng's house for several weeks[10] and to have had occasional meals at his office.[11] Under these circumstances, Lea might have seen Sun, for Ng was a logical conduit between the two. Hence, it is possible that they met in 1904, but not under the conditions described in Sun's article.

Nor is it likely, if we accept Sun's account of their first meeting, that this took place in Japan early in 1901. At that juncture Lea's name and person could no longer have been unknown to Sun because, in the meantime, Lea had been in contact with Sun's men in Hong Kong. In addition, as we shall see, by then Lea had had some involvement not only with the reformers' uprising of August 1900 but possibly also with one organized by Sun in October of that year. As a result there remains of the three possibilities only late July 1900 as the time of the first meeting. But in the face of Sun's explicit words, some serious doubts arise whether this was indeed the time and place when they first met. Such doubts result from the very words themselves. In the article Lea was identified as a "brilliant military genius" and a "master of modern warfare," accolades generally granted him only years later, after the publication of *The Valor of Ignorance*. In July 1900 his claim to being a military expert was known only to the California reformers and to their connections in the East. It is conceivable, however, that Sun's unnamed friend had heard about the newly found military man from Lea's acquaintances among the reformers.

Lea's penchant for self-promotion also gives cause to question the veracity of Sun's account. The article was published as a result of an interview Sun gave to the editors of the magazine when both he and Lea were in London in November 1911. Although it was stated in the foreword to the story that it had been "taken down from Sun Yat Sen's own lips," it is more than probable that Lea had a hand in its editing. It has even been suspected that he wrote it for Sun,[12] but there is no conclusive evidence for that belief. Whatever the extent of Sun's authorship, there are good reasons for supposing that Lea collaborated in formulating the text and determining the format. For example, the article as published is accompanied by photographs of only three persons. Two photographs show Sun, one his father, and the picture of the third person is that of Homer Lea himself in the uniform, of all things, of a general in the army of the reformers.

The reference to Lea as "Colonel" and "now General" also raises a question. Lea had never been called a colonel nor had he ever spoken of himself as such. In accordance with his own account, he began his military career as a general. In a 1901 interview after his return from China, he said he "went to China and offered his services" and "was made a lieutenant general."[13] In England, however, in November 1911, when the magazine article was written, it was of great importance to Lea if he could imply a regular military career with successive ranks he had held. At that time he was consorting with British officers of the highest rank and negotiating with government officials, international bankers, and other businessmen. With British military experts, he was discussing his strategic concepts as laid down in *The Day of the Saxon*, which was about to be published. Hence, it was in his interest to make himself a professional instead of being considered the rank amateur that he was.

Finally and, perhaps, most importantly, there was another reason why Lea might have wanted to put abroad this particular version of his first meeting with Sun. Lea was to embark shortly with Sun from London to China where he hoped to be accepted by Sun's colleagues and followers as a military expert and Sun's chief of staff. It would greatly buttress his position if he could establish an association with Sun that went back as far as 1900, his earliest days as a "China hand." Such an early tie with Sun would also help to gloss over his long association with the reformers, by then a grave drawback in the eyes of Chinese revolutionary politicians.

Given this background of the story as presented in the article, it does not come as a surprise that J. O. P. Bland, the respected China correspondent of the London *Times*, and author on China, called Sun's "Reminiscences" a "constructive memory as fantastic as the libretto of a musical comedy."[14] Bland pointed particularly to the account of Sun's first meeting with Lea. He had no reason to suspect Lea's hand in the description of that event, which Sun characterized as "important." For Bland it was Sun who he found had "learned in his travels abroad the gentle art of political advertising, together with a shrewd idea of the value of sensationalism in connection therewith. . . . The boyish bombast of his words and deeds is apt, indeed, to give us pause: as, for instance, when he engages 'General' Homer Lea to organize the Republican army of China."

It may be questionable whether Sun or Lea had the greater talent for political promotion and advertising. In any case, the account of their first meeting as portrayed in the "Reminiscences" leaves serious doubts as to its truthfulness. There is one circumstance, however, that appears to vindicate Sun's account of a meeting in July 1900: when he arrived in Hong Kong from Japan, Lea sought out Sun's followers and went with them to Macao, as Sir Henry Blake reported, to propose a combined action of the reformers and Sun's revolutionaries. Somebody must have given Lea the names and addresses of Sun's men in Hong Kong and that somebody could have been Sun. Likewise, Sun might have convinced Lea of the need for the two camps to unite, a strategy that Sun had intended to propose to K'ang in Singapore shortly before he returned to Japan in July of 1900. But as long as there is no conclusive evidence that supports the account in "My Reminiscences," that article alone cannot be used to decide the issue. Hence, there is no definitive proof that Sun and Lea met before 1910.

The inconclusive ending of Sun's account of his conversation with Lea and the uncertainty as to Sun's response to Lea's offer of military advice may have given rise to or at least contributed to questions that arose later with regard to Lea's connection with Sun. It was questioned whether Sun and Lea, after this supposed meeting in 1900, had become secret collaborators and whether Lea then began to act as a spy for Sun while ostensibly working for the reformers. Such a claim when made by a popular writer who has been absurdly wrong about innumerable points of Lea's life may be disregarded: "The first revolutionist Homer Lea met in China was Dr. Sun Yat-sen. This was secretly in Hong Kong, where Dr. Sun was living at the time in hiding. At this meeting the two men agreed on one thing: each was to go his separate way, but they were to keep in touch. It was also agreed that, for the present, Homer Lea should play ball with Kang Yu-wei and Liang Chi-chao."[15] More weight may be given to the words of a respected historian. According to this source, Homer Lea joined Sun and "the Chinese revolutionaries in 1904. . . .

Since then [he] served as Sun Yat-sen's military adviser. He accompanied K'ang in the latter's tour of the United States in 1905 serving, as many people suspected, as a spy for Sun Yat-sen."[16] This was an unambiguous statement labeling Lea as a spy, but the author, a grandson of K'ang, was perhaps biased when he made it. For when he was questioned, he conceded that it could not be corroborated and was based merely on speculation.[17] True, in 1904, when Sun expressed, in an appeal to the American people, the "hope we may find many Lafayettes among you,"[18] he might have been thinking of Homer Lea and his associates. However, according to Lea's wife Ethel, "it was not until the death of Kuang Hsu in 1908 that Homer Lea agreed to join Sun Yat-sen in his revolutionary plans, although Sun had approached him with that end in view some years previously."[19] Lea himself said in an April 1909 letter to Dr. Jordan that since the recent death of the Emperor he had severed all connections with the Chinese. He repeated this in another letter the following month: "The Emperor is dead, and as far as I am concerned, only the knowledge and experience I gained during these past years remain with me."[20] These statements were patently false because Lea was again engaged in Chinese political conspiracies. Thus, they cannot be used to prove that no prior collaboration with Sun existed. Nor can his wife's statement be considered proof. She only knew what he told her of events that occurred, or did not occur, before she knew him, and in any case she would have been anxious to conceal such a connection. The best argument against the spy theory and, indeed, against a meeting with Sun in 1900 is the fact that it was more than a year after the Emperor's death before Sun and Lea established contact with each other. With the Emperor's death, the focus of the reformers' cause had disappeared, and Lea was freed to work with Sun. That he did not and that the eventual initiative for a collaboration came from Sun in an unexpected way[21] should prove the nonexistence of any prior agreement between them.

The uprising in which Homer Lea expected to take part had been planned by K'ang, who was then in Singapore. Emissaries and circular letters had been sent to overseas Chinese in various countries, including the United States, to obtain financial support, arms, and recruits.[22] Negotiations for the acquisition and delivery of arms were carried on in several places. Thought was given to the enlistment of Philippine mercenaries. Members of the Chinese Empire Reform Association explained their cause in letters sent to the Governments of the United States, Great Britain, Germany, and Japan. Their goal was to obtain the powers' "aid in reinstating [the Emperor] on the Throne," have them "declare a joint Protectorate and undertake the government of the country through the Emperor."[23] Preparations for the coup were hastened by the outbreak of the Boxer Rebellion.

The reformers' campaign was to begin in the Yangtze provinces, where 100,000 men of the Independence Army were to spearhead the revolt. August 9 was set as the launching date, and once Wuchang and Hankow had been taken on August 22, 3,000 armed reformers, supported by 2,000 men of the imperial army who were expected to join the reformers, were to march to Shensi to rescue the Kuang-hsü Emperor.

Sun Yat-sen had also recognized the opportunities that the Boxer Rebellion provided for an armed insurrection. Anxious to assure the success of both undertakings, his and that of the reformers, he had gone to Singapore to obtain K'ang's agreement to coordinate them. When he was rebuffed by K'ang, he proceeded on his own.

Disaster overtook the reformers' enterprise. Because funds that were promised did not arrive on time, the starting date was postponed, but one of the leaders was not told of the delay. His premature start gave away the conspiracy and sealed its fate. Many leaders of the Independence Army were arrested and executed, as were many members of the secret societies involved and other sympathizers of the reformers. Sun's attempt at revolution that started in Waichow in October of that year ended just as unsuccessfully.

Where was Lea during these events, and what role did he play?

To begin with, nobody involved in the preparations for either uprising and nobody who took part in either one ever mentioned the name of Homer Lea, much less spoke of his active participation. Aside from Lea's own statements and except for one fairly reliable witness who states that Lea went to Shanghai after the debacles, all we have are hearsay reports. As a result, his role in the insurrections is quite uncertain. In addition, several reports that do exist are patently untrue or highly exaggerated. Dispensing with historical facts and dates, one fantastic tale has Homer secretly traveling from Canton to Peking to see K'ang Yu-wei. Although K'ang had fled China in 1898 after the coup d'etat of the Empress Dowager, the report describes him as her Prime Minister who, behind her back, is raising a volunteer army to overthrow her in order to restore the Kuang-hsü Emperor to the throne: "In the Forbidden Palace itself, [Lea] kept a prearranged midnight rendez-vous with the Prime Minister [who] was frankly surprised to see a crippled boy. 'Why have you come? What can you do,' he asked.

" 'I have come,' Lea said, 'to help you save China from the old Tigress. To rescue Kwang Hsu. To lead your armies to victory!'

"The Prime Minister smiled, 'You are very young to do all that.'

"Homer Lea replied, 'I am the same age Napoleon was at Rivoli.' . . . In the end, [K'ang] ordered Lea to proceed to Shensi there to take over a body of volunteers. . . . Within a hundred miles of his destination a runner brought him disastrous news. The Empress Dowager's palace spies and her eunuchs . . . had overheard the Prime Minister's interview with Homer Lea. She was at last aware that Kong [K'ang] was plotting against her. She instantly ordered the beheading of all his officers and sympathizers. But upon a whispered warning from a friend, the Prime Minister had fled the palace, with a prize of twenty thousand dollars on his head. On the head of the missing 'white devil' Homer Lea . . . the Empress had put a prize of ten thousand dollars. The Viceroy of Shensi, an appointee of the Empress, had already been apprised of the plot. He had lured all the officers of 'Leas's troops' into his palace, under pretext of surrendering the province to them. The next morning their heads had appeared in a grisly row on the city walls."

Lea was said to have ordered his volunteers to retreat into the mountains where he rallied them. "After several months, at the head of a few thousand pig-tailed, ill-disciplined 'Volunteers,' the American began his long-planned march on the Palace of the Empress Dowager. He now wore the uniform of a general with massive gold epaulets, the gold star of the Emperor about his scrunch-neck, and a sword almost as tall as he was. When he arrived outside the gates of Peking, the Boxer Rebellion was reaching its hideous climax."[24]

Another fanciful story published as recently as 1969 adds to Homer Lea's imaginary feats during the Boxer Rebellion: "In the midst of all this terrorism [by the Boxers], Homer Lea . . . was appointed a lieutenant general and ordered to take command of the Second Division of the 'Army of the Emperor.' . . . The 'shadow army' sworn to loyalty to the imprisoned Emperor . . . would take on the empress's Royal Manchu Army, while the combined expeditionary forces of the Western nations dealt with the Boxers besieging the foreign legations in Peking. . . . When the relief column entered Peking, Homer Lea and his Second Division of the Chinese Reform Army, about two thousand ragged and poorly equipped troops marched in on the heels of the expeditionary force. . . . When the dowager empress fled from her palace with a large bodyguard of the Royal Manchu Army, Lea was ordered to take his ragtag legion and pursue her. The Second Division marched out of the capital with Lea at its head, riding in a guilded palanquin and dressed in a mandarin's costume. The hardbitten old cavalryman, General Chaffee, must have shaken his head at that spectacle."[25]

According to this story, Lea's campaign failed when his division disintegrated after an attack from the rear. He found refuge in a Buddhist temple where monks nursed him back to health. The Empress Dowager put a prize on his head, but K'ang managed to have him smuggled to Hong Kong.

Whatever else Lea did in China, he did not take part in the relief of Peking. He never set foot in that city, neither at that time nor at any time later. Likewise, no contingent of the Chinese Reform Army, which at the time did not even exist, did any fighting. But the report did have some factual basis. The insurrectionist reformers had planned to send a force to the Shensi Hills to rescue the Emperor from the Empress Dowager. Lea is said to have claimed later that he set out from Kwangtung, where he had been drilling troops, for Hankow with two Chinese officers as his companions with the aim of joining the column that was to march to Shensi, at least 400 miles northwest. But the march to Shensi never took place. Lea claimed that before returning south he attempted to rally the troops who, however, had already dispersed.[26] As to General Chaffee, Lea did get to know him, although some years later and under quite different circumstances.

According to Dr. Jordan, who had seen Lea in Japan, the trip ended much less conspicuously. He maintained Lea had been barred from landing in China due to the notoriety that resulted from his unwise disclosures in the San Francisco newspaper before and after his departure. Lea had finally succeeded in getting to Hong Kong and Macao but, having run out of money, "appealed successfully to the Chinese in San Francisco for transportation home."

Dr. Jordan obtained that information from Ng Poon Chew, who confirmed it in a letter that Dr. Jordan published shortly after Lea's death.[27] It was the same letter in which Ng stated he had originally introduced Homer Lea to the San Francisco reform leaders. According to Ng, Lea stayed at the Palace Hotel in San Francisco before he departed "and we paid all his expenses and we raised enough money to pay his fare to Hong Kong and enough to last him for a few months." This is in conflict with a statement attributed to Lea after his return in which he claimed to have paid for the expenses of the trip himself.[28] As to Lea's stay in China, Ng contended that "Lea arrived in Hong Kong, tried to get in touch with the reform leaders there, and after a while he went over to Macao . . . and stayed there for a few months, but nothing was accomplished. After staying there for six months his money was all gone. He was without friends there, because the Chinese authorities were keeping a sharp eye on his movements, and the Chinese reform leaders did not dare to associate with him for fear of being found out. Lea wrote to the Chinese leaders here [in San Francisco] asking for money to return to the United States. Reluctantly, a few hundred dollars were raised and sent to him, and in time he returned to this country. After this his connection with the reform revolution was ended. . . . The Chinese here in San Francisco regretted very much that they had parted with their money in sending Lea to China in 1900."

The letter treats Lea's actions in China in very unfriendly terms, but Ng's words must be read with a good deal of skepticism. Dr. Jordan, the foremost U.S. proponent of pacifism and international arbitration, had reacted angrily to obituaries about Homer Lea that applauded his militarism. To counter what he considered propaganda for war, he appears to have convinced Ng Poon Chew to write the letter, which Dr. Jordan then sent to various newspapers and magazines. A man like Ng must have held Dr. Jordan in great awe and felt it necessary to defer to him. Otherwise it would be hard to explain why he should have changed his mind about Homer Lea. Only six months earlier, he had addressed a very friendly letter to Lea, in which he referred to their pleasant relationship of old and added: "I must congratulate Dr. Sun for winning you over in our behalf, and congratulate ourselves for your appearance in China during time of trouble. Thank you in behalf of my people and myself for the uplift of China."[29]

Another account painted quite a different picture of Lea's activities. This one was by the managing director of the Chinese Reform Association in San Francisco, Tong Chong, whom Ng Poon Chew undoubtedly knew very well. Tong Chong reported that Lea had been in Singapore, Hong Kong, Shanghai, and Yokohama and, finally, in the southern provinces of China "where he was well received."[30] To reorganize the reformers' army, Lea had been given the rank of lieutenant general with the command of all military operations in Kwangtung, Kwangsi, Yunnan, and Kweichow. "General Lea has now nearly thirty thousand men ready to take up arms for the Emperor. During the year of General Lea's absence, I have been in constant receipt of advices as to his success from the officers of the Imperial Reform Party, among them the president, Yung Wing of Macao, and many others whom the brave young Californian met. During the greater part of the time, he traveled with a guard of only half a dozen soldiers, as many sedan-chair bearers, and two aides-de-camp, who were graduates of both Chinese and foreign colleges and acted as his interpreters."

This report must also be accepted with some reservations. It appeared in the same issue of the newspaper that carried an interview Lea gave upon his return from China.[31] In it Lea also claimed that he "was made lieutenant general, placed in charge of affairs in the southern provinces, which include Kwangtung, and [had] thirty thousand men in that province alone." Thus, it is possible that at least some of Tong Chong's information came from Lea himself. It is also possible that Tong Chong needed to justify Lea's mission and the money spent on it in order to counter criticism of the venture and therefore felt it necessary to magnify Lea's role.

Tong Chong is the first to mention the name of Yung Wing in connection with Homer Lea's activities. This is interesting, for in 1910 the two men were to work closely together. However, in this earlier instance,

Yung Wing could not have given much information to Tong Chong that was based on firsthand knowledge. Yung Wing (1828–1912) was throughout his long life in contact with reform and revolutionary movements in China. He was the first Chinese to graduate from Yale (1854). As a young man he had a certain involvement with the Taiping Rebellion. From 1872 to 1881 he headed a Chinese educational mission to the United States and also served as Chinese deputy minister in Washington from 1878 to 1881. He married an American woman and became a naturalized U.S. citizen. The citizenship was later revoked and again reinstated. Returning to China in the 1890s, when he became involved in the reform movement, he had to flee after the "Hundred Days Reform Period."

Yung Wing was a prominent member of the Chinese Empire Reform Association, although he was not its president, as Tong Chong claimed. He was, however, selected to be president of the National Assembly of the reformers that convened in Shanghai prior to the uprising. Yung Wing also had good connections with Sun's group and, in fact, at one time was proposed as head of Sun's organization in place of Sun and as president of the new government to be established by the revolutionaries after Sun's people took power.

Yung Wing had to flee Shanghai when his involvement in the reformers' uprising became known. He arrived in Hong Kong on September 11, after the reformers' defeat.[32] Lea seemed to have gone from Hankow to Shanghai at about the same time.[33] It is possible that Yung Wing and Lea met briefly in Shanghai, but whatever knowledge Yung had of Lea's activities before and during the insurrection might have reached him from others or from Lea himself if, indeed, they did meet in Shanghai. In any event, Lea never mentioned Yung's name in connection with his experiences in the East. Nor did Yung Wing mention Lea in his biography or in a diary he kept from 1901 to 1902.[34] Yung Wing was in Singapore in March 1900, visiting with K'ang Yu-wei, when news arrived that Lea had proposed to the San Francisco reformers to organize a contingent of discharged U.S. soldiers. It was Yung Wing who told the British chief police officer in Singapore that 500 Americans were expected to assist in the uprising. Neither at that time did Yung Wing refer to Lea by name.

We will now consider the other point in Tong Chong's interview, that Lea received the rank of lieutenant general. After his return, Lea gave an interview that was headed, "How I Was Made a General in the Chinese Army."[36] But he said nothing about the circumstances under which this occurred or who gave him that rank. In an earlier interview, he was quoted as having said that "on arriving in China I was placed in charge of the southern part of China with the rank of a general in the

imperial army.''[37] According to still another report, he explained his role
in the military operation as follows: "My knowledge of military affairs
was of value to the organizers [of the uprising], and as the arrangements
progressed I gradually drifted toward the head of it, until I was looked
upon as the commanding officer of the Army of China in the Southern
Provinces.''[38] Years later, on his arrival in Shanghai with Sun Yat-sen in
1911, a reporter asked Lea how he had become a general. The answer was
unequivocal but the facts were not: "I was commander of four divisions
organized by myself for the rescue of the Emperor Kwang-hsu eleven
years ago." That army, he added, operated "chiefly in the South and
[was] commanded by American officers.''[39] However, no U.S. officer or
private was ever found to have fought for the reformers. Nor is it conceivable that Homer Lea assumed a commander's role in a campaign for
which plans had been completed well before he arrived. His name was
not among the five commanders who had been chosen to lead the Independence Army. Smaller units were scattered in various provinces, including Kwangsi,[40] and in theory Lea could have commanded one of
them. But he did not know the terrain or the local conditions, spoke no
Chinese, and had no prior military experience. If Lea were ever in command of any troops in the field during the uprising, aside from his aides,
his guards, and sedan-chair bearers, it could not have been a sizable de-
tachment.

    With respect to Lea's movements after he left Japan, Sir Henry
Blake's report[41] that he was in Hong Kong and went from there to Macao
may be accepted as true although the Governor may not have seen him
personally. Blake also gave details of Lea's plans that closely corresponded
to those he was said to have developed at the banquet given him by the
San Francisco reform leaders prior to his departure. According to Sir
Henry Blake, Lea's plan entailed "that Macao would form a convenient
base of operations; that 25,000 Coolies should be enlisted, under American Officers, and that Canton should be made the objective. It is assumed [by Lea] that all the Macao authorities could be bribed, and an
understanding arrived at with the Portuguese Governor on the basis of
territorial compensations. A new Government is to be proclaimed in
Canton announcing the annexation of the provinces south of the
Yangtze. The Governor and Governor General of Canton are to be seized
and held as hostages making them issue orders to surrender all forts, gunboats, and military stores &c., &c. When Canton has been captured a
circular is to be sent to all the foreign powers, stating the object of the
reform party and guaranteeing the protection of all foreigners and Chris-
tians." To be sure, the British Governor told his government in London
that "these were the views of the American delegate who advocated immediate action and pressed that the Powers are too busily engaged in the

North [with the Boxers] to interfere in the South." Perhaps unknown to Lea, the decision where to start operations had already been made when he went to Macao to present his plan. A heated debate had ensued among the reform leaders in the Orient whether to launch the uprising in the south or in the Yangtze valley. By the time Lea arrived on the scene, the issue had been decided in favor of the Yangtze provinces[42] where eventually the action began.

There is no definite information available on Lea's whereabouts after he travelled to Macao on July 30 until some time later when he turned up in Shanghai. He claimed even at the time that he did not remain in Hong Kong and other places on China's periphery but ventured inland. In its February 1901 issue, the *Stanford Alumnus* mentioned "a letter [by Lea] written recently from Hongkong . . . that he was to leave in a few days for the province of Kwang-Si, 800 miles in the interior of China."[43] The date of the letter was not given, but it must have been written about six months earlier. Years later, in 1908, he spoke of having been drilling troops in the province of Kwangtung when he learned of the Empress Dowager's flight to Shensi.

Anecdotes that appeared to corroborate Lea's claims flourished very quickly. An alumnus of Stanford and at the time a missionary in Honan (probably Hunan) province was said to have encountered Lea while in the interior. Will Irwin, Lea's friend from Stanford, who a few years later related this encounter, cited a letter written by the missionary to friends in the United States. One night at the mission house a white man applied for lodging. That man turned out to be Homer Lea. "Not a word did he say what he was doing in our corner of the world and next morning he was gone. What the blazes?"[44]

Irwin is the source for another encounter of this kind. This time, "Red" Wilson, a mining engineer and also a Stanford man, is said to have met Lea somewhere in the interior. In its embroidered form, the meeting became part of the Homer Lea lore, irrespective of the fact that in geographical terms it was impossible for Lea to have been where Wilson placed him, even if the account of his travel into the interior of China is accepted. According to this story, " 'Red' Wilson . . . was exploring formations to westward of Peking when a runner brought him news that the Boxers had risen against all Europeans. He started for Peking. That night he lodged at the compound of a friendly mandarin. Next morning, as he was saddling for what he knew the most dangerous stretch of his journey, out of a door came a white hunchback who addressed him by name. 'I have never had the pleasure of meeting you,' said this stranger, 'but I am a Stanford man myself—Homer Lea, ex-99— and I know all about you. Don't be worried about your trip to Peking. Word has gone ahead, and you won't be molested.' They chatted a little about acquaintances at Stanford. Then the hunchback, assuring him again that his way to Peking was guarded and greased, excused himself and disappeared."[45]

Other stories contend that after the debacle of the reformers Lea sought refuge in a Buddhist monastery where a monk treated a small wound on his arm. Disguised as a French missionary, he is said to have made his way to Hong Kong where a Chinese graduate from his Stanford days is to have nursed him back to health.[46]

If his own words are to be believed, Lea attached himself to Sun's forces after the defeat of the reformers. In May 1909 he presented General H. G. Otis, the owner of the *Los Angeles Times*, who had become his patron and supporter, with a sword supposedly from the Ming period. He claimed to have obtained that sword at the battle of Po-lo,[47] which was fought by Sun's men on October 11, 1900. No information is available that corroborates Lea's presence at the battle, nor any indication that he joined or was in contact with Sun's forces in the field. Finally, the only individual who ever claimed to have actually seen Lea in China, Tex O'Reilly, an American soldier of fortune, stated that Lea "had organized a little military company in Hankow, but he had to give it up . . . so he came down to Shanghai."[48]

Tex O'Reilly was at the time a member of the Shanghai international police force. He met Lea at the China Club in Shanghai and invited him to live at his house since Lea was out of money. According to O'Reilly, Lea was his house guest for about four months.[49] This could have been the case if Lea came to Shanghai early in September after the defeat of the reformers' revolt, for by January 11, 1901, he was already in Yokohama, Japan, on his first leg home.[50] On the other hand, if he took part in the battle of Po-lo, he might have been at O'Reilly's house only little more than two months. But O'Reilly's memory was somewhat weak when, three decades later, he entrusted his recollections to his biographer. For instance, he said he met Lea in Shanghai in 1902, which led a researcher in modern Chinese history to the conclusion that Lea returned that year to take part in still another uprising.[51] The historian had no other basis for the assertion of Lea's involvement with the planned revolt in 1902 and, when confronted with the fact that O'Reilly had made an error in the year, withdrew the assertion.[52] As a matter of fact, the year when he met Lea can be deduced from O'Reilly's own account, for he said that one of the "freaks" whom Lea frequently met at his house was the French writer and naval officer Pierre Loti. Loti had left France on board a French naval ship on August 2, 1900, destined for Shanghai and arrived there shortly after the end of the Boxer Rebellion, probably toward the end of August.[53] He described the aftermath of the Rebellion very vividly in *Les Derniers Jours de Pékin*.[54] Loti departed from China on June 15, 1901,[55] and since he never returned he could have met Lea only during the nine and a half months of his visit to China.

O'Reilly is the only source that mentions a meeting between Lea and Loti. The latter's name does not appear in Lea's surviving papers, nor did Loti speak of Lea in the account of his stay in China or in his published letters. But it can be assumed that O'Reilly, a roughneck, probably never heard of Loti before he met Lea. Moreover, there is some circumstantial evidence that lends credence to O'Reilly's report. As a result of his sojourn in China, Loti wrote a play, *La Fille du Ciel*. This play, according to O'Reilly, was inspired by Lea. It concerns a Ming empress, the last of the dynasty whose reigning heads had lived in hiding for the 350 years of Manchu rule and so escaped extinction at the hands of their enemies, the Manchu rulers. So far the story agrees with the legends that prevailed among those Chinese who awaited the return of their native dynasty. In the play the reigning Manchu emperor, whom Loti in the foreword to his drama identifies as the Kuang-hsü Emperor, learns of the secret existence of the Ming empress. He attempts a reconciliation of the two dynasties, prompted by his counselor, identified as K'ang Yu-wei. Empress and emperor fall in love, but the story ends tragically with her death. The time of the play is 1898, the year of the "Hundred Days of Reform," initiated by the Kuang-hsü Emperor at the instigation of K'ang Yu-wei.

The story was, of course, close to the heart of Homer Lea, who may well have told Loti of the legend and of the two real characters in the play, as O'Reilly maintained. The drama opened in New York under the title *Daughter of Heaven* on October 17, 1912, two weeks before Lea's death.[56] Loti came to New York for its premiere. There is no indication that he was in contact with Lea either at that time or before his arrival. But it can hardly be a coincidence that François de Tessan, a French writer who accompanied Loti to the rehearsals and to the premiere in New York, devoted a whole chapter (in a book he wrote about a trip to the western United States) to Homer Lea as a strategist of the Chinese Revolution.[57]

If there were a meeting with Loti, which seems most likely, it left an imprint also on Lea's own fictional venture, *The Vermilion Pencil*, a novel that he later attempted to make into a play under the title, *The Vermilion Spider*.[58] In his novel, Lea made the hero a Breton monk, the one priest whom "Fate had peculiarly redeemed . . . out of the whole utterly damned tribe of them all."[59] This may have been a tribute to Loti, a native of Brittany.

While Loti's stay in Shanghai can be verified, this is not so in the case of another visitor whom, O'Reilly claimed, Homer Lea met frequently at his house—Sun Yat-sen. "Night after night Homer Lea had him there, and they'd sit talking about Karl Marx and other socialists and their ideas. . . . Finally Sun Yat Sen moved out to my house and lived there awhile, and they never did stop talking.''[60] O'Reilly's memory certainly deceived him in this particular instance because, after the debacle of his uprising, Sun left Formosa and returned to Japan. He did not get off the boat when it stopped in Shanghai,[61] for he had been banned from landing there a few months earlier.

O'Reilly, a simple fellow about three years younger than Lea, was duly impressed by his houseguest, who in physique and mental alertness was his exact opposite. He considered Lea ''a prodigy, a genius, an intellectual giant.'' By the time he spoke to his biographer, Lea had become in his memory ''one of the greatest Americans who ever lived. . . . I heard him talk fluently in fourteen languages. He not only spoke Chinese, but he wrote it, and not only one dialect but a dozen.''[62]

While these statements cannot be taken seriously, O'Reilly's recollection of another characteristic of Homer Lea cannot be dismissed so easily. This concerns Lea's drinking habits. ''That marvellous mind was tied to a twisted, deformed little body, in constant pain. He suffered so horribly, that he was a most unpleasant companion, irritable and cranky. And he drank all the time. He was never drunk, but he drank from morning to night, trying to get away from the pain.''[63]

O'Reilly's observation of Lea's addiction to alcohol appears to be confirmed in both Ethel's and Homer's correspondence. In August 1911 Ethel wrote to her sister Agnes from Wiesbaden, Germany, that ''Homer is getting better every day. He has gone with some young army officers to a winery. The first time he's been out of my sight. Don't know how it will turn out.''[64] Later that year, when he had gone alone to London, he wrote to her: ''You must not worry. I have not entered a bar or taken a drink with anyone.''[65] Ethel was more explicit in a letter from Nanking written some months later, when Lea was seriously ill. She feared that alcoholism had contributed to the deterioration of his health and asked Agnes to ''tell Dr. Ferbert I make a pest of myself fussing over him about drinking and if it is within the possibility of humanity he will never be full again. He hasn't really been drinking. Has two drinks a day, but after he gets over this [illness] I'll try to eliminate even that. While we were in Germany he really didn't touch a thing.''[66] To judge from this letter, Lea's physician in the United States knew and had been concerned about his drinking bouts. A friend also mentioned a recurring drinking problem. ''He was wont, occasionally, to join a boon company on a spree. During these bibulous adventures, he sometimes became overenthusiastic, and although he lost his sobriety, he never lost his head.''[67]

Such ''overenthusiasm'' is apparent in a scene recounted by Dr. Jordan: ''Upon one of my visits to Los Angeles . . . I was . . . given a dinner by the Stanford Club of that city, containing about a hundred members.

Lea sent his regrets, but invited us all to dine with him at the Hotel Angelus the following evening. The young people paid little attention to the note, for the 'General' was never taken seriously by his former associates. Two of them, nevertheless, offered to go with me if I cared to accept the invitation—which I did. During the meal Lea told us wonderful stories of his adventures in China as commander of 'sixty thousand men.' If he found any general false to him—'off with his head!' But he 'made the mistake of his life' when he left China for Tokyo in a vain effort to induce the Powers to take up the young Emperor's cause, for during his absence the tricky 'Old Buddha,' Yehonola [the Empress Dowager], invited his officers to a conference under a flag of truce, and then seized and beheaded them all! He therefore found it quite impossible to reorganize another army, and so returned to the United States."[68]

It would seem that Lea's braggadocio was increased by alcohol, but it remains a question whether he drank primarily to overcome pain, as O'Reilly thought. Ethel's letters do not seem to indicate this. She might have expressed doubts about being able to turn him away from drinking if unbearable pain was the reason for it. Perhaps the cause could be found in a tense nervous system or in the frustration and limitations which his weak bodily condition placed on his ambitious mind.

Ng Poon Chew was probably correct in saying that Lea was out of funds before he returned. At least he was when O'Reilly met him at the China Club. It may be assumed that Ng Poon Chew also spoke the truth in saying that the reformers in San Francisco sent Lea money for the return ticket.

Lea probably left Shanghai in early January. The next we hear of him, he was to be found at the Grand Hotel in Yokohama where on January 11, 1901, he received a note from the secretary of Count Okuma confirming a meeting with the Count in Tokyo on January 13.[69]

Shigenobu Okuma (1838–1922) had been the Japanese prime minister during China's "Hundred Days of Reform" in 1898. He carried on a steady correspondence with the Kuang-hsü Emperor about the reforms needed. He greatly admired K'ang Yu-wei and after the coup d'etat of the Empress Dowager he helped both K'ang and Liang to come to Japan. In 1901 Count Okuma no longer held an official government position. It is not known how Lea approached him and whether he carried a formal introduction. K'ang would have been the most likely person to refer Lea to Okuma, but it is not known whether Lea had any contact, direct or indirect, with K'ang. At the time K'ang lived at Singapore, and, while it has been said that Lea went to Singapore, there is no evidence to that effect. At one point he is alleged to have said that he met K'ang but did not specify where that happened.[70]

In another interview given to a San Francisco newspaper upon his return from the Orient, Lea spoke briefly of his conversation with Count

Okuma. He said he felt indebted to the Count for telling him "the details and methods, the fine arts of law and statecraft by which such tremendous reforms [as K'ang's] were to be accomplished." Okuma, said Lea, called for reforms modeled on Japan's but modified by China's particular needs and circumstances. Such reforms should include the modernization of China's army "by Western methods of drill and tactics" and its "nationalization," that is, the formation of a national army under the central government instead of the existing regional armies under influential local officials and warlords.[71] Given Lea's interest in military matters, it is understandable that he should emphasize the reform of the military establishment as crucial in the regeneration of China.

In the same interview, Lea pointed to Russia as the chief opponent of China's unification and the main beneficiary of its weakness, which Russia was exploiting by steady expansion in the north. This caused concern in Japan, which harbored ambitions of political supremacy on the Asiatic mainland but was not yet ready to take up the fight for it. In the meantime, Japan considered a unified and strengthened China the best barrier to Russian encroachment and also to Western pressure upon the country. This view became known as the "Okuma Doctrine," which held that Japan had been the beneficiary of Chinese culture and civilization and, therefore, owed China an obligation to support its efforts for reform. To accomplish this, it was seen as Japan's duty to hold Russia and the Western powers at bay. Accordingly, the temporary interests of Japan coincided with those of the reformers.

Lea's statements, which may have reflected the view of the reform movement, were read as supporting Japan's policies in China. The day after Lea's interview was published, another San Francisco newspaper condemned Japan's assistance to the reform movement.[72] It held that only the continued existence of the Manchu government with the protection and support of the Western powers could preserve the integrity of the Chinese Empire. A reawakened China allied to Japan "becomes at once a menace to the peace of the world and the security and supremacy of the white race." It was a direct rebuke to Homer Lea's advocacy of a strong and united China with Japan's help and under its tutelage. It took Lea a number of years to reach the view that he finally expressed in *The Valor of Ignorance*, that Japan was as much a threat, and perhaps a stronger one, to an independent China as was the West. In any event, in 1901 Lea, a youthful amateur in the field of international politics, began by espousing uncritically the Japanese view of the China problem as presented to him by the foremost Japanese sympathetic to the cause of the reformers.

In a certain sense, however, Homer Lea's meeting with Count Okuma is significant more for the fact that it took place and under what circumstances than for what was said or not said. There was Homer Lea, an ambitious and grandiloquent young fellow who had gone to China to accomplish great things. As much as one may search, one does not uncover any evidence that he achieved any of the goals that propelled him into the venture, nor the expectation of the people who sent him. No hard facts have come to light to prove that the mission was of value to his supporters and their cause, nor any confirmation that he even met any of the leaders of the reform movement. But at the very moment when he was to come back empty-handed, when he might be dismissed as a braggart, "a schemer, pure and simple,"[73] and when his venture might be adjudged as an interesting but worthless stunt, with very little evidence that it took place at all, at that very instant he had a verifiable encounter with Count Okuma, an eminent, internationally recognized statesman. This prominent public figure earnestly discussed with our dubious protagonist the political situation in China. Nobody knows how Lea obtained the interview, whether it was granted to him as a matter of routine and courtesy or whether Count Okuma received him on the strength of the introductions by other men of prominence. Should one assume that Okuma had been informed about Lea by K'ang or Liang or known of him as a valuable ally of the reformers? Was there more behind Lea than we know? Did he play a larger role than the few facts that have come to light permit us to conclude? We will probably never find the answer. But however Lea approached and managed to have the meeting, once it had taken place and had been broadcast by him in a newspaper interview, it was forgotten and had no more consequences for his career. Count Okuma was never mentioned again in connection with the story of Homer Lea.

Although the meeting with Okuma had no sequel or, rather, because of that circumstance, it set a pattern for various encounters and other events that followed, some of them more important to Lea than the conversation with Count Okuma. Most of them, if not all, came about without discoverable preliminaries. Their preludes, the steps that led to them, remain hidden or obscure or were obscured by Lea himself or by the embroideries of others. The events themselves, however, were highly visible and were made even more so by Lea's fondness and need for publicity. Each time, the story of Homer Lea, which had flagged because of the dearth of discernible facts, came to life again, and the languishing curiosity in his person and his doings was renewed. But after each such episode, there still remained the question what it all would lead up to.

3

General of the Reform Army

On his return to the United States in April 1901 after an absence of ten months, Lea was much less voluble than before his departure. Not only did he fail to explain his accession to the high rank of lieutenant general and his part in the uprisings, he also remained vague about his plans for the future. He left one interviewer in San Francisco with the impression that he was "pass[ing] through here on a flying visit to Washington and London, whence he will return to China."[1] There is nothing to suggest that he went to any of these places. Still, as always with Lea, the possibility that he traveled to London cannot be dismissed entirely. It appeared later that he had some acquaintances in England, including Sir Bryan Leighton, who, in an undated letter, told him of an opportunity for purchasing a large quantity of Mauser pistols.[2] The tone of the letter indicates a certain degree of familiarity and a prior discussion of the Chinese cause. In 1904 Lea suggested to K'ang Yu-wei, who was about to go to London, that he see Leighton. K'ang replied that he made an appointment to meet the man,[3] but it is not known whether he actually saw him.

As to a return trip to China, there is an account that in 1902 Lea took part in another plot for the overthrow of the government in Peking. Yung Wing, then in the United States, was one of the leading figures in that conspiracy, while Lea was said to have been in Shanghai. This attempt at an uprising was said to have been undertaken by a radical, "leftist" wing of the reformers, with Homer Lea among them.[4] But Lea's participation is deduced entirely from O'Reilly's faulty recollection that Lea stayed with him in 1902, when in fact he was in Shanghai in 1901. Thus, there is no basis for believing that Lea returned to China.

After the interviews in which he mentioned further trips abroad, nothing was heard from Lea for two years. Some of his old friends in the

Chinese Empire Reform Association wondered whether he had abandoned their cause. A letter from one asked what he had been doing and whether he was still in contact with their old friends.[5] Apparently he was, for within a few months of this letter Lea emerged from his self-imposed silence with a petition in favor of two members of the reform movement in China. In the summer of 1903, the Peking government asked the authorities of the International Settlement in Shanghai for the extradition of the editors of an antigovernment reform paper. The British Government refused. Writing on August 6, 1903 to President Roosevelt, Lea argued for the United States to take the same attitude as the British. He maintained that he knew the editors personally from his stay in Shanghai from 1900 to 1901 as members of the Chinese Empire Reform Association and that the Association had, during the Boxer Rebellion, kept the peace in the Yangtze Valley and the southern provinces.[6] The latter point was not quite accurate since the society had attempted an armed uprising during that time. Perhaps Lea wanted to convey to the President that the reformers did not share the xenophobic attitude of the Boxers and that its members should not be delivered to a government that had made common cause with the Boxers during their war against the foreign powers. In any case, the United States Government also refused the Chinese Government's extradition request.

While the letter to President Roosevelt was a private communication, Lea was soon enough again in the public eye. Liang Ch'i-ch'ao, the most prominent reformer after K'ang Yu-wei and a vice-president of the Association, had arrived in the United States in May 1903 to visit the chapters of the Chinese Empire Reform Association in various cities.[7] In the course of his trip, Liang also went to Los Angeles where Lea, emerging from his seeming seclusion, played a prominent role in the arrangements surrounding Liang's visit. There is no evidence of Lea's prior knowledge of the trip and the visit in Los Angeles, but he was aware of the date of Liang's arrival in Los Angeles, which he could have ascertained only through reform circles unless he was in direct communication with Liang. There is no indication that he had any direct contact with Liang at any time prior to his arrival unless one assumes the existence of some kind of communication between the two men by the fact that both addressed petitions on exactly the same day to President Roosevelt in favor of the Shanghai editors.

Liang's speeches and his activities were widely reported in the U.S. press. In New York he had an appointment with J. P. Morgan, probably to discuss the financing of the work of the reform movement, but the young reformer, then 30 years old, felt awkward and tongue-tied in the presence of the financial tycoon and left after a few minutes without saying anything. He seemed to have been more relaxed in a talk with Secretary of State John Hay, which lasted for two hours. He also met President Roosevelt. After numerous stops he arrived in California in the middle of October 1903, and Lea acted as organizer and host of the Los Angeles part of Liang's cross-continent trip. Aside from the meetings in Washington, the visit to California was the high point of Liang's trip. In San Francisco and Sacramento he was received by brass bands and escorted through the streets by local dignitaries. He rode in a line of carriages decked with American and Chinese flags and spoke before large assemblies of Chinese from the local communities.[8]

Still the center of public attention, Liang then went down to Los Angeles, and, for a week or ten days there, Lea pulled out all the stops. Meetings, receptions, and banquets filled the schedule. Lea's preparations had been made early and with style. A month before he had asked the Governor of California, George C. Pardee, for permission to have a company of the National Guard escort "the Rt. Honorable Liang Chi Chao, formerly councillor to H. I. M., the emperor of China," from the railroad station to the city.[9] The request was referred to the local commanding officer of the National Guard who granted it. Lea's publicity of the visit started also prior to the event. On the eve of it, the *Los Angeles Times*, the city's leading newspaper, called attention to it under headlines designed to arouse the public's curiosity:

SILKEN ROBES TO BE WORN.
Reformer Liang Chi Chao Is Coming Tomorrow.
Prominent Citizens to Attend a Banquet in His Honor. Great Plans.

The plans, said the article, were discussed by Homer Lea with a committee appointed by the Chamber of Commerce. They called for an elaborate reception at the railroad station. Twenty carriages with local Chinese dignitaries in flowered robes were to gather. The Signal Corps of the National Guard, accompanied by a band, was to escort the distinguished visitor who, with the mayor of the city and General Homer Lea, was to ride in a four-horse carriage, "with attendants in livery." After a reception by the Chinese population of the city, "the guest [was to] be driven to his headquarters at the Angelus Hotel, over which the Imperial Chinese flag will be unfurled as he enters."[10]

The day after Liang's arrival, the *Times* published a lengthy article of several columns on the event it called "historic," "one deeply significant in its bearing upon the current events of nations, despite its insignificant setting." Liang was identified as "one of the leaders of the reform party in China, a councillor of the rightful ruler of the Chinese Empire" and "one of the greatest scholars of China." The procession that formed after his arrival at the depot passed through various streets until it came to the Chinese Board of Trade where a short reception was held for "a select few. . . including the representatives of the Los Angeles Chamber of Commerce and the officers of the military." Later, a lunch was served at the hotel for a small party, which included the guest and his secretary, four members of the Chamber of Commerce, and General Homer Lea. In the evening Liang spoke before a large crowd of Chinese of the need for a modern, enlightened government and the development of industry, business, and education of a united China.[11] In both reports, the members of the Chamber of Commerce present were identified as John Alton, G. G. Johnson, Newman Essick, and Archibald C. Way. Over the next few years the names of the four men would appear repeatedly in connection with Homer Lea's activities.

More stories covered the festivities of the second day. A lavish banquet was given by a Dr. Tom Leung, whose name, incidentally, would also reappear in the story of Homer Lea. Guests of the banquet included prominent Chinese from Los Angeles, San Francisco, and Sacramento. The only non-Chinese present was Homer Lea.[12]

A reception given by the Chamber of Commerce on a subsequent day was "one of the most attractive receptions given by the Chamber in some time."[13] Apparently the interest in it was so great that the members of the Chamber were requested to obtain tickets for themselves and their wives. Visitors to a bankers' convention being held in Los Angeles at the time were also invited. As a result of the publicity, the reception rooms were packed, and almost as many people filed into the large exhibition hall of the Chamber. Four policemen in dress uniform served as doorkeepers. "The richest merchants, the most solid and conservative business men, the city officials and the educators of the schools hereabouts mingled with the general public, white, black and brown, and with the scores of gorgeously appareled Chinese merchants. . . . The chairman of the evening, John Alton, introduced the guest. . . . President F. K. Rule of the chamber of commerce was the first speaker, and he welcomed the distinguished foreigner for the commercial and business interests of the community. Mayor M. P. Snyder followed for the city, [and] after a few words of thanks for the guest of the evening by General Homer Lea of the emperor's army, Liang took the floor. . . . At the close of the addresses the people passed one by one before the two Chinese [Liang and his secretary] and General Lea and were introduced. Fully 600 people met him and many more were unable to reach him during the evening."[14] Liang spoke about the business opportunities that a stable China would offer under the auspices of the reform party. He expressed hope for a peaceful change in his country, although he feared that force might be necessary.[15]

After the successful visit to Los Angeles, Liang left for Vancouver from where he sailed to Japan at the end of October 1903. There is no indication that he and Lea ever again had any contact with each other. Lea's extant papers do not contain a reference to Liang, nor did Liang mention Lea in his account of his U.S. journey. But the visit had provided Lea with an opportunity to get into the limelight and to manage public functions, for which he mobilized the support of the leaders of the community. It made him an accepted spokesman for the reform movement not only in the eyes of local Chinese but also of local dignitaries. Moreover, he was referred to in public for the first time and with consistent frequency as *General* Homer Lea, a title that until then had been used only by himself on his return from China.

Two years later it was said by K'ang Yu-wei that during his visit to Los Angeles Liang Ch'i-ch'ao had conferred on Homer Lea the title of commander in chief of the reformers' military organization in the United States.[16] That organization was the result of a new strategy that the reformers had adopted during and after the ill-fated reform period in 1898 and, particularly, after the defeat of their uprising in 1900. Liang alluded to it in an article that he published while in the United States. Under the heading, "The Educational Reformation of China," the article called education the only hope for political change and named the reform movement synonymous with the "Educational Movement." The reformers, he explained, carried on their educational work through their newspapers, through educational literature, and in numerous schools established by the Chinese Empire Reform Association.[17] Homer Lea said later that there were about 2,000 such schools in China alone. At one point it was decided to establish schools also in Chinese communities abroad, in addition to Japan where Liang was headmaster of a secondary school, which had a curriculum consisting largely of English and French political philosophy.[18] The other schools abroad (in Malaya, Java, Australia, and Canada, where there were no large groups of Chinese students who, as in Japan, had been sent by the Chinese Government to acquire an education in modern subjects not being taught in traditional Chinese schools) were probably concerned with a less formal education. They were "Patriotic Schools" that taught on the elementary level, including "physical culture," which had been part of K'ang's educational program since his first days as a teacher. One such school functioned also in New York. The other schools in the United States, in New York, St. Louis, Oakland, and other cities, were military schools.[19] In 1900 a leading reformer named On Wen Chew, who was probably Ou Ch'ü Chia, a vice-president of the Chinese Empire Reform Association, came to the United States to organize the schools. He and his secretary "traveled all over the United States" and "organized companies [military schools] in San Francisco, Los Angeles, Chicago, Pittsburg, Philadelphia, New York, Baltimore and elsewhere."[20]

Liang mentioned only the "numerous schools" established in China "where they are most needed" but did not mention the schools abroad, especially not the military schools in the United States. In 1905, however, K'ang Yu-wei, during a trip through the United States, not only visited military schools established by his Association but also reviewed their cadets. Furthermore, he did not hesitate to speak of them openly, although he repeatedly stressed that he looked forward to a peaceful change in China and maintained that "the military forces we are training in this and other countries is [sic] not for revolutionary purposes." But he added wistfully, "if when I was in power I had a military force, matters would be different now."[21] This statement leads to the conclusion that the men trained in military schools abroad were to help him to build a military power base if and when he would reassume his political role in China.

It is not known whether Lea met On Wen Chew in 1900 when the military schools were founded. Nor can it be established when he began to take an interest in this paramilitary organization. In May 1905 he stated, "our first school was organized at Los Angeles, Cal., more than a year and a half ago. Now in America there are 30 schools, patterned after this first one."[22] Accordingly, the founding of the military schools coincided more or less with Liang's visit to Los Angeles. If true, this would also refute K'ang's assertion, made a month earlier than Lea's, that On Wen Chew founded the schools in 1900. This discrepancy can perhaps be resolved by assuming that the latter laid the groundwork for the schools but that a nationwide organization under the leadership of Homer Lea was set up only after Liang made him the commander in chief of all the military companies in October 1903. There is an account that Lea became active in the military organization before the middle of 1902. This report came from Ansel O'Banion, one of the first men recruited by Lea to head a company in Los Angeles. Four decades later, O'Banion told a popular writer the story of Homer Lea's work for the Chinese Revolution as seen through his own eyes. The story, *Double Ten*, appeared with the subtitle, *Captain O'Banion's Story of the Chinese Revolution*.[23] These recollections were far from accurate. Moreover, the writer treated them, as he called it, in a "fictionalized" style, as he admitted to someone who questioned some of the facts.[24] The resulting farrago has been in turn responsible for many of the embellished and fictional accounts of Homer Lea's activities that followed.

O'Banion had served as a sergeant with the Fourth Cavalry in the Philippines from 1898 to 1902. He received his honorable discharge from the army on June 18, 1902, at Fort Riley, Kansas. On that occasion he was given a letter for Lea by his commanding officer, Colonel C. C. Carr, which, as reprinted in O'Banion's story, reads as follows:[25]

Lieutenant General Homer Lea
South Bonnie Brae Street
Los Angeles, California

The bearer of this letter is A. E. O'Banion, former 1st Sergeant of Troop A, 4th United States Cavalry, of whom I have previously written you. Without question he has all the qualifications you mentioned in your letter to the Auditor of the War Department.

Yours respectfully,

Adna R. Chaffee,
Major General, United States Army.

The letter, whose reprinted form bears no date, is not available in the original. At the time when it was supposed to have been handed to O'Banion at Fort Riley, Kansas, General Chaffee was serving in the Philippines as the commander of the U.S. troops fighting the insurgents. O'Banion had been a sergeant in the Philippines during General Chaffee's command. Colonel Carr, who is said to have handed O'Banion the letter of introduction, was indeed the commanding officer at Fort Riley at the time.[26] For the letter to be genuine, Lea would have had to be in correspondence with General Chaffee long before June 18, 1902. Lea's surviving papers do not contain the copy of such a letter to Chaffee nor of a letter to the Auditor of the War Department. Nor has anybody been able to find any reference to the matter in the archives of the War Department. We have nothing but the account of an untrustworthy source, who, knowing Lea's later relationship to General Chaffee, may have used the name of this high officer to make his own story more interesting and adventurous. Perhaps unknown to O'Banion, another connection between Chaffee and Lea was General H. G. Otis, the owner of the *Los Angeles Times*, who became a supporter of Lea and took a great interest in Lea's military units. Otis had served under General Chaffee in the Philippines and, therefore, could have acted as intermediary. It is more likely, however, that Lea used his old friends from Stanford, who served in the Philippines as officers of lower rank than General Chaffee, to refer to him noncommissioned officers such as O'Banion. In fact, Lea maintained connections in Manila for years to come. As late as September 1910, Sun Yat-sen asked him for introductions to his friends there.[27]

O'Banion said he waited a full year before he contacted Lea. When he did, Lea hired him as a captain in the Chinese military school in Los Angeles. This would have been, if O'Banion's statement is correct, in June 1903, which is before Liang's visit in Los Angeles. In December of that year and after Liang's visit, Lea engaged two more candidates for officers. One of them, George Whitfield West, kept a diary. On December 19, 1903, West, a retired civil engineer and ex-West Pointer, and Floyd Dessery, also an engineer, met Homer Lea for dinner at the Angelus Hotel in Los Angeles, where the interview took place. West and Dessery agreed to join the military unit. On April 30 the next year, West "attended interesting ceremony in Chinatown, saw a drill and was officially installed as captain by Gen. Homer Lea at the Poo Wong Hui [Pao Huang Hui] Hall." West was put in charge of Company B, while O'Banion headed Company A. On May 4 West and a Lieutenant Prescott started training Chinese troops. Dessery was appointed first lieutenant on May 20. On July 7 West's company was equipped with uniforms of "ill fitting and not too good material." On July 27 the unit "had a stiff competitive drill. . . . Sgts. Yip and Fong won first and second honors, respectively. Gen. H. G. Otis, Col. Fyfe and Schreiber [both of the California National Guard], Lt. Quinian, U.S.A., and several other celebrities [were] present."[28] Lea's school was clearly off to a good start. The presence of U.S. military men showed that, at least at that time, no objections existed to his paramilitary enterprise. Moreover, their material or moral support gave Lea the feeling that, in his capacity of commanding officer of the organization, he was a military man himself and the equal of the high officers sympathetic to his organization. Another question is whether these men looked upon his school, its organization and drill, as a serious military establishment or whether they saw in it an association akin to the Boy Scouts. We know nothing about the means and methods Lea used to gain their interest in his organization. We do know that they attended other functions arranged by Lea such as the receptions for Liang and later for K'ang. General Otis, in particular, remained in contact with Lea and tried to be helpful to him even after Lea's military career, if it can be called that, appeared to have ended.

Articles of incorporation were filed for the school in Los Angeles on November 28, 1904. It was to be called the Western Military Academy and was formed for "instruction in elementary and academic studies, in language and in military science and tactics." The charter did not mention that the students were to be Chinese nor that the school had a connection with any Chinese organization such as the Chinese Empire Reform Association. All of its five trustees were members of the Los Angeles Chamber of Commerce who had officiated or been present at the festivities in Liang's honor, including John Alton, a cashier at the Farmers and Merchants Bank, and Archibald Way, a cashier at the First National Bank of Los Angeles.[29]

The academy was established in an old armory on Marchessault Street, which also served as headquarters of the local branch of the Chinese Empire Reform Association. In addition to Companies A and B, there was a Signal Corps under Lieutenants Rhein and Fountain, with a total complement of about 60 men. A branch in Fresno under Captain W. S. Scott and Lieutenant Ben O. Young counted two dozen recruits. Drilling sessions were held every evening at 8 o'clock for several hours. As the number of men grew to about 120, larger quarters were required. O'Banion said that Lea purchased an old ball park of two and a half acres, which was surrounded by a high board fence. A rifle range was installed there for use on weekends. Occasionally maneuvers would be held in Hollywood on land rented for that purpose.[30] Eventually the academy was established at Carlsbad, San Diego County, on property which had formerly been used as a sanatorium.[31]

The Western Military Academy formed part of what called itself the Chinese Imperial Reform Army (CIRA) with companies in more than two dozen American cities. These companies were organized in conjunction with and attached to the local branches of the Chinese Empire Reform Association. Their commanding officer was Lieutenant General Homer Lea. There is no evidence that he was formally installed as such although, as was mentioned before, Liang was reported to have given him the position. Later accounts reported that Lea traveled all over the country to establish and inspect the units, but there is no proof to that effect, not even the assertion by Lea himself. He did, however, occasionally visit the units in California. The officers were mostly Caucasians, while the soldiers were all Chinese laborers, laundrymen, clerks, merchants, and farmhands. The headquarters of the army was in Los Angeles with Adjutant General George W. Schreiber and Col. Thomas A. McNerney, Supply Officer, serving under Lea. The military units were divided on a geographical basis into four regiments, the first plus the Signal Corps in California, the second in the Midwest, the third on the eastern seaboard, and the fourth in the Pacific northwest.

In addition to its three units in Los Angeles, the California regiment had companies in San Francisco, Fresno, Sacramento, Oxnard and Ventura, Santa Barbara, Hanford, Bakersfield, San Bernardino, and San Diego. The midwestern regiment under Major George W. Gibbs in Chicago had companies in Chicago, Denver, Philadelphia, Pittsburg, Phoenix, and St. Louis. The third under Major George McVickar in New York counted companies in New York, Baltimore, and Boston, and the fourth had units in Portland, Seattle, Spokane, Tacoma, Walla Walla, and Bellingham. There were also units in Vancouver and Victoria, B.C., which formed part of the regiment in the northwest. The officer corps consisted of 3 majors, about 20 captains, and 14 lieutenants. Overall, Lea's "Army" counted about 2,100 men.[32]

The army was financed by the local Reform Associations through the contributions and fees of their 40,000 members. Apparently the funds collected or part of them went to headquarters for defraying general expenses. Officers drew pay, with majors receiving $3,000 per annum with a liberal allowance for expenses, captains $2,800, and lieutenants $1,800. Payment was made in cash rather than by check,[33] perhaps a matter of precaution in case of questions about the legality of the enterprise. As for himself, Lea stated in 1905: "Since I have been connected with the movement I have not drawn a cent of pay, though I have been tendered a large salary. With this noble band working to get their Emperor out of prison and to lead 800,000,000 from the darkness into light, I would consider it criminal to accept pay. When the Emperor is restored, if he has anything to offer, I would then accept."[34]

It is not known how Lea managed financially, but since he was in charge of the funds at headquarters it may be assumed that at least his expenses as commanding officer and his living expenses were refunded to him. There were several reports, including one from O'Banion, that he administered the organization's funds, which were quite large. In a letter written decades later, O'Banion remembered that "Homer cared nothing about money. I first knew him [sic] he had a sizable fortune. He spent it all in getting the Revolutionary movement under way and organizing the Bo Wang Wai [Pao Huang Hui] Society, and when the money started coming in he did not want any of it for himself."[35] As far as is known, however, Lea did not have a fortune of his own. He seems to have inherited a modest amount of money when his father died in 1909, but in general he lived from hand to mouth. In 1904 he still lived at his father's house. After Lea's death his wife had to look for employment to maintain herself.

To return to the subject of the Army, it seems to have been well organized, with its units instructed to report regularly to headquarters on activities and attendance by means of "Parade or Morning Reports."[36] Headquarters mailed out printed "General Orders" signed by Adjutant General Schreiber "by command of Lieutenant General Homer Lea."[37] Pursuant to "G. O. No. 7," Lieutenant Rhein, "Comdg. Co. Signal Corps, First Brigade," submitted on January 16, 1905 a two and a half page typewritten report for December 1904. It noted that his men showed "an aptitude and intelligence that has been a wonderful surprise . . . having made very rapid progress in memorizing the code . . . and some having become very proficient in flag signaling. During the month I appointed three sergeants and four corporals, these men won their stripes upon their merits. . . . One sergeant I find is quite well versed in electrical lines, something that is entirely out of the ordinary with the Chinese. . . . Some recognizance should be taken into consideration in appointing subordinate officers for the Signal Corps." The report ended with a request for a $1,000 grant from headquarters for the purchase of greatly needed signaling equipment.[38]

Major Gibbs of Chicago wrote on stationery with the letterhead "1st BATALLION [*sic*], 2nd REGIMENT INFANTRY—1st BRIGADE, IMPERIAL ARMY," obviously a misnomer, and the Chinese Imperial flag in the left corner. He reported that uniforms had been ordered and a rifle and ammunition secured "whereby we may commence in rifle practice. Our academy has a golden sign 'American Chinese Empire Reform Academy' at the entrance to 311½ S. Clark St. We are painting and cleaning the school room which will be fitted with school equipment. A lady teacher has been secured and the regular daily sessions [of English classes] will be held. . . . I have ordered each company officer to prepare a roster of their companies . . . and to make their weekly parade reports."[39]

The company in Baltimore asked Lea to supply a drill master: "We beg to thank your generosity to arouse our new military spirits that will be a future result to our country through your work. . . . The whole career of our society is the military school that will strengthen our society [the Chinese Empire Reform Association] and country. Now we would like to inform you that we had organized a 'Chinese Military School' in Baltimore, Md. fully four months. We are all freshly waiting, hoping you will send us a teacher *soon*."[40] It is not known whether Lea succeeded in finding a military head for the school. He did so in a number of cases, mostly former noncommissioned officers of the U.S. Army, some of them from the Philippines.

With the exception of Lea's Western Military Academy, the organization in St. Louis was the only one for which incorporation papers were prepared though there is no record that the incorporation actually took place. Under the name "Chinese-American Educational Association," it was described as a night school with "a regular educational course in the common English branches." Its purpose was given as "the improvement and bodily health of the members by classes in drilling and calisthenic exercises." It aimed for "friendly intercourse with each other, and . . . information of its members by maintaining a reading room." As in the case of its sister school in Los Angeles, nothing was said about its political background or its military purpose.[41] General educational courses were, indeed, given in several schools. In the building of the Los Angeles unit, books were kept in the anteroom of the drilling hall to deceive unexpected visitors about the real purpose.

In time, all officers and common soldiers were required to procure uniforms. "General Order No. 8" commanded all men to obtain uniforms "without delay" from Pettibone Brothers Manufacturing Company, 628 Main Street, Cincinnati, or from the same firm at 19 Montgomery Street, San Francisco. The cost was $14 per man if ordered in company quantities. The uniform consisted of a dark blue cap and jacket with light blue jersey trousers. Dress uniforms for officers at $46.25 each were more elaborate and included shoulder straps, belt, saber, and optional saber knots. Fatigue uniforms were khaki coats and trousers, canvas leggings, and campaign hats.[42] As lieutenant general of the army, Homer Lea wore a resplendent blue and gold-braided uniform resembling one for an officer of the same rank in the U.S. Army. His gold buttons showed a coiled dragon surmounted by three stars. A gold star, suspended from his neck by a crimson ribbon, bore a medallion with the likeness of the Kuang-hsü Emperor and the words "To Homer Lea from K'ang Yu-wei." On the left side of his jacket was a medal with the emblem of the Chinese Empire Reform Association.[43]

At the time of Liang's visit, there had not yet been any publicity about the military schools, perhaps because their real work began only after Liang put Lea in command of the national organization. By the end of 1904, O'Banion and his fellow officers had drilled the recruits to the point where Lea, not one to pass up an opportunity for publicity, felt confident enough to have his cadets appear in public. The opportunity presented itself at the Pasadena Tournament of Roses on New Year's Day, 1905.

The initiative was taken by a close friend of Homer Lea from his Stanford days, John York. A native of Pasadena, he spoke to the mayor of the city and on December 14, 1904, confirmed the matter to John Alton, one of the directors of the academy: "I assure you, Mr. Alton, that it is the most earnest desire of the Mayor and the Committee in charge of the parade to have your cadets parade with arms as it will be the only military feature of the parade. If you can arrange for this it will be appreciated by the citizens of Pasadena in aiding to make this tournament a success."[44] The secretary of the academy, Roger S. Page, requested the necessary permission from the Governor of California, and this was granted on December 18 by the Adjutant General of the state.[45]

"A unique incident in history," said a newspaper report on December 31, "will be the appearance in the Pasadena Tournament of Roses Parade on Monday of Capt. O'Banion's Company of the Southwestern [sic] Military Academy. It will be the first time in history that a company of Chinese soldiers has marched on American soil and a great surprise is in store for those who may have looked upon the establishment of the school by Gen. Homer Lea as a burlesque. The Chinese soldiers will be one of the most striking features of the parade."[46] They marched, and march they did "in perfect alignment and cadence rigid as German dragoons."[47] They were "perhaps the most interesting among the marching clubs . . . in their new uniforms . . . and attracted much attention." Fifty-eight men were in "Capt. O'Banion's natty company . . . , leggined and musketed and grim,"[48] with their commander in chief, Lieutenant General Homer Lea, on the reviewing stand.

Next to Lea stood a Chinese official, Wong Kai Kah, a commissioner to the Louisiana Purchase Exposition held in St. Louis in the previous year. He had arrived at the reviewing stand together with Homer Lea.[49] The appearance of a Chinese official who had been sent to the United States by the government of the Empress Dowager T'zu-hsi at the review of a military band hostile to his government is one of the curious conjunctions that Lea's career often brought about. While the significance of such events is sometimes hard to determine, in this case the explanation becomes clear from other actions undertaken by Wong. O'Banion, usually not a very reliable source of information, reported a statement by Lea that "Envoy Wong is secretly on our side."[50] Indeed, quite a number of Chinese officials within and without China are known to have sympathized with the opponents of the regime in Peking.[51] Wong, a Yale graduate, may have been influenced by the reformer Yung Wing, who was the first Chinese graduate of Yale and considered himself the mentor of students who followed him.

Wong showed his sympathies toward the reformers on several occasions. A few days after the parade of Lea's men, Wong paid a visit to his academy. The papers speculated he was investigating the establishment for the Chinese Government. It was alleged that Wong wanted to learn of Lea's plans to train officers from among the Chinese in the United States, whom "he will pour . . . into China to take charge of the troops that are to overwhelm the arch adventureress [sic] of all ages."[52] But Wong's visit to the academy proved to be no threat to its existence. Nothing was heard of an investigation. Apparently Wong had come as a friend and not as an enemy.

That Wong was well acquainted with some reformers and Lea's circle of friends was revealed also by an incident a few months later. In an anti-Chinese raid he was arrested by an immigration officer at the house of Dr. Tom Leung, a reformer, one of Lea's associates and one of Liang's hosts half a year earlier. Another friend of Lea, the attorney John York, prepared the affidavits for Wong to use in his formal complaint about the harassment.[53]

Finally, Wong showed his true colors the following year at a banquet in Los Angeles for K'ang Yu-wei, at which "General Homer Lea presided as toastmaster. The main speaker of the evening, a surprise to all who reported on the event, was Vice-Commissioner Wong." He "voiced in sturdy terms the devotion of the Chinese people to the Emperor and to His Excellency Kang Yu Wei, whom he hoped to see again in power with the Emperor restored to his prerogatives."[54]

Early in 1905, Homer Lea found another opportunity for parading his troops. This time they paid homage to a man on the lower end of the Chinese hierarchy. Ah Mow, the old leader of one of the Tong bands in Los Angeles, "whose name once spread dread among enemies of his soci-

ety . . . had died . . . supposedly from poison administered by an enemy. . . . When the funeral procession was about to move, a group of
soldiers of the Chinese Reform Association, under the command of Gen.
Homer Lea, appeared as an escort. With their queues cut off, and clad in
a uniform not unlike that of the United States Army, the men made an
excellent appearance."[55] Nothing is known about Lea's relations to Ah
Mow and the Hop Sing Tong of which he had been the leader. It is possible that there were connections between that society and the Triads,
which would have made Lea and Ah Mow blood brothers. Or did Lea just
use this opportunity to show off his soldiers and to gain followers among
the Chinese population? That the men had cut off their queues was noticed not only by the newspaper reporter but probably also by the attendants and bystanders at the funeral. It was a sign of antagonism toward
the regime of the Manchus, who had introduced this traditional Manchu
custom among the Chinese people. O'Banion tells an apocryphal story
according to which, during a meeting in honor of Liang Ch'i-ch'ao, there
occurred a mass cutting of the queues of a great number of Chinese.
Liang was said to have been so impressed that he had his own cut too.[56] In
reality, Liang already wore his hair short when he came to the United
States.

     Liang's visit was followed more than a year later by one by K'ang
Yu-wei. In preparation for this event, Lea completed his organization
and had his officers proceed with the drilling of their troops in thorough
fashion. K'ang was not only the head of the reform movement and, as
such, also the chief of its military arm, the Chinese Imperial Reform
Army, but also a major political figure and, in time, a major historical
figure as well. After his arrival, Lea found himself busily engaged as host
for K'ang and as his travel companion during a tour through the United
States, while at the same time fighting off a challenge to his authority
from within the Reform Army. K'ang Yu-wei, too, became drawn into
the strife in Lea's military organization.

     Once before, in 1899, K'ang had tried to enter the United States
from Canada. At the time he had explained the object of his trip: "We
look to America for the realization of what otherwise will be impossible
to obtain—reform in China."[57] Specifically, he tried to obtain financial
help from the Chinese communities and political support from the U.S.
Government. He was not permitted to enter since the Chinese Exclusion
Law required nonlaborers to produce a special certificate issued by the
Chinese authorities. As an exile and an avowed enemy of the Peking regime, K'ang could not procure that paper. In 1905, however, he gained
entry by subterfuge.

     Lea knew of K'ang's intended visit long before he came. As early as
August 1904, he wrote a letter to K'ang in London that K'ang received

when he arrived there from the continent in October of that year. We know of Lea's letter only from K'ang's reply, as it has not survived. If it had, it might have shed light on the connections that existed between Lea and K'ang and K'ang's movement. Lea's letter might also have given a clue as to whether Lea and K'ang had met during Lea's trip to the Orient, which now is quite uncertain. K'ang's reply to Lea is vague on that point: "How thankful I am to hear that you are so kind as to render assistance for our cause. I shall leave for America in a very short time and I hope that I may soon have the pleasure of meeting you."[58] The answer suggests that this was to be their first meeting, but one cannot be sure because, judging from the handwriting, the letter was written by a Westerner for K'ang's signature. It thus may not have expressed K'ang's thoughts accurately. In a second letter, before they saw each other in California, K'ang used the phrase "my good and old friend,"[59] which seems to point to a long acquaintanceship. A few months after K'ang's arrival, Lea stated he knew K'ang because he had "met a friend who was also a friend of His Excellency. This mutual friend brought us together. I offered my services and they were accepted."[60] The identity of this friend and the time and place of Lea's offer remain conjecture. For example, it could have been Yung Wing in 1900. Moreover, after his return from the Orient, Lea spoke of a personal conversation with "Prime Minister Kanyerwa [K'ang Yu-wei]."[61]

At any rate, in his first letter K'ang promised to inform Lea of his arrival, which he apparently did. On February 13, on arriving at the railway station in Portland, Oregon, K'ang was greeted by about 100 local members of the Chinese Imperial Reform Army. This was presumably Company A of the Fourth Infantry Regiment under the command of Captain J. Francis Drake and Lieutenant William Grady. That company was said to have had 44 men, and so the newspaper figure may have been exaggerated. It was K'ang's first encounter with any of the Chinese military units in the United States. He seemed to have been taken aback by the military display for he was quick to explain through his interpreter the peaceful character of his mission in this country. He said that he had come "not to stir up strife and revolution within the Celestial Empire nor to create dissatisfaction among the Chinese in this country but rather encourage them to become better citizens and in that way carry the work of reform back to the mother country."[62]

During K'ang's weeklong stay in Portland, Lea's assistant at headquarters, Colonel Thomas A. McNerney, came to see him, surely at Lea's request. In a letter of February 15, which is no longer available, Lea proposed to come to Portland himself to accompany K'ang on an inspection tour of the military companies in various western cities. K'ang declined on February 18, pleading ill health and suggested Lea make the tour on his own. "I hope to get better soon and then will go to Los Angeles with the hope of seeing my good and old friend as you."[63] It is this phrase that implies he had met Lea before.

After a month in Oregon, K'ang felt well enough to travel. On the way south, he made stops in Fresno and Bakersfield but omitted San Francisco. San Francisco was the American city with the heaviest concentration of Chinese and was one of the six regional headquarters of the Chinese Empire Reform Association, but by 1905 the Chinese community in San Francisco was said to have turned away from the reformers toward the more revolutionary, republican policies of their rival, Sun Yat-sen.[64] But a more probable reason K'ang omitted that important community from his itinerary was another rivalry, that between Homer Lea and Richard A. Falkenberg. On account of that matter, Lea may have kept K'ang from visiting San Francisco all through his long stay in California. More will be said of that rivalry later on.

K'ang arrived in Los Angeles on March 16 with his secretary and interpreter, Chou Kuo-hsien, who had been educated in Great Britain, and Rupert Humer, an Austrian whom K'ang had met in Belgium and who acted as valet and interpreter. In addition, he was accompanied by two bodyguards from Lea's organization, Lieutenants Fook Sang of the Portland contingent and Ben O. Young of Fresno. "Mayor McAleer and several Councilmen, a delegation from the Chamber of Commerce, Gen. Homer Lea and a company of Chinese infantry under Capt. O'Banion and every notable in Chinatown in carriages" waited at the station when it became known that storms had delayed K'ang's train by three days.[65] The newspapers ran stories on the impending visit on each of the following days and fully covered the eventual arrival. The scenario was the same as that on Liang's visit. K'ang was met at the station "by large deputations from Chinatown, General Homer Lee [sic] of the Imperial army, and a company of the local Chinese military force."[66] The mayor was not at hand, however, nor were some of the other notables of the first delegation, but the welcome was "such as never before has been accorded to a man of his race."[67] K'ang was escorted to the hall of the Chinese Empire Reform Association where he found waiting for him "scholars, merchants and working men from Chinatown, ranging in clothes from the richest, gaudiest apparel of the Empire to the bloused field worker. Among these were scattered officers and men of General Homer Lee's [sic] Chinese military battalion, as swagger and correct as a lot of German lieutenants."[68]

A large banquet was held at a Chinese restaurant where "representatives of the bench, of the Chamber of Commerce and military men were present in his honor, as well as the elite of the Chinese colony. . . . Kang Yu-wei came in between rigid lines of Chinese cadets, perfectly disciplined and 'set-up' like West Pointers. . . . Behind him came Gen. Homer Lea in a gorgeous uniform of blue, heavily laced with gold, and with a shoulder cape and spurred riding boots."[69] Among the notables were found Governor La Grange of the Soldiers Home, Colonel C. M. Moses, formerly of the First Colorado Volunteers, Colonel W. J. Fife of the First Washington Volunteers, Judge Waldo M. York, John York, John Alton, G. G. Johnson, A. C. Way, Newman Essick, President Wong Quong of the local Chinese Empire Reform Association, K'ang's entourage, and 150 others. It was at that banquet that Lea acted as toastmaster and Wong Kai Kah gave his astounding speech in favor of K'ang and his reform movement. "This coming from a member of the present government [of China]," concluded the newspaper report, "was startling and portentous of the force of the hold Mr. Wei [K'ang Yu-wei] has on his people."[70] A few days later K'ang paid a visit to Mayor McAleer accompanied by his interpreter and by General Homer Lea.[71]

—4—

The Army under Attack

During his two months in Los Angeles, K'ang fully recovered his health, but during that time he was buffeted by dissension and rivalry within the Chinese Imperial Reform Army, which severely tested his equanimity. These annoying events also put an end to the public functions that had been planned for him in Los Angeles.

On March 23, the day after the visit to the mayor, K'ang was the guest of honor at a luncheon given by Mr. and Mrs. A. B. Hotchkiss of Los Angeles. Present were also K'ang's secretary, Chou Kuo-hsien, and Dr. Tom She Bin, a leading member of the San Francisco chapter of the Chinese Empire Reform Association and one of the small group of reform leaders before whom Lea had presented his plan for a revolutionary war prior to his trip to China in 1900. Lea was not mentioned as one of the guests.[1]

Some days later the same society column reported on a dinner "given on March 27 . . . at the home of Mrs. A. B. Hotchkiss . . . in honor of His Excellency Kang Yu Wei, the Prime Minister of Emperor Kuang Hsu of China, and his military chief, Gen. R. A. Falkenberg, the commander-in-chief of the reorganized Chinese Imperial Army, who has come down from San Francisco to meet his eminent chief. Gen. Falkenberg was commissioned some years ago by Hon. Leong Kai Chew [Liang Ch'i-ch'ao], adviser in His Majesty's Cabinet of Ministers and colleague of His Excellency Kang Yu Wei." The item went on to report that K'ang "had decided to strictly uphold his colleague's—Hon. Leong Kai Chew—official appointment of Gen. Falkenberg, as the commanding general, expressing the utmost confidence in Hon. Leong's wisdom, and His Excellency added: 'I have the same confidence in our commanding general, Falkenberg, as a soldier and a strategist and I feel assured that China with General Falkenberg's help will be one of the foremost nations within a much shorter time than Japan succeeded in forging to the first rank.' ''[2] The notice was accompanied by full-length photographs of K'ang and "Gen. R. A. Falkenberg," the latter in a uniform not less resplendent than that of Lea.

In this seemingly innocuous way, by a polite announcement in the society column, the existing rivalry between Lea and Falkenberg first came to public attention. It was to remain in the open for some time, consuming much of Lea's and also of K'ang's time as it became increasingly confused and colorful.

There is a theory that great historical figures and events tend to occur twice, once as a tragedy and again as a farce. Homer Lea was certainly not a great historical figure, but the theory applies perhaps also to lower levels of historical significance. While Lea's bizarre life story contained certain elements of tragedy, Richard A. Falkenberg's just as surely presented aspects of a farce.

Falkenberg claimed to have been born in Louisiana, but he was probably a German by birth.[3] He said that he was educated in Prussian military academies and served with distinction as a lieutenant in the Franco-Prussian War of 1870–71.[4] In 1899 he gave his age as 45,[5] which would have made him about 16 during that war. In the United States, he first became known as a prize fighter under the name of Captain Dick and was once knocked out of the ring by the famous Billy Manning.[6] His entrance into the political arena came in January 1894 when, as Captain R. A. Falkenberg of the Arizona Territory, he wrote to the War Department asking for recognition of his services at the Battle of Little Bighorn. He claimed to have been the sole white survivor of that battle in 1876, Custer's Last Stand. He had joined Custer, he said, independently with his own men at his own expense and served as an Indian scout.[7] Recognition was not granted. Washington heard from him again four years later when he offered President McKinley his assistance in the war in the Philippines. He would bring his own contingent, the First South California Volunteer Cavalry.[8] As to his military experience, he claimed service in the Riel Rebellion of 1885 in Canada as captain and commander of army scouts, for which he was decorated with a silver cross and a gold medal. "Although mortally wounded I completely recovered in a few months."[9] He also mentioned an offer of a colonelcy in 1890 in the Honduran army by emissaries of the President of Honduras, but the war in which he was to serve "blew over" before he had a chance to show his military proficiency.[10] Less than two weeks later, the offer became an actual commission as a colonel in the Honduran cavalry.[11] To ingratiate himself with the Republican president, Falkenberg recounted how he had intended to serve in the Spanish-American War but was prevented from doing so by "Democratic Intrigues."[12] Although the government informed him that it could not make use of his services and troops,[13] he continued to bombard the President, the Secretary of War, and the secretary to the President with letters and telegrams, proposing, among other plans, to join his volunteers with the "dashing regiment" of "rough riders" of Colonel Edmund F. English of Yankton, South Dakota.[14]

With possible serious consequences to himself, he proceeded to send telegrams using the name of Senator George G. Perkins of California, recommending himself for service. The resulting charge of fraud by the Adjutant General implicated also an "Assistant Captain Fernand Parmentier." Falkenberg's claim that he was a "Major and Commandant" in the California National Guard was found equally fraudulent. Nor could he be found in the roster of men who had served in the Spanish-American War.[15] It seems the charges were not pursued, and the case was dropped. Eventually and amusingly, Falkenberg succeeded in his determination to go to the Philippines, if only on board an animal transport as an employee of the Presidio in San Francisco. This came to light when Mrs. R. A. Von Falkenberg of Brooklyn, New York, complained to the War Department that he had left without her "knowledge or sanction. Of course," she added, "I am not sorry that he engaged as a scout if he will be of service to his country. What I would like to know is, what rank does he come under and what his salary will be as a scout." She must have known Falkenberg as a member of the minor German nobility, as the prefix "Von" indicates. In any case, the answer to her letter was surely disappointing. He was a "first-class packer at a compensation of $50.00 a month."[16]

How and why Falkenberg became interested and involved in the affairs of China and, particularly, in the political efforts of the reformers is not known. The U.S. archives show that as early as September–October 1900 he started his efforts on behalf of the reformers. Once again he addressed himself to the highest ranks of government. On October 6, 1900, "R. A. Falkenberg, General CER [Chinese Empire Reform] Army and Representative Extraordinary of Emperor Kwong-Hsui [Kuang-hsü] and Chinese Empire Reform Association," sent a petition to Secretary of State John Hay to support the reinstatement of the young Emperor. Falkenberg's letter to the Secretary alleged that on August 27 he had written in this matter to the U.S. President but not received an answer. He attached to his letter to the Secretary a copy of a similar petition he said he had sent on September 14 to the Queen of England, the Emperor of Germany, and the Mikado of Japan, confirming cables dispatched to them.[17] The timing of these first actions shows that he may have heard in the Philippines of Lea's efforts to recruit army personnel or learned of it through Lea's publicity or from candidates in the United States. Apparently he did acquire some connections to reform circles in San Francisco and these may have enabled him to meet On Wen Chew in 1900, when this man came to the United States to found the military schools of the reformers.

There is no information available on Falkenberg from October 1900 until the summer of 1903. At that time, a few months before the arrival of Liang Ch'i-ch'ao, he started a campaign for the post as commanding general of the Chinese Empire Reform Army, a position he had already claimed to occupy in October 1900 in his petition to the Secretary of State. "I have had a position offered me as General in the Chinese Reform Army," he wrote to the Governor of California, George C. Pardee, "and they are investigating my military record, which is without a flaw, since 1872." The Governor could help him to obtain the coveted position by appointing him a colonel on his staff before the expected arrival of the Chinese commissioner who would hopefully make him a general. "If I could show the Chinese Commissioner a Colonel's commission on your staff," he pleaded with the Governor, "that would decide the question in my favor, even if I were to resign again almost immediately from your staff." He added an inducement to the governor: "I had a very decided [sic] and strong influence with the German voters, and as you saw by the returns, not one vote went astray." He gave the names of various people who could vouch for him, including "Mr. Washburne, of the Los Angeles Times, Secretary of the L. A. Republican Committee, an old friend of mine. [He] was my Lieutenant during the Spanish war in 1898 in the First California Cavalry Regiment (Provisional), founded by myself," forgetting that, when he wrote to President McKinley, he said he had been prevented from serving in that war. He also referred to an honorary membership in the German Sharpshooter Club (Schützen Club) of San Francisco and signed the letter as "Major." The Governor, however, did not find it appropriate to appoint him to his staff and put him off with a polite promise to reconsider in the future.[18] The Chinese Commissioner of whom Falkenberg spoke in his letter to the Governor must have been Liang, but Falkenberg's name was not mentioned in any of the reports on Liang's visit, nor did Liang mention Falkenberg in his account of his North American journey.

Some time after Liang's visit, in February 1904, Falkenberg addressed another letter to the Governor, in which he requested permission to form a Chinese company of the National Guard. "The California-born Chinese population [has] grown very rapidly within the past few years" and "Mr. Wong Kin, a bright, educated young Chinese, connected with the U.S. Post office here [in San Francisco], is at the heart of the movement and informs me, that he has now 35 Chinese in his company, who are all . . . willing to serve in the National Guard." Falkenberg signed the handwritten letter as "General."[19]

The Governor apparently refused because less than three months later he received another petition from Falkenberg, who this time asked for permission to organize a military company to be known as the "American Born Chinese Military Cadets." The petition was signed by about 40 persons with Chinese-sounding names, the first signature being that of Wong Kin. It also carried the signatures of the Chinese Consul General and the Vice-Consul General and a number of individuals, most of them with Western names, who identified themselves as businessmen and professionals. Falkenberg signed this time as "Pres. Standard R. Oil Co."[20] The second request was rejected with the explanation that it might set a precedent for similar demands from other groups.[21]

The next time Falkenberg was heard from was the Hotchkiss luncheon and the famous dinner by the same hosts on March 27, 1905. The announcement of the dinner in the local newspaper's society column was meant as Falkenberg's challenge to Lea's position as head of the Chinese Imperial Reform Army. The resulting battle between the two contenders continued to be fought out in the newspapers until its eventual denouement. The journalists had a field day in questioning and even goading Falkenberg and K'ang and the latter's secretaries and reporting the respective statements. Homer Lea gave no interviews and kept in the background. But he was active behind the scenes and, in particular, brought pressure to bear upon K'ang to resolve the controversy in his favor.

To begin with, Falkenberg's announcement that had been given to the press by Hotchkiss was read to K'ang by a reporter. "The chivalrous and stately ex-Premier got a boiling case of plain American 'mad,' " and sent his secretary to Falkenberg with a message that left the latter "nervous." A renewed call on K'ang by the reporter found K'ang "raging" and unwilling to be interviewed. Instead he let his secretary, Chou Kuo-hsien, and another secretary from his entourage do the talking. It appeared that the Hotchkiss release had been sent out behind his back, but it was conceded that K'ang had addressed Falkenberg as commander in chief. This was to have been "a slip of the tongue," because, in reality, "Gen. Lea is commander of all the military schools in America." The other secretary added, "I am the secretary of Mr. On Wen Chew who came from China to organize these military schools under orders from His Excellency, Kang Yu Wei. . . . We organized companies in San Francisco, Los Angeles, Chicago, Pittsburg, Philadelphia, New York, Baltimore and elsewhere. Falkenberg was made commander of the San Francisco military school; that is all the authority he has. Gen. Homer Lea was made commander of all the military schools in the United States. Mr. On Wen Chew ordered all to report to Gen. Lea."[22]

In what was called an "official gazette," Falkenberg clarified his position:

General Falkenberg is the only regularly appointed officer and military representative commissioned by the Emperor Kwong Sui's [Kuang Hsü] personal representative, Leong Kai Chew [Liang Ch'i-ch'ao], the second adviser in his majesty's Cabinet. The General is a strategist of renown, and his commission was duly signed on October 5, 1903 and sealed with the great imperial reform seal, although appointed in 1900. . . .[23]

However, when confronted by the statements made by K'ang and his secretaries and under pressure from K'ang, he modified his stand somewhat: "Why, this boy Homer Lea—oh I have no wish to be harsh with him. In fact His Excellency sent his secretary to me this morning with such a suggestion. The fact is he is the head of these military schools. I have nothing to do with them. Oh they are just boys' schools, have nothing particular to do with the army. . . . I suppose Homer Lea might be called a captain or major or even a colonel, seven or eight companies, you know these military schools are equivalent to. . . . I am supreme in my authority over all the troops of the Chinese Imperial Reform Army. I am the only one who has a commission over them all." The commission was to have been granted to him by On Wen Chew.[24]

Probably at K'ang's behest, he followed up this patronizing explanation with the release of a formal statement.[25]

The American public seems to labor under the misapprehension that the Commander-in-Chief of the Chinese Imperial Reform Army attempted to claim credit for having organized the Chinese Military Cadet companies in the United States and to have assumed command over these cadets. Such, however, is not the case and we desire to give herewith full credit to Homer Lea as the founder of these various companies and accordingly recognize him as the commander of these Chinese cadet companies, which, however, have nothing whatever to do with the Chinese Imperial Reform Army in China.

We may possibly in the future, in case of an emergency, accept them individually or as a body for our Chinese Imperial Army depending upon circumstances.

(Signed) R. A. Falkenberg,
General Commanding C.I.R.A.
F. Parmentier,
Lieut. General and Chief of Staff.

Lieutenant General Parmentier was identified in the paper as a young architect in Los Angeles.

By making a distinction where none existed, Falkenberg's statement "to the American public" conceded nothing while relegating Lea to a mere head of military schools. Falkenberg still considered himself in charge of the Reform Army, although he placed it in China. Nor could Lea have been satisfied by the "warm tribute" paid to him by K'ang's secretary, who called him "not a military man . . . but . . . a profound student of military science . . . a brilliant man, a deep thinker and a reader of philosophy. He is warmly admired by Kang Yu Wei whose appointment he holds."[26] The nature of that appointment in relation to the Reform Army was not specified, however, and that was for Lea the main issue. He wanted to be a military leader and to be recognized as such. To get a more specific answer, he had his soldiers in Los Angeles march the next day to K'ang's residence "begging for the truth." To give the demarche more weight, he arranged for Captain Chung, rather than a Caucasian officer, to act as their spokesman. K'ang explained "to Capt. Chung that Leong Kai Chew [Liang Ch'i-ch'ao] told him all about the appointment of Gen. Lea, but he said nothing of Falkenberg." He promised the men he would cable Liang for a confirmation. "This message was cabled," but the text of the cable is not available, nor is it known whether it was answered. Moreover, K'ang said he had not addressed Falkenberg as commander in chief at the famous dinner. He volunteered, however, that Falkenberg had offered the reform movement a loan of ten million dollars, to be paid in September when Falkenberg as president of the Standard Rock Oil Company would receive his dividends from that firm.

Chung offered the press, and possibly also K'ang, a few comments of his own on Falkenberg. Falkenberg had recently written unsuccessfully to Los Angeles asking for money because his activities for the Reform Army had landed him in jail. In the meantime, said Chung, Falkenberg had been fired from the command of the San Francisco company.[27]

In the meantime, too, Hotchkiss, whom Falkenberg had made a brigadier general, after the successful dinner at his house, fell ill "as a result of the unkind aspersions cast upon his triumphant banquet,"[28] and a few days later suffered a fatal stroke, "quite unexpected, following closely upon the reception . . . at his home to Kang Yu Wei." The next day, K'ang, who had become exasperated, left town until "the Falkenberg incident blows over."[29] The removal of Hotchkiss and K'ang from the field of battle did not stop what, by Hotchkiss's death, had changed from a farce to a tragicomedy. On Falkenberg's charge, O'Banion and a certain William R. Sager were arrested for attempted blackmail. Sager was said to have asked for $5,000, for which he would have someone supply Falkenberg with certain secrets of Lea's organization. If Falkenberg refused to pay, he would be subjected to a campaign that would injure him in his battle with Lea and drive him out of town. When arrested, O'Banion denied any knowledge of the blackmail and so did Lea when sent for by the police. Both maintained that, to the contrary, Sager had tried to procure information from them. In the end, O'Banion and Sager were released, and Lea, turning the tables, now accused Sager of collusion with Falkenberg.[30]

Finally, K'ang had no alternative but to take a clear stand in the controversy about the army's command and, on Lea's insistence, issued a proclamation on April 7 in his favor:[31]

> To the American People: I desire to announce that Gen. Homer Lea of Los Angeles is the only one recognized and appointed by me as the general of all Chinese military schools in America, and furthermore, I have appointed no one such as "General Commanding," or any officer of the so-called "Chinese Imperial Reform Army," which is not in existence, and any person claiming such rank or position in the "Imperial Reform Army" is considered an impostor.
>
> Kang Yu Wei
> Grand president
> Chinese Empire Reform Association

The proclamation was disseminated to local newspapers and to Chinese papers in both the United States and Asia and posted in Chinese on red rice paper in Los Angeles's Chinatown. Once this had been accomplished, "General Lee [sic] satisfied with his vindication left the same night for a visit of inspection of the Chinese military companies throughout the state, and Captain O'Banion put his battalion through the manual of arms as usual."[32] Lea may or may not have gone on an inspection tour; he may have given out that information only to escape the reporters. In fact, the same day it was stated, though incorrectly, he had left with K'ang on a tour through the United States with London as the final destination.[33] But Lea must have found K'ang's statement not to his entire satisfaction, since it denied the existence of the Reform Army of which he claimed command. K'ang's denial of the existence of a Chinese army on U.S. soil was designed to avoid problems with the U.S. authorities. The publicity over the Falkenberg controversy must have made him quite uncomfortable. Indeed, he might have preferred to release no public statement, but, pressured by Lea and beleaguered by the press, he had no choice. By then he may also have been informed that Falkenberg's army consisted merely of a certain number of commissions granted through the mails. Moreover, he must have recognized that he had been beguiled by Falkenberg's grandiose offer of a loan of ten million dollars. He may not have had the time or inclination to inquire about Falkenberg's business venture, the Standard Rock Oil Company. According to its letterhead, which listed Falkenberg as president, the company was capitalized at $500,000 and owned 320 acres of oil lands in Napa and Coalinga Counties and 6,000 acres of asphaltum lands in Santa Clara County. My search in various archives did not lead to any trace of the existence of the company. In any event, its business activities could not have been very extensive, given the time and efforts its president devoted to extraneous matters and his eagerness to serve in other posts. Its greatest asset was, perhaps, its well-chosen name, which might have led unwary souls like K'ang to confuse it with the Standard Oil Company, especially when its president spelled it as Standard R. Oil Co.

For all that, Falkenberg was not yet ready to give up. He sought out K'ang to protest the treatment he had received. He listed his services to the reformers' cause. In particular, he claimed that he, together with his second in command, Lieutenant General Parmentier, had saved the Emperor's life when the Empress Dowager was about to have him murdered. At his own expense, at the cost of $35,000, he had sent cables to King Edward VII, Kaiser Wilhelm II, and Czar Nicholas and dispatched Parmentier to the various courts and gotten them to intercede on behalf of the Kuang-hsü Emperor. At this point K'ang was said to have lost his temper and treated him as an impostor.[34]

But the question, who appointed whom to what and when, still remains unanswered. As we know, Falkenberg had earlier called himself a "General C.E.R. (Chinese Empire Reform) Army" in his letter to Secretary of State John Hay of October 1900, as he had done in letters supposedly sent the previous month to the heads of state of Germany, England, and Japan.[35] He explained later that the appointment had been made in 1900, which is when On Wen Chew was in the United States, but the actual commission was issued only in October 1903.[36] During the controversy with Lea, Falkenberg was reported to have shown K'ang's secretary "an imposing-looking document done in green dragons and red seals and dated San Francisco, . . . a commission as 'general' from Leong Kai Chew [Liang Ch'i-ch'ao] . . . given to him at a banquet in San Francisco in October, 1903." He added, "Dr. Tom Leong [Lea's reformer friend] passed upon the signature of Leong Kai Chew and pronounced it genuine. Gen. Falkenberg [also] produced a number of letters, some from Kang Yu Wei and some from Leong Kai Chew, addressing him as general and discussing the situation with him."[37] Falkenberg's claim to have been appointed already in 1900, is obviously spurious. If he were a general, he would not have asked Governor Pardee prior to Liang's arrival in 1903 to give him a commission as a colonel so that he could be appointed a general by the "Chinese Commissioner."

As to the document issued by Liang, we have only Falkenberg's untrustworthy statement that it was declared to be genuine. Even at the time when he produced it, there were voices that called it a forgery.[38] On the other hand, it is fairly certain that he was in charge of the military unit in San Francisco, as stated by one of K'ang's secretaries. During the controversy he was "fired" from that post not only because of the debacle with K'ang but also for alleged financial irregularities.[39] His requests to Governor Pardee for permission to form a Chinese company of the National Guard and one of "American Born Chinese Military Cadets" can be understood as attempts to withdraw the unit in San Francisco from Lea's organization and command. This would have been effectively accomplished if the company were attached to the National Guard or otherwise legally established as a separate unit. As it turned out, Wong Kin, the young Chinese who, as Falkenberg had said, was the driving force behind these attempts was a member of the existing company and later, together with the other soldiers, served under Lea.[40]

As for Lea, his title of general was self-given, just as much as Falkenberg's. But he had a valid claim to the position of commanding officer of the Chinese Imperial Reform Army. This claim was recognized by the Chinese Empire Reform Association in the United States, whose military units in the various American cities reported to him as their chief. His position was also recognized by K'ang even before he came to Los Angeles. While his official proclamation "To the American People" spoke of Homer Lea only as the appointed "general of all Chinese military schools in America," the denial of the existence of the army did not, in fact, diminish Lea's rank and position. To the contrary, in the proclamation K'ang expressly granted Lea the title of general, thus ratifying Lea's years' old use of it. Whether K'ang, a private individual and head of a private political association, had the authority to appoint him a general is another matter. However, other private organizations such as the Salvation Army also have their "generals."

Although the conflict between Lea and Falkenberg was widely publicized and its details were easily ascertainable, various erroneous or fictitious versions later found their way into print. A Chinese source reported that Falkenberg, supposedly a retired army officer, offered his services to the reformers during Liang's visit in 1903. Liang was said to have accepted the offer and given Falkenberg, in a sealed and stamped document, the title of a "Grand Marshal of the Chinese Reform Army." Later he was said to have granted Lea, who had also offered his assistance, the same title. Thereupon Lea and Falkenberg engaged in a controversy about whose commission was the rightful one. Lea's was found to be genuine as it bore not only a seal but also Liang's signature. Liang then conclusively appointed Lea as the head of the reformers' military organization in America.[41]

The author of O'Banion's memoirs presents two different accounts in his two books on events that led up to the Chinese Revolution. According to the first account, Falkenberg never had a commission from Liang. When K'ang came to the United States, Falkenberg fabricated a document with Liang's forged signature, appointing him head of the military organization. In addition to the forged signature, the document bore the genuine imprint of the "Great Seal of China." This seal, without which no edict of the Manchu dynasty had any validity, had disappeared when the Empress Dowager fled during the Boxer Rebellion and had somehow gotten into the hands of K'ang. K'ang was said to have had it in his possession when he was in Los Angeles, but Dr. Tom She Bin, a secret partisan of the Peking regime and a friend of Falkenberg, stole it from K'ang and used it on the forged document.[42]

In the second account, it was Liang who had the Great Seal when he was in the United States, having been entrusted with it by the Kuang-hsü Emperor. Falkenberg was said to have contended that Liang used it when giving him his commission. But Liang had asked him not to present the document until it could be proven that Lea, as was suspected, acted as spy for Sun Yat-sen. That time seemed to have come during K'ang's visit in 1905, when Falkenberg attempted to take over the reformers' military organization with K'ang's connivance. But it could be proven to K'ang, who had the Great Seal in his possession, that the document allegedly signed and sealed by Liang was a forgery. Lea won out while Falkenberg "sued Liang in the American courts, and exposed the whole plot to make him head of the Chinese Imperial Reform Army. The lawsuit, however, came to nothing. It was quietly hushed up."[43]

As fantastic and contrived as the stories sound, the author of the two books really believed in the existence of the Great Seal and its presence in the United States. He also thought it had been stolen from K'ang or had disappeared in some other way. In 1945 he became nearly convinced it had finally been found. Somebody who, as a young man, had been connected with Lea's organization claimed to have identified it in the Chinese collection of the Seattle Art Museum. But upon examination it was found that the object, while probably the seal of a Chinese emperor, could not be authenticated as the Great Seal of China. It was then speculated that the seal in Seattle had been brought to the United States following the looting of the Forbidden City during the Boxer Rebellion. And so the mystery of the Great Seal of China remained unsolved.[44]

Around the time of Falkenberg's second petition to Governor Pardee, the *New York Times* reported from St. Paul, Minnesota, that attempts were being made to recruit officers in the United States for a "Chinese Imperial Reform Army." Letters had gone out to a great number of individuals, mostly members of the National Guard and veterans of the Spanish-American War, from Edmund F. English of Yankton, South Dakota, the same man whose "dashing regiment" Falkenberg had offered to President McKinley in 1899. The letters implied that English was acting for the Chinese Government,[45] as the following correspondence indicates.[46]

Chinese Imperial Reform Army.
General Staff.
Yankton, S.D., 4/22,1904.

Dear Sir:

Will you accept appointment as 2nd Lieut. in above Army?
Modeled after U.S.A. Pay goes with rank. To modernize the Chinese
Army. Transportation furnished. Be three months before we go. You
are recommended by Frank Eberle. Must be no newspaper notoriety
whatever. Includes all branches of service. Commissions issued when
Chinese Government so orders. Span.Am. soldiers preferred. Making application in own handwriting. State age, married or single.
Experience, sign name in full. Have you any friends, qualified, who
will accept appointment?

I am very truly,
(signed) Edmund F. English.

English even asked the Governor of Minnesota for the names of
men he might recommend "for appointment in CIRA." The Governor
apparently complied, for English thanked him, stating he had "placed
them in a roster as Second Lieuts. of Infantry."[47]

Some of the recipients of English's letters got in touch with Secretary of War William Howard Taft. Others contacted the State Department, which in turn brought the matter to the attention of the Chinese
Legation in Washington. The Legation replied it knew of English's activities but disavowed his authority to grant commissions in any Chinese
army, much less in a nonexistent Chinese Imperial Reform Army.[48] The
Minnesota authorities also asked the Chinese Legation for information.
In addition, they communicated with the War Department, which referred them to the Attorney General. The Post Office, too, began an
inquiry for fraudulent use of the mail.[49]

At that point, Falkenberg may have felt that he was getting more
attention than he had bargained for. Lieutenant General and Chief of
Staff Parmentier interceded with the State Department on behalf of his
commanding general, R. A. Falkenberg, and, in effect, made a retrac-
tion. The letter, which was addressed to Secretary of State John Hay, bore
the heading "Chinese Imperial Reform Army, General Commanding"
and was accompanied by a press release supposed to have been sent to the
Associated Press four weeks earlier. Both the letter and the release, to
judge from their wording and style, appeared to have been drafted by
Falkenberg. Both communications denied that any laws had been violated and that any recruiting had taken place. Nobody, in fact, had any
authority to enlist anybody. What had happened was that the names of

U.S. citizens had been accepted for the commanding general's roster.
General E. F. English, a divisional commander on that roster, had been
indiscreet in talking and writing too freely. This indiscretion as well as
"some young, over-ambitious lieutenants and some unwise remarks
from Yankton" were to blame for the unfortunate misunderstanding.
Moreover, the Chinese Ambassador in Washington was "poorly informed as to denounce this movement as a revolutionary scheme of reformers. . . . Her Majesty, the Dowager Empress of China, is fully informed of this movement, possesses full details and data, and has the
matter . . . under consideration. The Chinese Imperial Reform Army is
by no means formed to depose the Empress, but to protect the Throne
against the Chinese Republicans under Dr. Sun Yat Sen . . . and other
revolutionary societies. This army is intended to be the proper protection
of the higher class of Chinese Merchants and officials, and will be offi-
cered by men of superior ability. . . . It is unjust and detrimental to the
characters of the generals in command" to consider them as revolutionaries because they "would not stoop to menace the Throne of China with
revolution and visionary schemes of adventurers. Neither need the Government of the United States have any cause to interfere in any shape and
manner." This appeal to the sense of U.S. officials for law, order, and
authority was coupled with an appeal to their political instincts. The
President could gain great political advantages from Falkenberg's activities because "the officers who have thus far been placed on our list, some
two thousand or so, . . . are all either influential business or professional
or else literary or newspaper men, controlling the minds and votes of
their immediate community. Every one of these men, some of them being democrats, are politically informed that General Falkenberg is a
strong adherent and admirer of President Roosevelt, and that he would
remove from the list the name of any officer who should be known to
speak or act in a manner prejudicial to the President's future welfare."
Furthermore, Falkenberg offered his services to the U.S. Government in
foreign policy matters and suggested that it use him in the impending
negotiations with China about a treaty of commerce, as "he alone is
posted what the Chinese reasonably expect." He did not consider, just as
Homer Lea was to do some years later, that such action on his part would
pose a conflict of interest. Falkenberg's lack of political principles
showed up in his indifference as to whom he served, the regime in Peking
or the reformers, the American or the Chinese government. Falkenberg
was well known, Parmentier asserted, to Chinese high officials as well as
the U.S. Government, but he requested "that the Government will not
make public the Commanding General's name."[50] He did not explain
his request for secrecy. Was it made to avoid, for the time being, a confrontation with Homer Lea?

For Lea's military units, the publicity caused by Falkenberg's attempts to create his "mail order army" and to usurp Lea's authority as head of the Reform Army, was almost a disaster. The government discovered that it might have a subversive foreign army on its soil. For almost a year, Lea found his army under attack. In December 1904 the *Philadelphia Inquirer* reported that the Secret Service, under the personal direction of its chief, John E. Wilkie, had uncovered a conspiracy "by a large body of Chinamen" in the United States to overthrow the rule of the Empress Dowager. Great dissatisfaction was said to exist in the army of the Manchu government and in certain court circles. European officers were believed to be training sections of the Chinese army to support the overthrow of the regime, and now U.S. National Guard officers in "a score or more of the states have been offered huge salaries to go to China and train certain regiments." The revolutionaries were training Chinese soldiers at the Philadelphia headquarters of the Chinese Empire Reform Association, as they were in many American cities and, indeed, all over the world. This revolutionary movement, the paper reported, was connected with others in certain Chinese provinces.[51]

The investigation was followed by more government action. Lea's companies came under the scrutiny of the Governor of California and the state authorities of New York. In California Lieutenant J. Alexander in the office of the Adjutant General came to the conclusion that the Chinese military company in Fresno was violating the law by carrying arms without proper license. In April 1905, during K'ang's visit in Los Angeles, Governor George C. Pardee became involved when a lawyer for the Fresno branch of the Chinese Empire Reform Association, W. D. Crichton, claimed that the Governor had issued a permit for the unit to carry arms.[52] The situation was discussed at length in several San Francisco papers. Additional transgressions of the Fresno unit came to notice: "The State military inspecting officers to-day condemned a local company of Chinese soldiers and intimated that their commander, Curtis Neal, who also holds the office of second lieutenant of Company C, Sixth Regiment, National Guard, California, would be courtmartialed for the offense of being connected with a foreign military company. The Chinese organization is known as Company D, First Regiment, Chinese imperial army. It was organized here six months ago, supposedly with the consent of the Governor. Lieutenant J. Alexander of the Governor's staff declared to-day that no such consent had ever been given and that the whole company was subject to fine and imprisonment."[53]

The Governor now requested that Crichton produce any document purporting to be a license to carry arms. Crichton explained that he was acting for a group of Chinese merchants, presumably the Reform Association, not for the military organization, with which he had no connection. He had been in contact with the latter on only one occasion, when he had asked Homer Lea whether the company had permission to carry arms. Lea had told him it did, but that there had been "some considerable difficulty in persuading the Governor that it was a school." Of course, Crichton assured the Governor, the members would be ready to desist if the Governor believed that the company was not acting within the law. A local politician, Dr. Chester Rowell, gave the Governor the same assurance. The latter told both Crichton and Dr. Rowell that the law was being violated and instructed the District Attorney in Fresno to "take such action as [he] may see proper for the enforcement of the law." As to Lea's contention that a license had been granted, he rejoined, tongue in cheek, that "Homer Lea must be a 'diplomat.' I [saw] him once, but he did not 'persuade' me to do anything, and he did not even ask for a license for the company in question."[54]

The meeting referred to had been requested by Lea as soon as he heard of the difficulties at Fresno. On April 25 he sent a telegram to Governor Pardee: "Would be Honored if your Excellency Could Dine with me tomorrow Evening Eight Oclock Palace Hotel in San Francisco to meet Imperial Chinese Consul General Informal Answer."[55] A telegram with the same invitation went to Dr. David Starr Jordan, president of Stanford University, with the added note that several army and navy officers would also be present at the dinner.[56] Answers to the telegrams cannot be found, but from the Governor's statement it appears that the meeting did take place. Lea, too, referred later to a conference with the Governor in which he "told him [that he] would welcome an investigation."[57] Lea did not say, however, that he had taken the opportunity to ask permission for the academy's soldiers to carry arms.

Lea's actions show his indirect way of trying to overcome obstacles. He knew the Governor had not granted a permit, but, instead of confronting the problem directly, he relied on public relations to soften the Governor's attitude and to mitigate the impact of the District Attorney's investigation. Since he needed respectability for himself and his project, he invited Dr. Jordan and various military officials. Moreover, the presence of the Chinese Consul General was designed to show a certain measure of official Chinese countenance of the military organization. His presence, if indeed he were present, is further evidence that this official of the Manchu government was friendly with its opponents, which he had shown previously by his support of Falkenberg's petition for establishing a company of Chinese-American cadets.

Lea's indirect approach, however, was unsuccessful. The District Attorney persisted in his demand that the Fresno company abstain from further drilling. Even though the Reform Association replied that "the officers supposed and had been informed by one General Lee [sic] that

the permission required by Section 734 of the Penal Code had been procured," it agreed to discontinue the questioned activities temporarily,
until an official permission had been granted.[58] Lea for his part per-
severed, and now took the position that the Fresno company was part of
the legally established Western Military Academy and that the latter was
an institution of an educational nature founded "for the purpose of
teaching elementary and academic studies, as well as Military tactics."
Studies were carried on in the evenings because the young Chinese students came from modest backgrounds, which forced them to earn a living during the day. While military drill figured prominently in the curriculum, the students made progress also in their other studies. It
sounded almost like a military command when he asked, "Should you
not consider [that] the filing of the Incorporation papers in your County
gives the right to conduct an Academy in Fresno, you will at once kindly
inform me." In any case, a permit to parade in Pasadena had been obtained from the Governor half a year earlier, while a permit was not necessary for their work behind closed doors.[59]

The District Attorney was not swayed by Lea's arguments and
maintained that the school's activities were wholly military in nature and
hence in violation of the statutes. The articles of incorporation filed in
Los Angeles had no bearing on the matter, and so on May 30 the Governor stated that no permit existed and that the permission given for Pasadena was restricted to that single occasion.[60]

By that time Lea was in St. Louis, accompanying K'ang Yu-wei on a
tour through the United States. The local papers picked up the California controversy. One of them added the rumor that "the officers and
privates in the Chinese army in the United States . . . have marching
orders and . . . by July fully 50,000 will be mobilized in Pekin. Whatever
the result, the movement has attracted a large number of soldiers of fortune on the coast who declare they are getting good pay for their services."[61] Lea denied that he intended to take his men to China to overthrow the government there. "That would be an absolute physical
impossibility, even if we were so inclined. There are not enough trans-
ports on the Coast to carry that many Chinese away, and the Government
could prevent any such movement before we could move 100 men." The
whole affair, he stated, had been provoked by opponents of his organization who had waited until he left California.[62]

Lea had in mind Falkenberg, who indeed tried to take advantage of
Lea's difficulties. In a letter to Governor Pardee, Falkenberg distanced
himself from Lea's army and belittled it as well as Lea personally: "Several times of late I have seen my name mentioned in connection with the
so-called 'Chinese Imperial Army' of 'General' Homer Lea, who is a
young ex-student, hunchback, 27 yrs. of age, 4'6" high." Falkenberg

stated that he never had anything to do with the Chinese cadets as he considered them "entirely illegally organized." A year ago "the San Francisco boys" had asked for his advice, and "being a military man I at once told them 'to ask permission and a license from our Governor, who himself is a soldier.'" This was a reference to his petition to form a Chinese-American company in San Francisco. "I would thank you," he added, "if you would inform the papers that I have had no dealings with Homer Lea's cadets at any time. My organization of 3000 American Officers is entirely legal and has nothing to do with these Chinese Military Companies in America."[63]

Falkenberg also had one of his men, W. H. Eckley of St. Paul, Minnesota, write to the Governor, calling attention "to the fact that there are a number of Chinamen belonging to an organization, of which Kang-Yu-Wei, one time Minister of War under the present Chinese Emperor, Kwang Hsu, claims to be the Grand President, who are armed and drilling in different cities of this country. The men are drilled three times a week by Americans who are under the command of one Homer Lea." The Governor replied that Falkenberg should make his own announcement to the papers because "then it will be more authoritative," and asked Eckley for more definite information on drilling activities in places other than Fresno. Falkenberg continued to press the Governor for action and told him a month later: "In spite of your peremptory strict orders, remarks are being made in the different Chinese Colonies [in California] that 'everything is all right' and the Chinese military Companies in Los Angeles, Oakland and San Francisco are still drilling regularly with Rifles every week. In fact a new American Captain and Lieutenant was [sic] engaged recently for the San Francisco Company."

The Governor's reply that action would be taken if these allegations could be proved did not satisfy Falkenberg, who continued his charges. He had been informed, he wrote, "by an excellent Chinese authority that Mr. Homer Lea is going to start a Chinese Military Academy in Los Angeles for the drilling and educating Chinese in military matters. 500 young Chinese will be asked to join and each will pay $100 to Homer Lea, who is said to have remarked: 'I don't care what they say up there, I am going to start up anyway, they won't interfere with me.' He says that because the other Chinese military companies in Los Angeles and Oakland are still running full blast." Governor Pardee advised Falkenberg to bring the matter to the attention of the District Attorney in Los Angeles. There is no record of any action from that agency.[64] In his desperation Falkenberg wrote one more letter, this one to the State Department in Washington, denouncing Homer Lea's illegal drilling of Chinese soldiers in the United States. To give weight to his complaint, he identified himself as "a member of the present Federal Grand Jury," but lowered his rank to "Major."[65]

This letter was Falkenberg's swan song in connection with the story of Homer Lea, but his own was not yet at an end. Early in 1908 he surfaced again, this time as president of the Wild Horse Mining and Milling Company in Cottonwood Creek, Nevada, and "Colonel, Military Staff, Governor of Nevada." According to the mining company's letterhead, the Governor of Nevada, the Hon. John Speaks, was its vice-president, and the State Bullion Tax Director a director of the company. At the time, the miners at Goldfield, Nevada, had gone on strike. In a statement to the Senate of Nevada, Falkenberg, as "Colonel and Brevet Brig. General," offered "a body of seasoned veterans over 3,000 in number, all of whom have seen active service [and] in many ways are much superior to U.S. regulars." He would select 260 of the men to "protect Goldfield and its citizens, mine owners as well as law abiding union miners, against the radical and anarchistically inclined and other disturbing elements." With his eyes still on Washington, and forgetting that he had just questioned the value of U.S. regulars in breaking the strike, he proposed, "as a large mine owner myself," to President Roosevelt that U.S. regulars be stationed in the county affected by the strike.[66] There is no record of an answer, and nothing further is heard about Falkenberg.

Homer Lea, before leaving with K'ang on the tour, successfully reasserted control over the company in San Francisco and appointed two new officers, a captain and a lieutenant, as Falkenberg had reported to Governor Pardee.[67] But Lea needed to shore up also his position with the local reformers who, like Dr. Tom She Bin, had come under the influence of Falkenberg. Again he used the way of public relations to accomplish his objective. In this case he sent two of his men in uniform to General Frederick Funston, Commander of the Department of California, U.S. Army, with an invitation to dine with him at one of San Francisco's "swell restaurants." The two were Captain Faneuf, a Caucasian, and Captain Kim Wong, the latter the same Kin (Kim) who had figured prominently in Falkenberg's attempts to establish a separate company and had since switched his loyalty to Lea. Apparently, Lea also planned to invite a dozen or so of the members of the local Chinese community, probably reformers, who would be impressed by his connections with the U.S. military. But the plan misfired when General Funston recognized the uniform of Lea's officers as a copy of the U.S. uniform and questioned Lea's right to call himself a general. The dinner never took place, Lea left the city in a hurry, and General Funston proposed to close the military school in San Francisco and seize its arms with a provost guard. When informed, however, that federal neutrality laws had not been violated, Funston left the matter to the state authorities for further prosecution.[68]

The troubles of the Chinese Imperial Reform Army were repeated in New York. There Eckley, Falkenberg's man in St. Paul, had brought the drilling of Chinese to the attention of the Governor of New York, Frank Higgins. The Governor referred Eckley's letter to President Roosevelt's secretary, who in turn forwarded it to the War Department. It finally got into the hands of General Chaffee, then Chief of Staff of the U.S. Army. At his request, the Los Angeles Chief of Police investigated the Western Military Academy and confirmed "that a Company of Chinamen, numbering thirty-six men, under the personal supervision of Homer Lea, and drilled by a white man by the name of Capt. Ansel O'Banion, formerly of the Philippine Army [are conducting exercises] on Wednesday and Friday nights. Their uniforms are blue with yellow stripe, shoulder straps and brass buttons with a Chinese dragon on them. They use unloaded guns when drilling. These Chinamen are operating under a charter, issued by the Secretary of State of California, under the name of Western Military Academy. The drill master informs me that they do not drill in public, except with permission from the U.S. Government, and that their object is the betterment of their condition, as they expect to occupy responsible positions in the Chinese Army at some future date." These findings were reported by General Chaffee to the Judge Advocate, who found no violation of federal laws. The Secret Service had also become involved in this investigation.[69]

Governor Higgins also had the New York City Police Commissioner make an investigation. The latter reported the Chinese had been drilling for the last ten years every Thursday evening in the hall of the Chinese Empire Reform Association in Chinatown, under a Major McVickar who was also an officer of the National Guard. They used discarded National Guard muskets and dressed in uniforms resembling those of the Sixty-ninth Regiment of the New York National Guard. The Commissioner, who had just been made an honorary member of the National Guard, did not take the situation very seriously. "If the Chinamen," he said, "generally can't shoot any better than Mock Duck [a known Chinese gambler] and the others we have arrested in Chinatown, they couldn't do any harm if they go back to China, and it will be a good way of getting rid of them." But some action had to be taken, and so he forbade any drilling and carrying of arms outside the hall.[70] But Major McVickar refused to stop the drilling. "There were about eight thousand Chinamen drilling in different cities of the United States. They had been drilling for six months in Philadelphia with rifles used in the regular army, and . . . for a year in San Francisco. They had no intention of returning to China to engage in any rebellion against their mother country, but drilled to build up body and mind and to gain military carriage."[71] The president of the New York Chinese Empire Reform Association, J. M. Singleton, a respected citizen and owner of several businesses, blamed Chinese adversaries of the reformers for their woes, the forces of "Dr. Sin Yat Mun [Sun

Yat-sen] . . . , the head of the Gat Ming Society [T'ung Meng Hui], . . .
the friend of the gamblers, the Highbinders, the secret society members
and the revolutionists."[72]

Singleton's statement deserves attention because, in connection
with Homer Lea's activities, it is the first reference to the differences between the moderate reformers under K'ang who were constitutional
monarchists and the revolutionary republicans who followed Sun Yat-
sen. In any case, McVickar's and Singleton's efforts succeeded. The New
York unit was permitted to continue drilling though forbidden to parade
with rifles.

In California, however, the situation continued to be critical. Even
though Governor Pardee's answers to Falkenberg had been noncommittal, he insisted upon the disbandment of the Western Military Academy.
Ralph Faneuf, postmaster in Oakland and member of the National
Guard and one of Lea's trusted men, who had been one of the two captains sent to invite General Funston to dinner, on September 28 "severed
all connection with the nefarious movement."[73] But Lea did not concede
that easily. To avoid further difficulties, he changed the character of the
Los Angeles school to make it appear to be a regular military academy, a
move that Falkenberg had denounced to the Governor. The school was to
be "open to all who wish to come and when they have acquired a degree
of excellence as sanctions the issuance of a diploma, it will be given to
them. The tuition for each student is $100." The curriculum was
changed, with greater emphasis laid on instruction in English. Otherwise, "the course of instruction will be as given in a practical Military
Academy," except that the school was to cater to "young Chinese students in this country, who have neither the money nor sufficient general
knowledge to attend college, [and] also on account of their timidity
[refuse] to submit themselves to treatment which is by no means pleasant." The form of a military academy was selected because "there is [sic]
in China greater opportunities for military students than in any other
line."

Lea explained all this to Governor Pardee in a second meeting on
his return from the tour with K'ang. He followed up with a letter a few
days later requesting the Governor's approval for the institution to conduct its business on property recently secured at Carlsbad, which formerly had been used as a sanitarium. Lea used the word "secured,"
which makes it appear that the property had been bought, but in reality
it had only been leased.[74] He emphasized that "no Chinese have anything to do with the management of this academy; it is solely in the
hands of Americans who are trying sincerely to help the deserving youth
of that Empire." He listed as directors the same individuals who had
been directors for the Western Military Academy and mentioned as refer-

ences several prominent individuals, Dr. Jordan, General Otis, and Judge York, as well as three members of the National Guard, Major Snyder, General Prescott, and Colonel Schreiber. Most of all, Lea insisted on the nonpolitical character of the school. "I am very well aware that misrepresentation has been made to your Excellency and your advisers, connecting this school with a revolutionary party. It is quite true that a political party did claim to have instituted the Academy, in order to gain credit among the Chinese people in the United States, but this is not true."[75]

Unlike the military units in other cities, the Western Military Academy in Los Angeles and its Fresno branch had been legally established. By carefully limiting the discussion to that Academy, Lea left the Governor with the impression that all the companies in California were part of it and either had no connection with the Chinese Empire Reform Association or had severed it. He clinched his argument by dropping the name of the highest authority of the land: "I expressed all this to President Roosevelt in June, and he expressed his approval."[76] This was, at best, a half-truth. K'ang Yu-wei had met the President, with Lea being present, and had spoken of the Chinese companies in various U.S. cities, established by his Association for physical training along military lines. The President was reported as having expressed his approval of the project.[77] Lea's version seemed to have made an impression upon the Governor. After asking the state's Adjutant General for advice, the Governor found that military schools and colleges did not require special permission for their students to use and bear arms in the course of military instruction, except for public parades. Accordingly, he informed Lea that it was "not my duty to issue licenses in cases as that which you call to my attention."[78] Homer Lea finally won his case.

──5──

With K'ang Yu-wei

On April 8, 1905, Homer Lea was reported by the *Los Angeles Examiner* to be "on his way to London, traveling with His Excellency, Kang Yu Wei. Their tour has extended as far east as St. Louis. Everywhere they are received with acclaim and high honor. . . . On his present trip, Lea will inspect the various Chinese military companies. No one seems to know how long he will be gone."[1]

This news item, however, appeared more than a month before K'ang's tour began. At that time, the newspaper reporters were pursuing Lea day and night in connection with the Falkenberg affair. The report, then, appeared to have been planted by Lea. According to one of his boyhood friends, Lea learned this ruse from the Chinese in Los Angeles. "They had a technique of giving out the information that they were going somewhere when as a matter of fact they had just been to the place; or, giving out the information that they had been there when they were about to go there."[2] In fact, K'ang and his entourage, including Lea, left Los Angeles May 10.[3] While the group did not travel as far as London, they did inspect Chinese military units in various American cities and indeed were received "with acclaim and high honor" wherever they went. Clearly, the trip had been prepared meticulously, and, to judge from the premature news item, it was Lea who had made the arrangements and knew in advance what awaited the travelers.

K'ang's and Lea's "triumphant tour" lasted about two and a half months. It extended to St. Louis, Chicago, Washington, Pittsburgh, Baltimore, Philadelphia, New York, Boston, and New Haven. It was triumphant because it was filled with applause from local Chinese as well as other residents, with dinners and banquets, parades and meetings, speeches that aroused the throngs, and interviews that were avidly sought and widely published by reporters who followed the trip's progress from city to city. Its high points were two meetings with the nation's chief executive and other high government officials. Lea shared with K'ang the limelight and the platforms. Upon arrival he rode with K'ang in the lead carriage dressed in his splendid uniform. The uniformed soldiers of his "army" cheered him as their general. He gave speeches and made himself the spokesman for the group by giving "authoritative" statements to the press. Local dignitaries greeted Lea no less than they did K'ang, and he accompanied the latter to the White House. A great career seemed to have opened to the 29-year-old self-styled military man and politician.

St. Louis, the first stop, inaugurated the fanfare and the attention the tour received. A banquet was arranged by the local Reform Association and attended by such prominent citizens as the former Governor of Missouri, Charles P. Johnson, Judges Benjamin F. Clark and Hiram M. Moore, and the officers of the reformers' military organization. K'ang made an address, and among the speakers who followed was "General Homer Lea, who has spent seven years for the realization of the reformer's dream."[4]

The visit coincided with a convention of the American Baptist Missionary Union. K'ang was invited to speak before the assembled delegates who, when he entered the hall with his secretary and Homer Lea, rose from their seats and greeted him with great applause. K'ang spoke of the Chinese youths who are "receiving education along modern lines." But, he said, "they desire to complete their studies under American influence, and they would do so were it not for your rigid exclusion laws. I have no objection to these laws," he added, "in so far as they relate to the undesirable classes [uneducated Chinese laborers]," but he objected to the consequent indignities to which scholars and students were subjected on entry to the United States. He also promised that "in the event of my return to Peking, I will do my best to encourage missionary work in China." After K'ang it was Lea's turn to speak. "General Lea followed His Excellency with an eloquent address in which he expressed the language of Mr. Kang and pleaded strongly for additional educational facilities for the denomination in China."[5]

This speech showed Lea as a pragmatic politician willing to ignore principles to gain some immediate advantage, for he was far from being a friend of missionary work in China. Only a year later, he published his novel *The Vermilion Pencil* in which the work of missionaries in China was criticized. An American Methodist minister in China interested mainly in women and treasure and a Catholic bishop willing to condone murder if it would help the church in its quest for temporal power were the two villains of his tale. Lea's hope was that the novel would be widely read and lead to an end of the China missions.[6]

In St. Louis Lea gave an interview that was published under the heading "American Hopes to be Lafayette of China—Leads Army." According to the reporter, "the man who feels that he is destined to command the 'military forces of [a nation of] 800,000,000 people' explained . . . the work and how he came to be a part of it. . . . 'We [K'ang and Lea] studied and planned together . . . the reformation of China. . . . I saw China was a nation of dough. What it needed was yeast. That yeast is western energy. I realized that I could be of vast service.' " The solution was education, hence the military schools in the United States. Lea said that their system should be adopted by the 2,000 schools of the reformers in China after the Emperor's restoration to power. In the meantime, Americans should support the movement for reasons of fair play as well as for business reasons in view of China's large population.[7]

More interesting than what Lea had to say about his role in the reform movement were some remarks that foreshadowed theories he developed later in two books, *The Valor of Ignorance* and *The Day of the Saxon*. Incidentally, the attention that these books eventually received in military and political circles made his contemporaries as well as later reviewers of his work take him and his activities on behalf of the Chinese revolutionary movement more seriously than would have been the case otherwise. He told the reporter in St. Louis that he had made a study of military science when he was a student at Stanford (where, according to the report, he had graduated in 1898). "I realized that no nation was ever in the ascendancy, no powerful dynasty ever fell save through the degeneration of its military. The military is and should be the fundamental science of all sciences, for it is this that develops manhood to its highest perfection."[8]

As it turned out, Lea's military unit in St. Louis was kept out of sight. The reason was probably that the local papers were then reporting on the troubles of the military companies in California. In Chicago, however, the next stop of the tour, the local military unit was very much in evidence. A contingent of 400 uniformed men with a band greeted the traveling party at the station. A carriage drawn by four white horses brought K'ang, with Lea riding alongside him, to the headquarters of the Reform Association, where K'ang made a speech and both he and Lea passed the military unit in review.[9] There was no mention in the news of any speech by Lea, nor, it appears, did he speak at a meeting of another missionary group that invited K'ang and his party.[10]

On June 8 the travelers arrived in Washington, D.C. Lea gave an interview to a reporter for a Los Angeles paper. "It is only a question of time when China will throw off the yoke of tradition and conservation [*sic*] that keep her in a backward condition and that is why I am bending all my energies to educate young men of that race who will go home and assist in the reform movement that is sure to prevail ultimately." The chief thrust of Lea's words was directed, however, against the Chinese exclusion laws, which he called a monstrous injustice. With an eye toward his Californian readers, Lea did not propose a privileged status for Chinese students and scholars but referred specifically to laborers badly needed by Californian fruit growers and vineyard owners. The exclusion laws were to be the main topic of the conversation that K'ang expected to have with President Roosevelt, and that visit was, Lea stated in the interview, the reason for their arrival in Washington.[11]

A Chicago newspaper had already reported on May 23 that K'ang was to meet the President.[12] It is not known in detail who arranged for the meeting, but Lea must have had a share in it. On the day he left with K'ang from Los Angeles for, as he put it, "Eastern cities, Washington, and Europe," Lea had asked Dr. Jordan for letters of introduction to the President "and such other persons as you would deem advantageous to meet in regard to the preservation of China's progress and integrity." Dr. Jordan complied.[13]

June 15 was set for the meeting with the President. Lea accompanied K'ang to the White House and was present at the meeting, and so was Acting Secretary of State Loomis. The scene was quite unusual. Here was the President of the United States receiving the head of a political movement directed against the legally established government of a country with which the United States was at peace, a man who had been declared an outlaw by that government and on whose head it had put a prize. That man, who held no official position, discussed with the U.S. Government at its highest level a matter that should have been handled by the foreign government's accredited diplomat. And, finally, present at the meeting between the President and the unauthorized Chinese spokesman was Homer Lea, the self-styled general of a private army on the territory of the United States, composed largely of aliens, that, in possible violation of the U.S. Neutrality Laws, had as its aim the overthrow of a friendly government.

The main subject of the conversation was the existence of the exclusion laws and, according to K'ang, the President pledged a change in their application, though not their abolition.[14] Lea's military units were brought to the President's attention in a second meeting on June 24, when Secretary of State John M. Hay was present and K'ang was accompanied by Yung Wing.[15] Lea claimed that he, too, was present. "Mr. Kang said that he told President Roosevelt of the military training the Chinamen in different cities of the United States were receiving and how it was teaching them the English language, to all of which the President said, 'Good!' "[16] Lea's version of the president's answer, as reported by O'Banion's author, was the word "Bully!"[17]

From Homer Lea's point of view, the discussion about the military units was the most important item because of the attacks that had been mounted against them. The President's approving exclamation was for him an authoritative consent to their existence. For K'ang, the main purposes of the conversations were a suggestion that the United States press for the abdication of the Empress Dowager and for a change in the Chinese exclusion laws.[18] Roosevelt did not accede to the first and, while he did nothing about the exclusion laws, on the very day of the second visit he issued instructions that Chinese visitors as opposed to labor immigrants should be treated with courtesy.[19]

The two meetings with the President were the high points but not the end of a tour that promised to be most successful. Earlier, while waiting for the first meeting with President Roosevelt, the party had gone to Baltimore, where they were met by a large band and escorted in a parade to their hotel. K'ang made addresses in which he stressed the need for technical schools in China. On the evening of June 11, before returning to Washington, "Mr. Lea made an after-dinner speech, praising the work of the Chinese soldiers who were trained in America."[20]

Between the two presidential visits K'ang and his retinue went to Pittsburgh, where they were received with the usual parade and band. No fewer than 800 Chinese crowded into the Fourth Avenue Baptist Church where, in his speech, K'ang mentioned the first meeting with the President and his hope for a modification in the exclusion laws. He also expressed hope for changes in the Chinese government, which, he was careful to say, could come only through political propaganda and the acquisition of technical proficiency on the part of its opponents.[21]

After the last meeting with the President, the party proceeded to Philadelphia, home of one of the largest companies formed by the local Reform Association. That unit even had a chaplain, the Reverend Frederick Poole, head of the Chinese Mission in Philadelphia, who had been instrumental in obtaining a parade permit against the opposition of the Chinese Imperial Consul.[22] Perhaps due to the two meetings with President Roosevelt, the visit in Philadelphia was very widely covered, and elation among the local Chinese community ran very high. The throng at the railway station was so great that the police had to clear a passage for K'ang, dressed in traditional silk robes, and for Homer Lea, who had donned his resplendent uniform. The parade was preceded by a platoon of mounted police, followed by a band of the Pennsylvania National Guard, more than a score of carriages, and two companies of Chinese-American soldiers, one of them from New York. "The Phildelphia contingent consisted of about forty men of Company G, Second Regiment, all of whom are being trained for the cavalry service under the command of Captain Thomas Wichard, formerly of the Fourth United States Cavalry, who served with that regiment in the Philippines," probably together with O'Banion. The group from New York, about the same size, consisted of Company B, Third Infantry Regiment, under a "native" commander, Lieutenant W. Lee. The standard bearers carried the Stars and Stripes, the Chinese Imperial flag, and that of the Reform Army. The same flags fluttered also from the hotel where the travelers were staying.[23]

Both K'ang and Lea spoke at a large gathering of Chinese and at a banquet. When K'ang asked at the meeting, "Who will join with the reformers? Who stands ready to sacrifice his life, if necessary, for the future of China?" he got an enthusiastic answer. "With loud cries every Chinese in the room and many of them belong to General Lee's [sic] organization, sprang to their feet and declared that their lives were at the disposal of the reform leader. It was evident to the spectators that the Chinese soldiers, despite the declarations that the reforms can be brought about quietly, meant to signify that they were willing to follow their leaders and if necessary secure reforms at the point of bayonet."[24]

When speaking about the success and growth of the military organization, Lea "was applauded to an echo." He was similarly greeted at a banquet of 200 prominent Chinese of the city. In fact, Lea aroused in Philadelphia no less curiosity than K'ang. He was described as "the most skilled military leader of China. He is exceedingly short, being a trifle deformed, but his ability in military affairs is conceded in all countries and at present he is the head of seventy-two Chinese battalions that are being drilled in this country."[25] Another report in the same paper embroidered in more detail: "Students of Chinese affairs . . . believe that it is possible that some day the American may be at the head of the armies of the Chinese Empire. The General himself disclaims even the remotest thought of such a possibility, but his constant companionship with Kang Ye We [K'ang Yu-wei] and the enthusiasm which he is arousing among the Chinese here and in Europe has a deep significance to all observers. . . . Military men who have had long conversations with General Lee [sic] say that they are impressed by the depth of his knowledge of military affairs and his power of organization. . . . In the course of his travels investigating military systems in various countries he reached China and made a study of the army system. Kang Ye We was at the time a member of the Chinese Cabinet and personal instructor of the Emperor. He took an interest in General Lee's work and assisted him in every way. When General Lee was visiting in Europe the Chinese reformer had to flee from China to save his life, and the two met later in London and joined hands. . . . Three years ago General Lee again visited China and since that time he and Kang Ye We have traveled through much of the world together."[26] However, at the same time, a Chicago newspaper ran a dispatch from Philadelphia that called "Lee" a soldier of fortune and an exile from China, probably misled on the latter point by the misspelled name.[27] These reports, anything but correct, were never denied by Lea. In his quest for publicity, he seemed to have welcomed any statements that enhanced his stature, whether or not they were true.

The reception in New York, the next stop on the tour, was equally impressive, though marred by the controversy over the legality of Lea's army. When K'ang's arrival was delayed by the second meeting with the President, the honor guard that was to receive him held a parade in Chinatown anyway.[28] By the time the group arrived, on June 27, the local military unit was no longer permitted to carry arms. Thus, when the soldiers met K'ang and his party, they carried instead massed flags, those of the United States, China, and the reformers. The party arrived at the Pennsylvania station in Jersey City. The two New York companies, joined by the Philadelphia one, accompanied the travelers to the ferry and, then on the New York side of the Hudson, to the headquarters of the Reform Association in Chinatown. Homer Lea in full uniform sat with K'ang and the local reform leader, J. M. Singleton, in the first carriage. They were followed by about 20 others carrying the leaders of Chinatown and were preceded by the cadets and a band. The streets of Chinatown were crowded with people, but the drill and Lea's inspection of the troops had to be held indoors because of the prohibition to carry arms in the streets.[29]

In New York Lea gave several interviews about the situation in China and his and the troops' role in it. "It is a bosh to say that I am the head of a revolution," he was quoted as saying. "This is not a revolution. Quite the contrary. We are drilling and teaching these young men to help the empire. She needs above all things an army if she is going to work out her salvation."[30] In another "authoritative" statement he explained, "I am educating many of these men to become officers. If the government of China should ask to-morrow for competent officers, I should recommend these men. I have set out to help China to preserve her ancient rights. It is immaterial to me who is at the head of the Chinese government. If the Empress Dowager should say the empire was to be attacked, I should give aid to her as freely as to the young Emperor. I am not governed by any political party in China." He denied being an enemy of the Empress Dowager and her party, although he stressed that China would be better off and stronger under the Emperor. Reiterating a proposal he had submitted in 1901 on his return from China, he called for a centralized Chinese government: "China should become a nation, not a group of provinces. Her finances and her army should be controlled by a central government. China has only a provincial army. In fact, there is nothing national in China. The future of China depends upon a truly national army. . . to maintain her entity as a nation" and "to withstand the aggressions of Russia, Germany and France." He added, "I would not tolerate the political corruption that exists in China to-day," as if he were to be the leader of the new, national army. "I have given officers to these troops at my own expense. The only object I have is that they shall be at the service of their country. I consider it best to educate them until the Chinese government realizes the necessity of introducing a homogenous system into China."[31]

These statements appear to represent a new stance toward the Chinese political situation. Not only did Lea disavow any thought of overthrowing the Empress Dowager; he also declared his neutrality in the struggle between her regime and the reformers. The change of attitude appeared to be dictated by several tactical considerations. A week earlier, the Imperial Chinese Minister to the United States, Chentung Liang Ch'en, had been shown a dispatch from Los Angeles that a Chinese army was being organized, drilled, and supplied with modern arms in the United States, with the purpose of overthrowing the present Chinese government. His comments sounded like a suggestion that the United States take action against any such attempts throughout the country: "The idea that an army for a hostile movement against China could be recruited in a friendly nation like the United States is absurd. In a time of peace, this country would not tolerate the formation here of such an army, but would suppress it at once. Evidence of that can be found in the action taken some time ago by the Governor of California, who had occasion to suppress some such movement which was being organized within his jurisdiction."[32] By declaring his neutrality, Lea sought to obviate any need for action by the United States Government. Moreover, the investigations by the Governor of New York and the New York City Police Commissioner were culminating and were widely discussed in the press. Thus Lea tried to blunt these inquiries by ascribing a peaceful and neutral role to his army.

The visits to the last three cities were something of an anticlimax. In Boston, K'ang was acclaimed by hundreds of Chinese and met the mayor of the city and the state governor. Lea's presence was mentioned in the press, but little was said about his activities except that he was the only non-Chinese among more than a thousand at a meeting where K'ang spoke. He was also referred to as the man "who drilled the Chinese of this city in military tactics." The visit in Boston was marred by a heat wave that made K'ang ill.[33] In Hartford, where he arrived on July 16, K'ang was faced with dissension within the Chinese community. A large part of the city's Chinese considered themselves enemies of the whole Manchu dynasty, including the Emperor. They belonged to a society "similar to the Boxer organization in China,"[34] probably Free Masons allied with the Triad Society and followers of Sun Yat-sen. These men stayed away from the functions organized by the reformers, and, as a result, only an automobile and a few carriages brought K'ang and his party to a meeting of 30 people at the local headquarters of the Reform Association. There were no fanfares or brass bands. K'ang did not even attend a dinner given by the reform leaders of Hartford, excusing himself by his recent illness. Lea, too, did not attend and instead had a private dinner with Yung Wing, who lived in Hartford. While K'ang spoke later at another meeting, nobody there seemed to have paid special attention to Lea.[35] The one report on him, which appeared in the local newspaper, may not have been entirely to his liking. He was "called 'general' by courtesy" only. But it was also stated that "he is a student of warfare and is said to be a genius in military tactics. He matriculated at Harvard and graduated at Stanford University. General Lea belongs to the Lee family of Virginia, noted for its warriors. . . . General Lea has charge of all the Chinese military companies in this country and there are about fifty of them. The reformers have no idea of having these men go to China to fight for reform, but it is desired to teach them modern military tactics so that when they return to China to live they will be of assistance to the military authorities."[36]

K'ang, together with one of his daughters who had joined him in New York, and others of his party, visited the Colt arms factory at the suggestion of the mayor. Colt's president had "the latest patterns of weapons . . . displayed to the visitors. The military automatic revolver claimed the attention of General Lea at once and he examined the mechanism, measured and cocked it like a practiced hand. The little Derringer 41, of bulldog shape, and short, intended as a pocket pistol, caught the eye of Miss Kang and she wanted to try it at once. Mr. Kang looked over all the kinds and made numerous notes upon a pad. General Lea was the only one in the party, who knew anything about a revolver and he didn't have to ask questions."[37]

The visit in Hartford was cut short so that K'ang could attend a national meeting of reform leaders that had been hastily called in New York. On the way to that meeting, K'ang stopped in New Haven to visit Yale University. Lea had left Hartford a day earlier to wait in New York for the rest of the group.[38]

At the Waldorf-Astoria in New York, Lea gave another noteworthy interview on July 22. The time was shortly before the convening of the Peace Conference at Portsmouth, New Hampshire, which, under the sponsorship and mediation of President Roosevelt, was to end the Russo-Japanese War. The fates of Manchuria and Korea were at issue in these negotiations. Russia had penetrated Manchuria and forced China to grant a 99-year lease on the Kwantung Peninsula, which included Port

Arthur. In Korea, Japan held a dominant position since the Sino-Japanese War a decade earlier, although China still claimed nominal suzerainty. From the Chinese point of view, there was the danger that the peace treaty would disregard China's interests and also legalize Japan's annexation of Korea.

In the interview Lea called for China's participation in the peace negotiations insofar as they involved the disposition of Chinese territory. Lea supported the Imperial Chinese Government on this point because, as he had said in an earlier statement in New York, his purpose was to "preserve China's ancient rights," and in this respect it did not matter to him who ruled China. Thus he, a spokesman for the Chinese reform party, became a spokesman for the Chinese Empire. "If this country, insisting on the integrity of China, permits other nations . . . to dispose of Chinese property as they see fit, . . . then the contention of the United States for Chinese integrity is nullified. And even though the Chinese had representation in this peace convention and the convention did dispose of Chinese territory, regardless of Chinese protests, yet it would show the United States consistent in trying to preserve the integrity of the Chinese Empire. In regard to warlike measures and the disposition of armies and fleets, the Chinese representative would not wish to have anything to say. This is my personal point of view, and I believe that it coincides with the point of view of the Chinese people. It should certainly coincide," he added, appealing to the American sense of fairness, "with that of all men who believe in justice."[39]

Whether Lea's plea made any impression upon the United States Government is very doubtful. It certainly did not affect the attitude of the warring parties or the course of the peace conference. His assuming the role of spokesman for the Chinese Empire did draw, however, an acerbic comment on the editorial page of a Hartford newspaper that a few days earlier had reported on him during the visit to that city. " 'General' Homer Lea . . . cheerfully chips in with his views about how China ought to be represented at Portsmouth, and as to whether Port Arthur should 'revert back to China,' just as if he were the present government of China, or at least the 'chief of staff' for that government, instead of being, as he is, in the personal employ of a man who professes to wish to see that government changed or done away with." From there the editorial went on to criticize other actions of the reformers. "Mr. Homer Lea is of course only an ass in all this—and jackasses have not been noted as reformers or as promoters of reform, . . . but . . . as 'commander-in-chief' of the thousands of Chinamen drilling in many cities of the United States . . . his function . . . is not asinine. It is a violation of the hospitality of this country. . . . This country is living on terms of perfect amity with the existing Chinese government; and Mr. Kang and Mr. Lea have no . . . right to drill men here in the United States for use as soldiers or as military instructors in China." The editorial also berated K'ang for speaking out against the exclusion laws while a guest in the United States.[40]

K'ang's and Lea's answers to this attack are not known. Silence might have been the best policy, but, after the many accolades they had received, the hostile remarks at the end of a successful tour must have left a bad taste. But worse was yet to come.

The purpose of the national meeting of the reform leaders, so hastily called in New York in July, remains conjectural. Neither the reason nor the agenda was ever explained. It is quite likely, however, that the assembly dealt with the military arm of the Chinese Empire Reform Association. The companies were under attack in various states and in danger of being closed down by state or federal authorities. If they were to continue they had to disappear from public view, which had led to their scrutiny by various officials. Apparently, the reformist delegates in New York decided to remove the units from the streets of American cities, to abstain from parades, and to suppress any publicity about their existence. Whatever the deliberations and decisions of the reform leaders, after so much publicity and fanfare, a curtain of silence fell abruptly over the army's activities. Among Lea's surviving papers, no parade reports and no general orders are dated after the summer of 1905. Newspapers no longer recorded the doings of the military companies after the hostile Hartford editorial of July 26, 1905, except for a news item on the establishment of the new military academy at Carlsbad.[41] A faint echo of the controversy with Falkenberg was heard in the *New York Tribune* on January 20, 1906. Apparently, the United States Minister in Peking was still receiving inquiries from U.S. citizens about a Chinese Imperial Reform Army. The Minister asked the State Department to advise such persons that they should not have anything to do with that organization.[42] Official references to Lea's organization ceased after Governor Pardee's letter to Lea of October 13, 1905, when he agreed that Lea's cadets could bear arms as long as they stayed indoors. After that, the silence was so complete that the military units seemed to have disappeared from the face of the earth. There is not even a record that the schools ceased to function or that the military companies were disbanded.

Furthermore, no member of any of the local companies in the various American cities was subsequently identified as having seen active duty in China. One of Lea's friends believed that "many of the Chinese who had been drilled later became officers in the Chinese army."[43] Another source spoke of "some" who had been smuggled into China prior to 1911,[44] while the author of O'Banion's story claimed that in 1907 and 1908 all 2,100 members of the military companies, except for a few unable to go, were taken to China to help in the impending revolution. The soldiers, according to this account, arrived in San Francisco in small groups of 3 to 8 and were taken by smugglers in boats to Mexico, 28 to 32 men at a time. The same well-organized smuggler operation then took them from the Mexican port of Mazatlan to Kobe, Japan, from where Japanese connections of the secret network landed them at Amoy. "Slowly and carefully, one by one, the men scattered over China and enlisted as quickly as they could in the Royal Manchu Army. Some went into the hills and joined the brigands [units of the secret societies]. Some few others were used as go-betweens, messengers, to contact by devious ways the soldiers serving under the flag of the enemy. It was a vast and intricate system . . . a secret army within an army waiting patiently for the day when they could rise up and free China."[45] Transporting the army to China was said to have taken several years. What is more, the same secret means were used, according to O'Banion's story, to bring young men from China, mostly sons of high officials who sympathized with the enemies of the Peking regime, for training with Lea's military units.

There is, in fact, a tiny grain of truth in this farrago. Some Chinese, helped by O'Banion and a team of smugglers, did come to the United States, but hardly for political or military reasons. They were ordinary Chinese smuggled by boat from Mexico to southern California. Such illegal immigration was not uncommon during the first decade of this century and was frequently reported in Californian newspapers. O'Banion's version of his smuggling activities relates them to the reform movement and Lea's military units. "One of the men engaged in the smuggling of soldiers in and out of the country talked out of turn. Not knowing the real truth of what was behind it all, he told a garbled story. Rumors of this reached the ears of certain Federal officials. And O'Banion was accused of smuggling Chinese into the United States. An indictment was returned in 1912. O'Banion, of course, could at this time have told the truth in the matter and probably nothing would have been done. But it was too soon, and the whole story was still a secret to be kept and closely guarded. If he spoke, he would betray the trust the soldiers had placed in him, and the ideals Dr. Sun had for a free China. . . . O'Banion, like a true soldier, loyal to his oath of silence, accepted the judgment of the court."[46]

The court records of the case provide a different story. On May 22, 1911, O'Banion and six others were caught by the Coast Guard while smuggling 15 Chinese laborers from Catalina Island off the California coast to a point near the Bolsa Chica Gun Club at Huntington Beach, Los Angeles County. Homer Lea's widow, Ethel, posted a $2,000 bond for O'Banion on December 19, 1912, a month and a half after Lea's death, and again a $1,000 bond on July 6, 1914. All but O'Banion and one other of the conspirators pleaded guilty and were sentenced to 60 days in prison. O'Banion was finally sentenced to 18 months in prison on January 15, 1915. He began serving his sentence on April 1, 1915, and was discharged on April 19, 1916.[47]

Once before, O'Banion had come in conflict with the law. The information about this earlier case comes from a letter Lea wrote to Ethel, then his secretary, on September 20, 1908: "The Captain came down . . . and I returned to the City with him on account of his trial which took two days and I have not as yet heard the result."[48] Unfortunately, the records of this case cannot be found, and it is, therefore, not known whether the smuggling of Chinese was also the subject of that trial. Nor can it be established whether Homer Lea knew and, perhaps, abetted these activities or why Ethel twice felt obliged to post a bond for O'Banion. At the same time, it cannot be completely excluded that, at one time or another, Chinese were brought to the United States for training in Lea's military organization. A newspaper clipping that Falkenberg attached to his last denunciation of Lea in October 1905 contains this unverifiable statement: "While most of the attendants of Lea's schools are residents of America and sons of Americanized Chinese, there are a number who have come from the eastern empire to get the education these schools give."[49] While such trainees may, or may not, have been brought to the United States, it appears that Lea was aware of organized attempts to import Chinese laborers. In May 1909, about eight months after O'Banion's first trial, General Otis related to Lea an unsuccessful and costly effort to transport needed laborers from China via Japan to Mexico and California. This particular group of Chinese had only reached Yokohama when a competing organization planted the rumor that the American company for which they were to work had become insolvent. The group returned to Hong Kong. Otis made it a point to say that the project was "a legitimate labor immigration movement." Lea appeared to have played a certain role in the undertaking, since Otis offered to send him, when available, his agent's full report on the matter.[50]

Even 30 years afterward, O'Banion refused to talk about the court cases. Before entrusting his memoirs to his editor, O'Banion stated, "my wife and daughter object to any mention of my conviction or run-in with the law."[51] Whatever his reasons for secrecy, O'Banion's account of the smuggling operations is so inconsistent that its veracity is very doubtful. According to him, the shipment of troops to and fro ended in 1908. When the training "was over, and the soldiers had all been sent to China, . . . there was no longer any need for the boats," and therefore some of his friends and associates "returned to their former occupation of conventional smuggling."[52] If so, at the time of his arrest in 1911, he could no longer have been bringing in young Chinese for training.

Therefore, if O'Banion's own words are accepted as true, they lead to the conclusion that the smuggling for which he was convicted was just as "conventional" as that of his associates.

Moreover, Lea himself claimed as late as September 1910 that his four regiments were still in existence in the United States, though hidden from the eyes of the public and the authorities. He referred to them in a letter of September 18 to Sun Yat-sen. Fortunately, though the letter has not been preserved, Sun's reply is available. It seems that Lea had spoken with the Chinese Minister in Washington about the possibility of sending his military units to China. How he should have come to make such a proposal to the Chinese Imperial diplomat cannot be ascertained from Sun's letter. Earlier, in 1910, Sun and Lea had discussed the clandestine stationing of 500 American officers in China to train troops for the planned revolution. Sun's corevolutionary and comrade-in-arms, Huang Hsing, rejected the idea as impractical because it would inevitably draw the attention of the government.[53] Lea may then have conceived the plan to move his men there openly so that they could join the insurgents at the proper moment. Whatever the background of the matter, Sun rejected the second plan: "And about the Chinese Government in concerning [sic] the force you had trained in America, I think most likely, if such force is still under your command, they would like to get it over and transport it to China and to destroy it. . . . And for the present Government to maintain such force as your four regiments under [their] service is the most untenable thing under the present situation of China. And I think the whole thing is propped up by Chang Yim Fang, the present Minister in Washington, for his own good. Be careful for all Chinese you come in contact with in America."[54]

A letter to Lea by George W. Gibbs of Chicago, erstwhile major, First Battalion, Second Regiment Infantry, is another indication that Lea was in communication with his units as late as 1910. Gibbs wrote on September 4, 1912, that two years had passed "since I last heard from you," and he continued: "I have noted your return to America, after strenuous days in China. I am writing you for information, as to what has become of all the grand promises made to me and my sub officers by the Chinese. . . . General, you seem to be the only one who has shared in the glory. . . . In order to save their rights under the Statute of Limitations Cofts, Wood and Simpson [presumably subofficers] have commenced suit in the Civil Court against the Chinese Academy. Until I hear from you I still pin my faith in a Chinaman's word, and am still waiting. Some settlement ought to be given to us who labored in their behalf. The suits, at my request will remain in 'Status Quo' until I hear from you. I fear a great scandal if they are aired in court, which won't benefit the Chinese." He then added, as a hidden threat, that he had studied law for the last two years, "which I find has been of great benefit to me in my work."[55] At the time, Homer Lea lay stricken in California and had less than two months to live. He probably could no longer read the letter, or one may hope that his wife withheld it from him.

Thus ended somewhat sordidly the story of the Chinese Imperial Reform Army. History had passed it by. If the word of Homer Lea's widow may be accepted, it might have had a marginal influence on the situation in China. She said in a statement published in 1926 that "after the outbreak of the revolution in 1911 many of these young men went to China and were enrolled in the republican forces and did good work."[56] According to another source, "at least 24 American Chinese went to China and offered their services to the new government."[57] As early as November 1911, with the outcome of the Wuchang uprising still in the balance, it was reported that Chinese from Detroit and other parts of the country were leaving for China to assist in the final overthrow of the Manchu regime, but it is not known whether these men, if they actually went to China, were from Lea's units. It was reported also that several airplanes were shipped to Sun's forces from Cleveland, Ohio, and Albion, Michigan, with materials for ten more ordered in Akron, Ohio. Ray Wilcox of Albion was to have left for China as constructor and instructor.[58] Incidentally, the planes were never put to use due to lack of pilots. It is not known whether Lea had anything to do with this matter. A month later, when Sun and Lea had arrived in China and the victory of the revolution seemed assured, U.S. military circles were said to be astonished that revolutionary bands could have overcome the large and well-organized armies of the empire. They came up with the answer that the victory was due to Homer Lea and his U.S. noncommissioned officers. They had trained Chinese in the United States behind locked doors, and a number of these soldiers had gone to China.[59]

While Lea's army may not have made a contribution, or only an insignificant one, to the Chinese Revolution, Major Gibbs was not entirely wrong when he pointed to Lea as the chief beneficiary of the army's existence. It had conferred on him fame or notoriety as its commander in chief and permitted him to assume the rank of general. Though the legitimacy of the title was subject to doubts and many put it between quotation marks, it eventually helped to increase its wearer's renown as a master strategist and military genius after he added the pen to his sword. But that was to be in the future. As it turned out, after the national meeting of the reform leaders in New York in July 1905, Lea's situation underwent a drastic change. Of course, he continued as the head of the military companies of the reformers in the United States, but he commanded an army of which the world no longer took any notice. To be a military leader meant to Lea to be recognized as such. The recognition that he craved had disappeared with the disappearance of the publicity. It was an abrupt shift from the triumphant marches and parades in the streets to vacuous anonymity. Now even his victory in the argument with Governor Pardee over the military companies' right to exist had a hollow ring for him.

Moreover, after the national meeting of the reform leaders, K'ang and Lea went their separate ways. They said goodbye to each other at the end of July 1905. Lea returned to Los Angeles via Canada, according to a postcard he was said to have sent from Toronto to a friend.[60] A Hartford newspaper reported that K'ang intended to visit Montana and from there travel to South America in order to establish branches of the Chinese Empire Reform Association in various countries. Lea was not expected to accompany K'ang as "he is sufficiently tied up with his duties in this country."[61] In a 1940 letter that has since been lost, Sun's son, Sun Fo, told somebody interested in the story of Homer Lea that Lea proceeded secretly from California to join Sun in French Indochina. In another letter, also no longer available, Sun Fo said that two years later, in 1907, Homer Lea again joined Sun Yat-sen in French Indochina to assist in a campaign in China's southern province of Kwangsi.[62] There is no other corroborating evidence for these assertions. Sun Fo's statements, if indeed they were made, are of very dubious value. He was 15 or 16 years old at the time of his father's activities in Indochina and living in Hawaii and could not have had firsthand knowledge of these events. But in spite of their improbability, Sun Fo's statements later contributed to the rumors that linked Lea with Sun Yat-sen as his spy in the reform movement.

As far as is known, K'ang and Lea never met again after their parting in New York. Some kind of contact may have continued, or, at least, Lea seemed to have been aware of K'ang's whereabouts. About three years later, Lea told a mutual acquaintance, Charles B. Boothe, who had inquired about K'ang, that K'ang might come to the West Coast "later in the spring or summer but I am not certain."[63] In June of the following year, 1909, when Lea hoped to have K'ang use his influence in China on his behalf, he approached K'ang through Boothe rather than directly, even though Boothe knew K'ang only from one meeting in St. Louis in 1905. It appears that there was no longer any direct communication between Lea and K'ang. "I see General Lea frequently," wrote Boothe to K'ang, "and we often speak of you, and I wish that circumstances were such that we might be able to converse with you on the situation in China. General Lea is informed of my writing this letter, and desires to extend to you his compliments."[64]

The silence between these two men, who appeared to have been political allies and maintained almost daily contact during four to five months in 1905, may indeed have represented an estrangement. There could have been several reasons for it. The Falkenberg affair and Lea's lingering disappointment or anger at having nearly been dropped in favor of a man whom he considered an impostor were possibly a big factor. The unfavorable publicity and the investigations that followed and the disappearance of the military units from public view, a possible result of the investigations, may have added to Lea's resentment and affected his faith in K'ang. In addition, K'ang's financial moves and integrity became suspect after he and Lea parted. K'ang left the United States with a large sum of money from the treasury of the Reform Association to invest in business schemes abroad. Part of the money—some speak of $400,000—came from Lea, who controlled membership fees.[65] But while Lea was said to have been displeased at K'ang's departure with the money, in principle he agreed with the decision to invest the funds in Mexico and South America.[66] The investments were made to obtain sources of income for the work of the reformers, but when the schemes failed K'ang's personal reputation was severely damaged. Boothe, for example, blamed K'ang for the use of the reformers' funds "in a way that is not approved of."[67] Yung Wing made more specific accusations: "Kang Yu Wei is under a cloud of doubt. It appears that while in this country he raised about $800,000 from laundrymen and others and that he has appropriated the same to his own purposes, it is known that he bought property in Mexico which now stands in his daughter's name who is a student at Barnards [sic] (Columbia). . . . He was called on for an accounting which has not been rendered."[68] The losses may also have affected Lea's opinion of the man. Sun Yat-sen's "Reminiscences" of November 1911, in the writing of which Lea appears to have helped, said the following, though without mentioning K'ang by name: "One man is now universally denounced as a traitor to the cause for having appropriated a huge sum of money entrusted to his care. He will meet with his due reward."[69]

There is also a theory that Lea and his cadets belonged to a radical wing of the Chinese Empire Reform Association, which opposed K'ang's more moderate views.[70] If so, the estrangement could be traced at least partly to ideological differences. But evidence that Lea and his military organization belonged to such a wing, if it ever existed, is not available.

Of course, one cannot be sure who dropped whom, whether Lea abandoned K'ang or vice versa. But given the pragmatic character of Lea, it is also not impossible that he deserted K'ang when K'ang's political fortunes declined. Over the years, Sun Yat-sen's influence and that of his revolutionary group increased among Chinese abroad at the expense of the reformers. When Lea first became involved in Chinese political affairs, the reformers dominated the scene, and he joined them. But when the reformers lost ground to the revolutionists, he readily switched his loyalties and turned to Sun Yat-sen. It would take him a number of years to complete that change. Now, in the fall of 1905, he suddenly faced the prospect of commanding an army that did not even make a stir in the newspaper columns, not to speak of the battle field. At the same time, his future relations to K'ang, the head of the worldwide reform movement, became questionable. The heady days of his joint tour with K'ang were fading into oblivion. Later he would say plaintively: "Every thing I lean on breaks; every hope I conjecture up vanishes before the realities of each new day."[71]

——6——

Interlude

The silence that engulfed Lea's army after Governor Pardee's letter of October 13, 1905, also seemed to have fallen over him personally. Available records do not show a sign of life from Homer Lea for two and a half years from the date of his last letter to Governor Pardee of October 7, 1905, to his letter of April 7, 1908, in which he informed Boothe that K'ang might come to California in the spring or summer of that year. That last letter makes it clear, however, that he had been in contact with Boothe for some time, for he had sent him a copy of his novel, *The Vermilion Pencil*, which was published early in 1908.

Lea must have worked on the book already in 1906, which is the year of the copyright notice, and it is possible that he made a trip to China before its completion. The novel contains such a vivid and detailed portrayal of Chinese life, conditions, and landscape that one would think he could have acquired that knowledge only by personal observation. The few months he spent in southern China and Shanghai from 1900 to 1901 may have been sufficient for him to absorb some of the local atmosphere, especially since he passed part of that time in the company of Pierre Loti, an experienced traveler and travel writer, from whom the young, impressionable, and eager Lea may have learned a great deal. But it is more likely that he gathered the material for his novel during a longer stay in China in the fall and winter of 1905–6. There is no proof that he went there, but there are indications. In his letter to Governor Pardee of October 7, 1905, in which he requested permission for his academy to continue its work, Lea asked for an answer "by Wednesday . . . as I must go away on Thursday."[1] The words, "must go away," make it appear that he was not just thinking of leaving San Francisco to go to Los Angeles or some other location in the United States where he could be reached if necessary. In a previous instance, when he set out with K'ang on their joint tour, he asked several individuals, Dr. Jordan and the Fresno District Attorney, to forward their letters to him in New York,[2] but in this case it seems obvious that after that Thursday he was going to be incommunicado and unable to receive mail. On that Thursday, October 12, the steamship *Korea* departed from San Francisco on a voyage to Japan and Shanghai. The list of passengers is no longer available, and a partial list published in a San Francisco newspaper does not list Homer Lea as a passenger. But that partial listing contains the name of "Wong Kai Kah, Trade Commissioner and servant."[3] This was the same Wong Kai Kah who, together with Lea, reviewed the Chinese company at the Pasadena Tournament of Roses; came to Los Angeles to visit the Western Military Academy; was arrested at the home of one of Lea's friends; and for whom another friend, John York, prepared legal documents in connection with his problem with the immigration authorities. At the time of his arrest, Wong Kai Kah had been described as a high provincial official in the "Quang district,"[4] probably a garbled version of Chekiang, the locale of Homer Lea's novel. Though it is by no means certain, under these circumstances it is quite likely that Lea traveled to China in the company of Wong who, notwithstanding his strong relations to the reformers, was at the same time in the good graces of the Peking government. Lea's friend, Will Irwin, remembered that some time after Lea was in New York with K'ang Yu-wei—actually Irwin mistook him for Sun Yat-sen—"the mail brought from China to my desk at *McClure's Magazine* the manuscript of a novel entitled *The Vermilion Pencil*, with a note of enclosure from Homer Lea. . . . The manuscript was not 'serializable,' but it had a sense of authenticity unique in fiction about China. I recommended it to the book house annexed to *McClure's*, which accepted it."[5] If Irwin's recollection did not deceive him, Lea completed his novel while in China, where he may have stayed for some time under Wong's protection.

The novel deals with a beautiful Chinese peasant girl who was discovered by a traveling mandarin. He heard her singing while passing her father's farm. It was "an outburst of song not unlike that of a mocking bird in its sweet intensity and freedom but vibrant with the melody of human passion [rising] with supreme impulse and passion above the tea thicket." Willfully, she refused the mandarin's request to sing for him. "I never sing for mandarins. . . . My song, 'she replied in cold, careless tones,' is for the birds and tea-pickers of the Valley, but not for wolves and tigers of the Yamen [government office]."[6] But she was drawn into the Yamen when the provincial viceroy, who had heard of her beauty from the mandarin, married her. Marriage to a high official, however, did not change her view of the world. She continued to favor the com-

mon people among whom she had grown up, despising wealth and prod-
ding her husband to rebuild decaying Buddhist temples, found hospi-
tals, and provide food for the poor. An uncorrupted child of the people,
she wrung good deeds from the Confucian government in the person of
her weak husband.

To educate her, her husband engaged as a tutor a young, tall, blue-
eyed Breton monk who had been recommended by the bishop of the
local Catholic mission. The monk had come under the influence and followed the steps of an older missionary who, while scrupulous in the per-
formance of his religious duties, was never known to have made a convert. Instead, he ministered to the poor and sick without recompense,
either spiritual or material. At first, the young, temperamental woman
ridiculed her somber, taciturn, and unworldly tutor but soon admired his
quiet strength and fell in love with him, while he also became attached to
his strong-willed, beautiful pupil. He tried to escape the violent conflict
between his vows and his desires and for weeks stayed away from the viceroy's palace, only to be pulled back by his ardent love. When away he
lived among the common people in the countryside. One night a Westerner, a "derelict, . . . one of those nameless Europeans whom Fate had
utterly cast adrift in those mysterious currents of the Orient Seas,"[7] lay
dying in a poor fisherman's hut. The Breton was called to minister to
him, and before dying the stranger put around the Breton's neck a sacred
medallion of the Deluge Family—the Great Seal of the T'ien Ti Hui or
the Triad Society. Anybody wearing that seal commanded the loyalty and
unconditional support of the society's members. The monk made use of
this power when, after his elopement with the viceroy's wife, the pair was
captured in a grotto from the Ming period and the unfaithful woman was
condemned to death by a Chinese magistrate. The court acted in concert
with the Catholic bishop and the French consul, who both had been
promised territorial concessions for their cooperation. Just when the condemned was to be beheaded, the Breton monk with the Great Symbol of
the Triads around his neck went out of the mission gate followed by the
soldiers who had been guarding him. "And as he went along there rose
at certain intervals that terrible cry, 'Hung Shun Tien!' Men stopped in
their labor at the sound of this, and when they saw the tall black-robed
Breton with the Great Symbol [and] the stern, armed array behind him
holding overhead their right arms with thumbs pointed upward," they
joined the marching band. "Beggars peeped out of their holes and
joined them. Merchants came from their gilded shops. . . . Thieves crept
out from their hidings and sentries left their stations. Hucksters put
down their trays and scholars their brushes. Itinerant barbers, physicians,
woks, fortune-tellers, robbers, clerks, silk robes and tatters; youths and
tottering old men; from mansions and cellars came the Children of the

Deluge to follow the black-robed man."[8] At the moment when the executioner raised his knife, the deluge of humanity overflowed the square of execution. French marines, stationed there to protect the French consul, were unable to get their cannon in position. The Chinese troops fled when they heard the cry of the Hung Society, and thus the aroused Chinese people, represented by the secret society and led by a Westerner, saved China in the person of a woman who had rejected the Chinese official order personified by her husband. The people defeated not only the government establishment but also the military might of the foreign powers and the hypocritical Christian missionaries allied with them.

In coded form the novel portrayed Homer Lea's views of China and the way of its salvation. He wrote to a friend that it was the real China expressed in literature.[9] "There is but one way to reform China," he said some years later, "the way they themselves have done these six times in the past, the extirpation, root and branch, of official corruption. . . . The West has nothing whatever to do with the reformation of this nation. . . . China can be reformed . . . without the introduction of a single occidental idea."[10] In the novel the West contributed only the leader, tall, taciturn, of quiet strength, a man unlike Homer Lea but, perhaps, the man he would have liked to be.

Contemporary reviews of the novel could not, and did not, penetrate Lea's code, and so it did not make the impact for which Lea had hoped. Above all, the novel did not mark the end of the Christian missions in China, which, Lea believed, deflected the country from its own path and made it subservient to foreign ways and powers. But the novel's authenticity was recognized by several reviewers. One of them found that Lea had "done for China what Rudyard Kipling and A. E. W. Mason have done for India—given a sense of it, a feeling for it," and called it "the first real Chinese novel in English."[11] Another read it as "an exceedingly singular and almost mystical romance of China."[12] But its style turned others away: "The atmosphere and a certain wealth of words and invention recall Hugo's wildest excursions. Nature is wrenched asunder and the dictionary deracinated. . . . 'The Vermilion Pencil' is a lurid and grotesque impression of China."[13] Posterity also considered the novel a failure, "a very bad novel . . . about which the less said the better."[14] But its literary value and its authenticity, or the lack of them, are of less importance than its veiled portrayal of Lea's ambitions for China and, above all, for himself.

The manuscript of *The Vermilion Pencil* is no longer in existence, and there are few clues as to where it was typed. Will Irwin's recollection that it came from China may or may not be correct, and so may be the recollection of Homer Lea's stepson, Joshua B. Powers, who in the 1950s, wrote a note stating that his mother, Ethel Bryant Powers, typed the manuscript in Los Angeles in 1906. With Ethel's assistance, Joshua B. Powers added, "began a colaboration [*sic*] that made it possible for Homer Lea to do his work."[15] It also marked the beginning of a relationship that was to last throughout the rest of his life.

    Little is known about Homer Lea's relations to women, aside from those to Ethel. There are reports that he and his friends visited bordellos on their excursions to Chinatown. His sister, Ermal, saw "him unhappy because he could not marry the girl he loved" but did not say whether his deformity spoiled this love affair.[16] To judge from a story told by his friend Marco Newmark, Lea had a low opinion of female intelligence. Lea was said to have recounted an accident he had in the mountains with a burro, when he fell and hurt his ankle so badly that he could not rise. Having no water, he was resigned to dying of thirst when the burro began running to and fro, whinnying excitedly. Lea managed to crawl after the animal, which, lo and behold, led him to water where he could still his thirst. "After the conclusion of his recital of this adventure," Newmark continued, "he wagged his fingers up and down at my wife, looked her straight in the eye, and said, 'And do you know, Mrs. Newmark, that burro is the most intelligent female it has ever been my pleasure to meet.' "[17] If the account is true, Lea, in addition to his unfavorable opinion of female intelligence (perhaps a case of sour grapes given his unattractive appearance), had little feeling for the sensibilities of women and, for that matter, of men. His derogatory view of females shows up also in *The Valor of Ignorance*, where he continuously equated femininity with lack of reason and with weakness.

    Ethel, of modest background and education, may not have tried to disabuse him of these notions. Born in a small Tennessee town a year before Homer, she was seven when her mother died and, as the oldest girl of several, had to take care of the household. For that reason she had very little formal education. At 15 she married a young man of 21. She had her first child at 17 and two more within the next five years. Her husband tried his hand at several trades but had a hard time feeding the family, and so, after they settled in Memphis, Ethel decided to earn money for her family. She took a one-month course in typing and stenography, which helped her to find a position as secretary at the local office of the Illinois Central Railroad. In 1906, at the age of 31, she was given a free railroad pass, which she used for a trip to Los Angeles on the Southern Pacific. The pass was for one person only, and thus she went alone on the first holiday of her life. At a family hotel in Los Angeles, she met a woman from Mississippi, who was acquainted with Homer Lea and knew that he needed help for the typing of his book, *The Vermilion Pencil*. Ethel took the job, and on its completion she returned to her family in Memphis.[18]

The following year, "when hard times hit the family,"[19] she went back to Los Angeles to work again for Homer Lea. She took care of his correspondence and typed several articles and most of his next book, *The Valor of Ignorance*. From a typist she developed to a secretary and from a secretary to a friend and confidante. She had a great capacity for work, and, indeed, during the winter of 1907–8 she worked so hard that she fell ill. By September 1908 Lea could no longer afford to pay her salary and thus she returned to Memphis. "I wish I knew of some way to fix it so you could come back," he wrote to her, but, he added despairingly, "every thing I lean on breaks; every hope I conjecture up vanishes before the realities of each new day."[20] He wrote this letter in answer to hers in which she apparently told him of having found employment in Memphis. It also seems that she was no longer living with her husband and was trying to find a boarding school for her two boys, the oldest and the youngest of her three children.

In 1909, when Ethel left Memphis again for Los Angeles to live with Homer Lea, her husband divorced her. Ethel was with Lea in February and March of 1910 when Sun Yat-sen visited with him. In his subsequent letters, Sun almost never forgot to add greetings for Ethel. In 1911 Lea planned to go to Germany with Ethel for the treatment of his failing eyesight. They then found it advisable to get married. The wedding is said to have taken place on June 10, 1911.[21]

Ethel was but a trifle taller than Homer, plain-looking, quiet and sensible, endowed with a good sense of humor, as was he, and of natural intelligence. By reading she had made up for her lack of formal education. She had a keen sense of observation, as shown in the letters to her family, and some writing ability. Had she acted as Lea's editor, she might have improved, by her simple and direct style, his grandiloquent and sometimes convoluted manner of writing. An acquaintance called her "a remarkable wife . . . solicitous, attentive, intelligent, sympathetic, sweetly managerial."[22]

According to her oldest son, Joshua, she served Lea as secretary and confidante, nursemaid, housekeeper, and motherly friend.[23] There may be a question as to the intensity of their relation. A 1908 letter to Ethel, after her second period of working for Lea, does show a certain degree of emotional involvement on his part: "Almost two weeks have passed since you left but it seems tenfold longer. . . . Write to me often, Ethel, regardless of my neglect to reply at once. You know how much I want to hear from you yet how difficult it is to answer as soon as I might wish."[24] A letter from London in October 1911 reveals more passion: "I have never been so miserable and lonesome in my life. . . . I have been dreaming of you every night. I certainly will devour you with kisses as soon as I get you here."[25] On the other hand, Ethel does not seem to have been convinced of the strength of his attachment for, in March 1912, a month after the onset of his last illness, she wrote to her sisters from China: "If I am away from the bed for ten minutes he begins to get excited and nervous, seems beset with fear that I'll *never* come back. He didn't know how much he cared for me until he got sick."[26] Illness and physical dependence on Ethel may have changed Homer's views of marriage and domesticity. In the same letter Ethel told her sisters, "he says now he wants to go back and build a home and 'adopt' Al, Sis and Bryant [her children]—so we can be happy." A few months later he remarked to his friend, Marco Newmark: "Do you remember that time when you became engaged to be married, I told you you were a damn fool, that now you will have a family, that you will lead a monotonous life and be of no use to anybody? Well, I wanted to say to you that I made a mistake."[27]

Shortly after Ethel's first stay in Los Angeles, Homer Lea began work on *The Valor of Ignorance*. The book was to make him known as a military strategist in the United States as well as abroad. It also appeared to reinforce its author's claim to the rank of general and to give him respectability as a military expert, which he so avidly sought. Much more than his work for the Chinese Imperial Reform Army and for the Chinese Revolution, the book was responsible for the survival of his name.

In 1907, before Ethel's return to Los Angeles, Homer Lea spent considerable time away from the city. He had been very ill during the winter of 1906–7 and, as Marco Newmark was said to have remembered, during the summer of 1907 went "to Bear Valley in the San Bernardino mountains east of Los Angeles, partly to recuperate and partly to explore the passes and mountains in that vicinity with the object of using his knowledge [of the terrain] in the proposed book—'The Valor of Ignorance'—showing military conditions in connection with the Pacific Slope's undefended position."[28] A report from a half-brother of his father, who stayed with the family in 1907, confirms Lea's excursions. On his arrival he was told that Homer had gone with friends to the mountains and, as a result, the two never met.[29] Lea himself stated in the epilogue of his book, published in 1909, that he "spent nearly seven months exploring from a military viewpoint, the San Jacinto, San Bernardino, San Gabriel and Tehachapi mountains, the Mojave and its adjacent deserts, traversing between one and two thousand miles."[30] However, he did not give the time when he undertook these explorations. It has been said that he made the strenuous excursions through mountains and deserts on O'Banion's strong shoulders, but this was vehemently denied by his sister, Ermal.[31]

He continued to work on the book during 1908. In April of that year he wrote to a friend that he hoped to finish it in the latter part of

June,[32] but it took him longer. In September he wrote to Ethel that he had changed the ending and had added another chapter but could not complete the work until he had obtained the material for the appendices.[33] He probably finished it during the winter of 1908-9, for in early February 1909 Boothe mentioned its completion to a New York friend, W. W. Allen. In the same letter Boothe reported that the manuscript had been read by Lieutenant General Chaffee and Major General Story; the latter had been Chief of Artillery of the U.S. Army and Chairman of the Board of Coast Defense. According to Boothe, both men were enthusiastic about "the remarkable work," which "marked the author a military genius." On the basis of these endorsements, Boothe asked for Allen's help in finding a publisher. In a second letter he mentioned that both generals expected the book to be "a good seller and create a vast amount of discussion in the country, not only in military circles, but among the people generally."[34] Allen succeeded in placing the book with Harper's. The publishing contract was signed on June 17, 1909,[35] and the volume appeared later that year with one foreword by Chaffee and another by Story. Originally, Lea wanted President Roosevelt to write a foreword, but Boothe advised against it because Roosevelt had already endorsed so many books "as to cheapen the value of his endorsement."[36] As long as he could not grace his work with the name of the country's chief executive, Lea dedicated it to another national figure, "The Hon. Elihu Root," who, until 1909, was the Secretary of State and thereafter a U.S. Senator. Lea did not use the general's rank with his name as author, but the frontispiece showed him in a general's uniform, which, to the average reader, could have been that of a U.S. Army officer rather than that of a general in the Chinese Imperial Reform Army.

It is not known how and when Homer Lea got acquainted with General Chaffee who, upon his retirement, went to live in California. General Otis, who had served with Chaffee in the Philippines, probably introduced the two men to each other. It is also possible that Lea got to know General Chaffee through Charles Boothe. Later, in a letter to Boothe, Sun Yat-sen spoke of "your friend, the former general in the Phillipines [sic]," although he failed to make it clear whether he referred to Chaffee or Otis.[37]

The Valor of Ignorance did cause a stir when it appeared but was not the immediate success that had been anticipated. In March 1910 Allen had a conference with Harper's chief editor about better promotion and distribution of the book. Allen assured Lea that Harper's was doing its best. Though sales did not reach spectacular numbers, they continued steadily for several years.[38]

Extracts were translated into French, and there were plans for Chinese and German editions, which, however, did not materialize.[39] A Japanese edition under the title *The War Between Japan and America* was published in November 1911. Sun Yat-sen arranged for the translation through his Japanese friend, Koki H. Ike (Ike Kyokichi), and Lea arranged that the royalties were to go to Sun for political purposes. The book had forewords by four Japanese generals[40] and underwent three printings during the first week alone. Ike expected a "wild sale," and, indeed, 84,000 copies were sold within three months.[41] Even before its publication, a pirated version had made its appearance. A publicity release by the authorized publisher called it "the most popular book in the world." Its author was referred to as a U.S. staff officer. The U.S. Government was said to have bought copies "from the first edition down to the tenth," while the German Kaiser was reported to have distributed tens of thousands of copies among his officers.[42] These exaggerated claims spawned similar, extravagant assertions by popular writers for many years to come.

The success of the book in Japan is understandable because after the Russo-Japanese War the United States was the foremost potential rival of Japan in the Pacific area. According to Lea's book, Japan was consistently and energetically preparing for conflict with the United States, which was neglecting to build a sufficiently strong navy and a large enough army combined with an effective transportation system. Lea predicted that Japan would proclaim its own "Monroe Doctrine" in the Pacific, which eventually occurred decades later under the name of "Greater East Asia Co-Prosperity Sphere." By the establishment of strong naval bases in the Pacific, Japan would gain temporary supremacy in the area, and through its efficient and large merchant fleet Japan would rapidly deploy its well-trained armies at strategic points. The outcome of the war with the United States would thus be decided by the Japanese army.

An immediate war objective of the Japanese would be the conquest of the Philippines, a relatively easy task. Lea described in detail Japan's strategy in that case, the disembarkation points of the Japanese army and the routes from there to Manila, which, as history showed, would fall in a very short time. The prize objective of a Japanese war effort would be the islands of Hawaii. The occupation of these islands in the heart of the Pacific area would open up the South Pacific as well as provide an eventual basis for the invasion of the United States' Pacific coast. The military could not prevent the loss of Hawaii, where there was no strong U.S. naval or army base to protect the islands against the qualitatively superior Japanese navy. The Japanese navy also had a quantitative advantage because that of the United States was divided between the Pacific and the Atlantic. In addition, the U.S. inland transportation system, the railroad network, was unable to take a sufficiently large army to the West early enough to repel the Japanese troops disembarking rapidly from their numerous transport vessels. On the basis of detailed maps, Lea described the Japanese strategy for invading the population centers in Washington, Oregon, and California. And, finally, Lea predicted—correctly, as it turned out—that Japan, to gain time and the advantage of surprise, would start the war without a prior formal declaration of war.

Lea's assessment of the strategic value of the Philippines was called the basis for U.S. military strategy in the Pacific area until World War II. Indeed, his fame among many rested on his prediction of a war with Japan and of Japanese designs on the Philippines and Hawaii, although he was not alone in making such forecasts.[43] U.S. military leaders were also of the opinion that the country was ill-prepared for defending the vast Pacific area. General Chaffee, when Chief of Staff of the U.S. Army, suggested after 1904 the drafting of various plans for meeting the defense needs of the country. The plan dealing with a possible war with Japan was given the code name "Plan Orange."[44] In 1908 the Joint Army and Navy Board that discussed Plan Orange came to conclusions not dissimilar from those that worried Lea. It was also thought that the base in the Philippines would be taken by Japan at the beginning of the war, thus depriving the U.S. Navy of its capacity to operate in that area. Furthermore, the Hawaiian islands were considered in danger of occupation, which would imperil the western states. Japan's success depended solely on its shipping and transportation facilities, while the United States faced the incredibly difficult task of countering the attack by sending its fleet from the Atlantic to the Pacific, a distance of more than 10,000 miles.

Lea was unknown to the War Department when his treatise appeared. The Chief of Staff of the U.S. Army, who had followed Chaffee in that position, called Lea's ideas "certainly interesting to all students of military affairs."[45] Other military circles also took much notice of it and applauded his ideas, including British Field Marshall Lord Roberts,[46] who started to correspond with Lea and became a good friend of his. In the United States a whole generation of army and navy officers were influenced by the book. A dissenting voice came from Dr. Jordan, a leading pacifist, who considered it without value from the military point of view, singularly worthless, and possibly mischievous. An English-language newspaper in Japan published the same negative opinion under the heading, "The Impudence of Charlatanism," with an endorsement by Dr. Jordan.[47]

Sun Yat-sen is reported to have read the book in 1909 while in London. Impressed by Lea's views, he is said to have written to Lea, which led to their meeting in California early in 1910.[48] Whether this is true or not, *The Valor of Ignorance* established Lea in Sun's eyes as an authority on the military and strategic problems of the Pacific area. Before leaving the

United States, he met somebody who had in his possession numerous secret military papers of Japan. The identity of Sun's contact is not known, and his earlier letter, in which he told Lea of his find, has not survived, but a second letter written a few days later is available:

> On Sea, March 24, 1910
>
> My dear General:
>
> In my former letter I informed you that someone posessing [*sic*] some very important documents of a certain military Power. Just before my sailing I received a list of the same, herewith I am [*sic*] enclosed with a translation. The list only given [*sic*] 12 kinds but there are others besides, all amount to more than thirty big books. All are the latest work of the General Staff of the Power. I think it is the most valuable thing that any rivalry Power could get. Would you try to find out whether the War Department of this country would avail this opportunity of obtaining these secret documents?[49]

Though Lea's answer is not available, it is quite conceivable that he asked Sun to obtain the documents and eventually turned them over to the War Department. A search for them in Washington has not been fruitful. O'Banion claimed he obtained the papers for Lea through a secret contact in Japan against payment of a sum of money.[50]

The Valor of Ignorance, which made Lea a defense expert among interested circles in the United States, also made him, in November 1910, one of the delegates from southern California at the Pacific Slope Congress in San Francisco. This meeting, which was attended by western governors, politicians, army officers, and other notables, had been called to discuss the defense of the Pacific coast and the protection of U.S. trade routes. Lea, a prominent member of the Congress, spoke at great length "to reiterate assertions . . . anent the futility of depending on the coast fortifications, and criticized the American people generally for their selfish attitude and indifference to affairs of national importance."[51]

In later years, a revolutionary exile in Switzerland, Vladimir I. Lenin, read Lea's book and was said to have commented that "this book will some day be studied by thousands of people." Among the people who studied the book not so much later was General von Seeckt, the driving force behind German rearmament between the two world wars, who pronounced Lea an astounding writer.[52]

The book was rediscovered after the Japanese attack on Pearl Harbor. Before the Japanese invasion of the Philippines, a young American journalist, Clare Boothe, visited General MacArthur's headquarters and heard his officers talk of Homer Lea and his projections for a Japanese attack on the islands. According to these officers, "MacArthur . . . knew what Homer Lea had written in *The Valor of Ignorance*" and " that general staffs everywhere, including the Japanese, had read Lea's extraordinary forecast. In many a pre-Pearl Harbor staff conference at the general's Manila military headquarters in gloomy old Fort Santiago, Lea's 'invasion map' of the Philippines—a pincer movement on Manila beginning with landings to the north at Lingayen Gulf and to the southeast at Polillo Bight—was discussed. The name of Homer Lea popped up most prominently when the whole of Manila society was buzzing about a Japanese espionage case and an alleged betrayal that involved a Filipino officer, a graduate of West Point. In pleading for lenience toward the Filipino West Point graduate on the ground that his 'secrets' were public knowledge that 'could be had in a bookstore,' MacArthur's staff had reference to [a] particular passage" in Lea's book.[53] After the war, MacArthur's chief officers called Lea "clairvoyant to the point of specifying the precise bays and beaches the Japanese would use to debark their troops."[54]

When the attack came, Clare Boothe remembered the conversations at MacArthur's headquarters. In 1942 she arranged for the reissue of *The Valor of Ignorance* and of Lea's second work on military strategy, *The Day of the Saxon*. She wrote lengthy introductions to the books and also published a magazine article about Lea.[55] Unfortunately, she had to rely on the legends that had grown up among Lea's friends, to which she added her own unsubstantiated embellishments.

Lea completed his last book, *The Day of the Saxon*, in China during the hectic days of Sun's short term as Provisional President of the Chinese Republic. In Lea's own words, "This book has been written under numerous difficulties. Begun in America, parts were written upon every continent and every sea, being finally completed in Asia. Begun in profound peace, the concluding chapters were finished upon a recent field of battle. Nanking, China. H.L."[56]

The last chapters reached the publisher, Harper & Brothers, shortly before the onset of Lea's illness in February 1912. Originally, Lea wanted to dedicate the book to King George V, but, in case the King's consent could not be obtained, he suggested Harper ask Lord Roberts for permission to dedicate it to him. The publisher considered it "a rather impracticable thing to secure the necessary permission for a dedication to the King," and, therefore, procured that of Lord Roberts.[57] Lea seemed to have forgotten that he had already obtained Lord Roberts's permission when in London in November 1911.[58] The book appears to have been published rather soon after the last chapters were received in London, for in October 1912 the publisher reported that both *The Valor of Ignorance* and *The Day of the Saxon* continued to sell steadily. Although sales of the second book had not yet caught up with the earlier one,[59] it was said to have sold 7,000 copies in England alone. It sold well in Germany when, a year later, a German edition appeared, followed by three more during the next six years. By contrast, a second U.S. edition had to wait until 1942. The success of the work in Germany paralleled that of *The Valor of Ignorance* in Japan. The latter book had dealt with the political and military problems between the United States and Japan, while the new book treated largely the situation of the British Empire in relation to the growing power of Germany. The German version was translated and prepared by the German ultranationalist and Anglophobe Count Ernst zu Reventlow,[60] who later became a prominent Nazi.

In the preface Lea had mentioned a third, not yet completed, volume. Indeed, on June 8, 1912, while still an invalid, he had Ethel write Sun's secretary, Chockman, to obtain for him material for this last part of the planned trilogy.[61] However, when in the fall of 1912 the editor of the *American Magazine* asked for the rights to the serialization of the third volume, Lea confessed on October 7, less than a month before his death, that the manuscript was not advanced far enough. Due to illness during the last nine months, he explained, he had been unable to continue his literary work.[62] No sign of the manuscript, which was to have carried the title *The Swarming of the Slavs*, has been found among his surviving papers.

That book would probably have been an elaboration on the theme of the growth of Russian power and its impact upon the other great powers, which he dealt with in two chapters of *The Day of the Saxon*. Having been blocked in its expansion toward the north Pacific through its defeat by Japan, Russia would turn south and threaten India, the crown jewel of the British Empire. From there, on another line of expansion, Russia would approach the Bosphorus through Persia. During and after the Cold War period many asserted that Lea had predicted a direct Russian attack upon Europe. This is not evident in *The Day of the Saxon*. To the contrary, he spoke of a *Dreibund*, a tripartite alliance between Russia, Germany, and Japan, as a threat to the British Empire and with it to the dominion of the Anglo-Saxon race, which to him meant the United States and South Africa as well as Great Britain. He had mentioned this threat already in his first letter to Lord Roberts, in which he called his forthcoming book, *The Day of the Saxon*, "but introductory to the general work I have in mind to bring about: (1) a change in form and spirit of the American government," and "(2) conscription," a job that he compared to cleaning an Augean stable.[63]

In *The Day of the Saxon*, Lea proclaimed the need for the British Empire, if it were to survive, to restructure its military, naval, and political systems. He advocated making the empire one military unit, politically as cohesive as a single state, with the individual parts subordinated to the unified whole and military and political supremacy of the Saxon over its constituent parts. To attain this, compulsory military service was required to obtain large and strong expeditionary forces, in addition to the mighty British navy. The expeditionary forces were to be distributed in size and geography according to the potential and the location of adversaries. Above all, he called for a revival of the militancy of the "race" and the abandonment of complacency and self-deception in favor of greater militancy. This meant increased military organization concurrent with the increase of political and economic development of the individual territories and proportionate to the military, political, and economic growth of other nations. Unless the Saxon people and their empire chose this path they were doomed. "At this late hour or never," he preached, "must the Saxon people arouse themselves to the somber consequences of their neglect and break away from the pleasant security of their delusions. To them has now come that gloomy dawn so familiar to man throughout all the nights and dawns he has bedded and risen together, falling asleep upon a peaceful earth and getting up to find it a place of strife. . . . This has ever been the fate of nations as they have laid themselves down to sleep throughout the ages much in the same manner as the Saxon race, in all their glory and vanity, only to awake at a predetermined hour to find themselves upon a savage dawn, stripped and desolate."[64]

Lea's main thesis concerned the relation of land to sea power, a theme that he had already touched upon in *The Valor of Ignorance*. Ever since Mahan, naval power had been considered the key to dominion. Command of the seas ensures national supremacy. Like Mahan, Lea used the British Empire as the example to prove his theory, and without mentioning him—in fact, in none of his two books on military matters and strategy did he mention or quote other authors—Lea set out to correct Mahan's theory. For Lea, sea power cannot bring a continental power like Germany to its knees. Ultimately, wars are won by land armies transported, if necessary, by the navy and supplied by it. For that reason, a strong navy alone does not preserve a nation's dominant position, much less assure its expansion. A land army placed in the empire's strategically located bases and equal to that of a potential adversary or a coalition of adversaries is needed in addition to naval power to maintain superiority.

As for Germany, whose expansionist drive threatened the British Empire, the occupation of Belgium, the Netherlands, and Denmark and sovereignty over Austria would make it an invincible power both on land and on sea. With a strong fleet Germany could challenge Britain's rule of the seas, put it in a defensive position, and, eventually, use combined sea and land power for an invasion of the British Isles where victory was assured since there would be no land forces opposing the invaders. To posterity this sounds like a prescription for the strategy tried by the German High Command in World War II. That Germany's "Sea Lion" campaign did not succeed, was due, to a large degree, to a factor that Homer Lea disregarded and belittled, air power.[65]

Lea's dissent from Mahan's theory, "the most articulate and also the shrillest,"[66] appears to have been vindicated in the Pacific area when, during World War II, the British and Dutch possessions and the Philippines were lost to Japanese land armies. But in another, and larger, sense his theories did not stand the test. For Mahan and others, sea power was not a value in itself, but mastery of the seas meant the protection of the nation's trade routes, the security of its economic lifeline, and expansion of foreign commerce necessary to national power and prosperity. Expansion to which the navy was a mere handmaid, meant, in the colonial period, also the expansion of overseas business. But such mercantile considerations had no place in Lea's scheme of things. He saw the world in narrow military concepts. He did not realize that "military questions are so interwoven with economic, social, and technological phenomena that it is doubtful if one can speak of a purely military strategy."[67] While Lea acknowledged a connection between these spheres and the military, he reversed their order of importance. "Military activity," he postulated, "is a condition of national life, in the same sense as industrialism, but with this difference: though military development and industrialism are both factors subordinate to the ultimate aim of national existence, the militant spirit is a primordial element in the formative process and ultimate consummation of the nation's existence; while industrialism . . . is [merely] national alimentation."[68] In the end, therefore, Lea's thoughts were divorced from the realities of his times due to his disregard of the contribution that industrial strength and commercial development and penetration make to a nation's power in world affairs.

The Day of the Saxon found its readers among military personnel, politicians, and scholars perhaps more than among the general public. In 1942, upon publication of the second edition, it was said, with a considerable degree of exaggeration, that Lea's "strategic analysis now seems remarkably up-to-date," but it was certainly true that "his writings have lately received—after some thirty years of oblivion—the awed attention bestowed by posterity upon departed prophets."[69]

The book was widely reviewed, but some of its reviewers faulted its style as pedantic and dull with a stentorian quality that made it sound like a protracted oration. Due to its ungrammatical, involved, and empurpled phraseology, Lea was called a master of uncouth and untutored eloquence that infrequently achieved a lucid period of great force while mostly stumbling over a simple descriptive phrase. Lea's habit of raising even simple observations to the category of universal laws found its

critics, as did the pseudoscientific and pseudophilosophic pronounce-
ments of the self-made scholar. Count Reventlow, in a long introduction
to the German edition, also criticized the heavy-handed style and the
laborious thinking of the self-made military expert. Indeed, Lea's style
and thinking, the tendency to systematization and abstraction, the com-
pulsive stress on underlying and invariable principles and trends of national existence reminded him of typically German thought processes
and manner of writing. He called Lea a quite un-American American.
But he, as well as American and British reviewers, even when they disagreed, acknowledged the seriousness of Lea's arguments and noted his
genuine insight into many problems of political and military power.[70]

Homer Lea as General of the Chinese Imperial Reform Army

Homer Lea in a Mandarin Costume

Soldiers of the Chinese Imperial Reform Army in Training

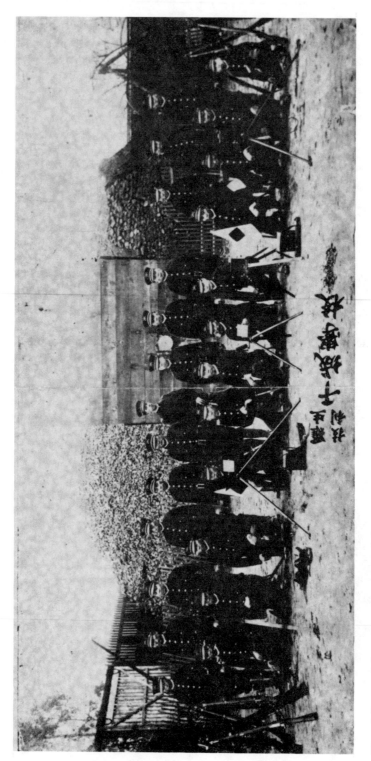

Signal Corps of the Chinese Imperial Reform Army

The Kuang-hsü Emperor

The Dowager Empress Tz'u-hsi

K'ang Yu-wei

Liang Ch'i-ch'ao

Sun Yat-sen and his son, Sun Fo

Arrival of Sun Yat-sen and Homer Lea in Shanghai, December 25, 1911

—— 7 ——

Conspiracies

By the end of summer 1908, Homer Lea's activities had come to a dead end. K'ang had come and gone, but his presence in the United States had not brought Lea nearer to his goal of active participation in the political and military affairs of China. In the intervening years, Lea had completed his novel and nearly finished *The Valor of Ignorance*. His military organization, while still in existence, had become a blunt instrument in his hands due to the need for secrecy and the lack of opportunities for putting it to use in the struggle for China. Therefore, if he were to become a factor in that struggle, he had to devise other means to attain his objective. And so he conceived a new and audacious plan, one that he hoped would take him to the theater of action and let him play a prominent role in the political changes to be brought about in China. In short, Lea proposed to go to China in an official capacity for the U.S. Government, establish direct contact with revolutionary groups in the country, and lead them in a revolution against the existing Chinese government. Lea discussed this plan with Charles Boothe, who agreed to lend his support.

Charles Beach Boothe (1851–1914), a businessman from Connecticut, had moved to Los Angeles in 1892, where he continued to be active in business and in matters of public concern such as irrigation. In May 1905 Boothe happened to be in the Midwest during K'ang's and Lea's joint tour. At the time he met K'ang in St. Louis.[1] It has been reported that his sons were friends of Lea,[2] which, if correct, would explain the meeting. It was Boothe who early in 1908 asked Lea about K'ang's whereabouts and the possibility of his coming again to the United States. He asked the same question in September 1908 when he left for the East Coast, where he hoped he could meet with K'ang.[3] It was probably not

K'ang the reformer but K'ang the man in whom Boothe was interested because it is not known that before that time he had ever concerned himself with the political affairs of China.

In September 1908 Boothe was about to travel to Washington and New York. Lea saw this as an opportunity for Boothe to help in the realization of his plan, and so he revealed it to him. Lea wanted to be appointed the U.S. Consul in Canton, a strategically important southern city where revolutionary trends were more active than in many other parts of the country. Boothe was to use his connections to obtain that appointment for Lea. If given the post, Lea's official duties would include the promotion of trade between the United States and China. This would entail ending the Chinese boycott of U.S. goods. That boycott had begun in 1905 after the renewal in 1904 of the Chinese Exclusion Act. Lea believed it was particularly effective against U.S. textiles, hence his proposal to Boothe to work through trade organizations in that field, which included cotton growers, cotton piece goods trade, and shipping interests. The "proper person" among them should then talk to President Roosevelt to get his approval for the appointment. On his part, Lea would, if necessary, enlist the help of Dr. Jordan, General Otis, Senators Flint and Perkins of California, the Governor, and the heads of the Chamber of Commerce and the Bankers Association of Southern California. He would also obtain the endorsements of the governors of the southern states interested in the cotton trade.[4] Eight years of futile wait for effecting a political change in Peking seemed to have blinded Lea to the embarrassment that his double role as U.S. official and Chinese revolutionary might cause his sponsors and his government.

The choice of Canton was dictated not only by the relative strength of the city's revolutionary forces but also because it was the hub of the boycott. "The Canton merchants," said Lea, "are the most active of any in the Empire; their Guild-houses are to be found in every large city, from Manchuria to Singapore; the ramifications of their trade interests and power are, in the Orient, without end."[5] Any effort to end the boycott had to begin in Canton.

A few months before disclosing his plan to Boothe, Lea had published a lengthy magazine article about the historical background of the boycott.[6] He explained it as an action by the Chinese people against the injustice of the exclusion laws. It was a protest by the "unorganized democracy of the Chinese people," which was "a form of government independent of Imperial power," and was "exemplified in the word, *whui* [hui], meaning association." Associations of the Chinese people existed for purposes of "self-protection, education, diffusion of knowledge, business, or political purposes," and comprised secret as well as non-secret societies, the former mostly militant and revolutionary, the latter including merchant guilds. Past efforts to end the boycott had been un-successful because U.S. officials did not understand its nature. It was not a measure adopted by the Chinese Government, but the instrument of voluntary associations of the people. Homer Lea who for years had had contact with Chinese associations, both secret and nonsecret, believed he possessed the key to the solution of the problem that others had been unable to solve.

Lea took pains to assure Boothe that his educational background was adequate for the coveted appointment. He said he had studied eco-nomics and sociology "under Prof A. E. Ross [a noted sociologist] with whom the President [Roosevelt] is acquainted. This course of study for my B.A. degree gave me the best possible education that one could have as far as academic knowledge is concerned in a position of this kind." By mentioning the course leading to the degree, he left the impression that he had actually obtained it.

He also pointed out that his knowledge of the Chinese people equaled that of any U.S. citizen with long and varied experience in the Orient. "Politically and racially, in a personal and sociological sence [sic] I do not think it possible to find anyone in this Nation who understands more thoroughly the Chinese."[7]

Homer Lea had not formally studied China's history and people. He may have studied the language for several years as Chinese sources maintain,[8] and he had learned a good deal through private reading and personal contacts. His writings on China are replete with facts from Chi-nese history. In the foreword to one of his articles, which deals with Chi-nese society under the first emperor of the Sung dynasty, he listed the works he had consulted: an encyclopedia by Ma Twan Sin [Ma Twan Lin] entitled *Profound Researches into Ancient Documents*, "similar Chinese works not translated into English," Demetrius Boulger's *History of China*, Abbé Huc's *Travels in China*, Abel Remusat's *Nouveaux Mé-langes Asiatiques*, and Mailla's translation of *The Chinese Repository of History*.[9]

But more significant than the facts he may have gleaned from the literature about China were his attempts at understanding the historical development and the social structure of the country. The distinction he drew between the official rule of the dynastic government and the unof-ficial, unorganized institutions of the people as represented in the so-cieties are also the views of more recent writers on China. His analysis of the boycott as a popular movement rather than an action of the Chinese Government has been confirmed by a researcher half a century later.[10] In *The Valor of Ignorance* and elsewhere, he spoke of the cycles of Chinese history, the successive rise and decay of dynasties combined with the de-terioration of bureaucratic order and the weakening of social bonds.

Some historians are also wont to recognize such cyclic patterns of dynastic rule.[11] Homer Lea further maintained that Western assumptions about the immobility of the Chinese governmental structure and societal life throughout thousands of years did not agree with the historical facts.[12] Scholars will concede to him that China, in the course of its history, went through numerous diverse phases, politically, socially, and institutionally. While many of Lea's contemporaries spoke of the effete celestials, he showed, by examples taken from Chinese history, that the people had a long and extensive martial tradition[13] and that, if properly trained, were equal to others in military prowess, a view shared by contemporary professionals and modern historians.[14] Finally, he submitted that, until the advent of modern science and technology, China was superior to the Occident, politically and intellectually, and continued to be so in those spheres of life unaffected by scientific progress,[15] a thought shared by many in the West during the latter part of the nineteenth century.

His novel, *The Vermilion Pencil*, leaves the impression that, in addition to a certain understanding of China's historical development, Lea was also familiar with Chinese society. The story does not deal with everyday life, but it does allow the conclusion that its author knew in a general way the lifestyles of the Chinese people, even though he had spent only a limited time in the country and faced the disadvantage of the language barrier. His eager and receptive mind helped him to overcome these failings, just as he tried, by his total and unreserved engagement, to compensate for the lack of formal studies. Therefore, whatever the merits of Lea's assumptions and propositions about China and the Chinese, and they may have been neither unique nor profound, one must recognize the sincerity and earnestness of his efforts to know and understand the country.

Boothe discussed the question of the appointment while in Washington and reported on his endeavors to Lea in a letter that has not been preserved. In acknowledging it, Lea voiced his pleasure at the favorable progress of the matter.[16] However, he was never given the appointment. In fact, the Chinese boycott was not very effective, or no longer so, as was explained to Boothe a few months later by his friend W. W. Allen, whom he had enlisted on Lea's behalf.[17] With the boycott's failure, Lea's main argument for obtaining the post in Canton was also bound to fail, but he was not entirely unprepared for the unfavorable outcome of the matter. Writing to Ethel in September 1908, after she had left for Memphis, he told her, "I have gotten the Canton affair started and my friend C. B. left for Washington and New York Wednesday. . . . I shall use every [*sic*] to gain it but may fail as I have so many times before."[18]

The failure did not daunt him, however. Half a year later another, even greater opportunity beckoned when the ministership in Peking became vacant. Again he mobilized friends and acquaintances. It was then that he got Boothe to write to K'ang on his behalf. After the death of the Kuang-hsü Emperor, K'ang was rumored to be ready to make his peace with the Manchu court and to end his exile: "General Lea's friends having knowledge of his kindly feelings towards the people of China feel it to be most appropriate that he should be appointed to the now vacant post of Minister to China. All who know him feel that it would be beneficial to both countries to have a man of his capacity, and with his knowledge of the traditions and temperament of your people as the representative of the United States Government in Peking." Lea's name was, of course, anathema to the government in Peking, and, as K'ang was expected to establish good relations with the Prince Regent, Lea thought he could smooth the way for the appointment. Moreover, if K'ang, the erstwhile enemy of the Peking regime, were to be accepted by it in good graces, so could Lea, who for years had been close to the reformer, although Boothe expressed this thought with a certain ambiguity: "It has occurred to me," wrote Boothe, "that possibly [General Lea's] friendship and loyalty to you might operate in some quarters in China to bring out an unfavorable comment upon his filling this post. It seems to me, however, that if the Prince Regent is advised of General Lea's past history, in connection with Chinese matters, and his true relation with those who are faithful adherents to the late Emperor, that any opposition to him from unfriendly quarters would be unlikely."[19]

K'ang, however, did not return to Peking at that time. Nor is there any record of an answer to Boothe or to Lea, and thus this approach failed. Equally fruitless were Lea's efforts to gain support for the nomination in Washington. Even before Boothe's letter to K'ang, Lea had approached Generals Chaffee and Story and suggested that they send a joint telegram to President W. H. Taft recommending him for the ministership. But both declined to intervene unless "a political person" would take the initiative, in which case they, as military men, would be able to support it.[20] General Otis might have been such a political person as the owner of the *Los Angeles Times*, but after taking some steps to that effect he "satisfied himself by further inquiry that the project as undertaken was not feasible of accomplishment and so informed Gen. Chaffee" as well as Lea.[21]

Dr. Jordan of Stanford was another prominent man whom Lea approached in connection with the appointment. *The Valor of Ignorance* had not yet appeared, and, therefore, Lea could still fully count on his goodwill and support, which may not have been proffered as readily once Dr. Jordan was aware of the depth of Lea's militaristic leanings. In asking Dr. Jordan for a letter of recommendation to the President, Lea suggested that his "experience of the last ten years concerning Oriental politics and knowledge of the peoples of the Orient should be utilized, not only for the benefit of our own country, but also for the furtherance of a juster understanding between the two nations." He added the assurance to Dr. Jordan that "you will have no reason at any time in the future to regret the interest you may have taken in aiding me to secure [the appointment]."[22] Although Dr. Jordan did write the letter of recommendation, Lea failed again in getting the post.

Lea's letter contained a further assurance: "Since the death of the Emperor Kwang Su [Kuang-hsü], I have entirely severed all affiliation with the Chinese, inasmuch as my sole efforts in the past ten years have been to secure his reestablishment, and with his death I felt at liberty to entirely withdraw from any further services in that country." After he received Dr. Jordan's letter of recommendation, he repeated that deceitful statement and gave the additional dubious promise "that my past affiliation will influence me in no way nor affect to the slightest degree the impartiality of my judgment."

These assurances and promises were false because, for six months before they were made, Lea had been engaged in a conspiracy with three other individuals in the United States with the object of starting a revolution in China. The scheme of the four men, to which they gave the code name "Red Dragon," presupposed a cooperation between K'ang's group, the Pao Huang Hui, which was still in existence, Sun Yat-sen's Revolutionary Alliance, and the secret societies in China. Lea was to be in charge of the military operations. One can hardly assume that plain naiveté prompted him to seek an appointment to a government that he was plotting to overthrow. Nor can one deny the deviousness with which he approached Dr. Jordan for support of his diplomatic ambitions. However he may have explained and reconciled in his own mind his conflicting attitudes, he does not appear as a man burdened by scruples in the steadfast pursuit of his goals.

On his trip east in the fall of 1908, Boothe was to accomplish two missions for Lea: first, he was to enlist support for the appointment in Canton; and, second, establish connections that would help to start and further the planned revolution in the southern Chinese provinces, Kwangtung, of which Canton was the capital city, and Kwangsi. Yung Wing, of whom he had known as a prominent member of the reform movement since his trip to China in 1900, appeared to Lea as a man who could help him to reestablish contact to the reform movement abroad and to win support for his scheme among other insurgent leaders. Yung, then 80 years old, was respected by all factions as a sincere patriot and archenemy of the existing regime in Peking. Accordingly, Lea asked Boothe to visit Yung and discuss the project for a revolutionary uprising.

In particular, Boothe was to ask Yung Wing whether he and other leaders were prepared to support Lea's plan for a revolution; and whether

Yung could secure backing by the most powerful opposition groups in southern China, provided that Lea succeeded in obtaining the finances needed for a military campaign. Yung, when approached by Boothe, gave positive answers to both queries.[23]

Since his return to the United States in 1902, Yung Wing had remained an implacable enemy of the Peking court and from time to time had drafted his own plans for its overthrow.[24] As far as the financial side was concerned, Lea counted on the funds in K'ang's hands, as yet unaware that they had disappeared in the latter's unfortunate business ventures. In addition, he had discussed with Boothe the possibilities of obtaining financial support from U.S. business interests desirous to increase their share of the large Chinese market. In this respect, Boothe expected to get help from a boyhood friend, W. W. Allen in New York, a consulting engineer well connected with financial circles in Wall Street and in London and with direct access to J. P. Morgan. Among other business ventures, Allen was said to have organized the Guggenheim Exploration Company. Boothe described him as "a hard-headed businessman with but little sentiment who strikes at the heart of things in business, . . . rather brusque and . . . more likely to make short cuts to the point at issue than to advance after the manner of diplomats."[25]

Allen, too, was impressed with the Red Dragon scheme and decided to take part in the venture or, as he called it, the "business between the United States and China," if he were given sufficient details.[26] These were to be provided to him by Yung Wing, who was most eager to proceed with the enterprise. After his return to California, Boothe wrote to Yung, he had apprized Lea of his discussions, and Lea had expressed his satisfaction with their outcome. Yung replied enthusiastically, "Glad you have heard from the General, that he is ready to go into action. He has much to see to, before harnessed for the field."[27] He congratulated Lea on having picked Boothe to manage the affair and in having selected the right spot "to plant our standard." He added magnanimously, "for these two things, you are entitled to no small credit. The first province you take in China, I shall make you a Viceroy, & Boothe a Baron, if I had the power of dubbing you both."[28] Thus, these four men, Homer Lea, Charles B. Boothe, Yung Wing, and W. W. Allen, entered into a conspiracy to bring about a revolution in China. As proposed, Lea was to be in charge of the military aspects of the undertaking. Yung's role was to establish contact and maintain liaison with the leaders and the revolutionary forces in the country. Allen was to obtain the financial backing and keep in contact with Wall Street financiers, while Boothe would act as general manager, organizer, and coordinator of the enterprise.

Such a venture into high, international politics, it was felt, had to be kept secret, hence its code name, the Red Dragon. Code books were to be used between the four plotters and code names given to them and others involved. China was to be called "the old country," the Manchu government, "Jingo," Yung Wing to be identified as "Memento," Booth as "Memorial," Homer Lea as "Melting," and K'ang Yu-wei as "Menace." But after a while these precautions were dropped, and the four used their initials in the correspondence between Los Angeles, New York, and Hartford. Lea usually appeared as Gen. L. or L. or as the General. Only once, and that in a matter of less than capital importance, Lea was given his conspiratorial name when Boothe wrote to Allen, "I have not seen Melting for several days, as he has been ill with a severe cold."[29]

As the initial step in the plan agreed upon, Yung Wing was to approach K'ang and other leaders and have them come to Los Angeles where they would constitute themselves as an Advisory Board, later referred to as the Grand Council, of the revolutionary undertaking. The Council would then appoint a provisional government to which it would act as adviser. Perhaps in consideration of Lea's role and that of Allen, Yung Wing added a caveat that the War and Treasury Departments should not be headed by Chinese nationals for at least ten years.[30]

When it came to sending out the invitations to the various leaders for the meeting in Los Angeles, Yung Wing addressed them, instead of to individuals, to four associations that were requested to send representatives for the formation of the Grand Council. These associations were K'ang's Pao Huang Hui or Protect the Emperor Society; the Ko Lao Hui or Society of Elder Brothers, a secret society that had supported K'ang's revolt in 1900; the Cheng Ch'i Hui or Society of the Righteous Spirit, another secret society that had been involved in K'ang's unsuccessful uprising; and, finally, the Chung Kuo Ming T'ung-men Hui, the Chinese Alliance, formed in 1905 under the leadership of Sun Yat-sen.

The letter of invitation as drafted by Yung Wing required the four associations to give assurances for amalgamation into a single body so that they could form a unified army, and asked them to give their representatives full power to make any decisions of the Grand Council binding upon all their members and officers. These requirements were based upon both naiveté and ignorance. It was naive to expect the two political groups, reformers and revolutionaries, to merge by the simple decision of a few representatives without prior consultations and negotiations. It betrayed woeful ignorance of conditions in China to consider the two secret societies "political associations" like the groups of K'ang and Sun. They were social organizations and, at that, amorphous congeries of many local groups not organized and held together by statutes but formed by regional customs, rites, individual loyalties, and common, yet inarticulated, economic and social interests.

The proposed letter contained an assurance to the four associations that a financial syndicate could "be promptly organized to command at once adequate capital for the sinews of war commensurate with the magnitude of the undertaking." That financial syndicate would have the right to designate three members of the Grand Council, and "as soon as the Provisional Government is organized, the sum of one million, five hundred thousand dollars ($1,500,000) (gold) will be raised at once by the financial syndicate and delivered over to the Treasurer of the Provisional Government. At the end of from six to twelve months another sum of $1,500,000 (gold) will be paid and so on. When the Grand Council is satisfied that enough funds are raised authority will be given to begin revolutionary operations."[31]

The letter of invitation was not sent, however, because "upon further consideration" Yung changed his mind again. To avoid "endless discussions and personal selfishness ad infinitum," he now proposed that first a common plan of action be worked out with a specific place for each of the leaders to limit any rivalry among them. This could be done only by sending somebody to China to establish "a skeleton organization of the component factors in the most practical, expeditious and inexpensive manner, as well as obtain a reliable secret business report in writing of the exact status of the affairs there at the present time."[32] In principle, he would be prepared to go personally, but, fearing to draw the attention of Peking, he proposed that one of his sons proceed as his personal representative. The young man, born and raised in the United States and without direct knowledge of conditions in China and the political ramifications of the undertaking, possessed the qualifications of a Yale graduate and a practical businessman as president and general manager of the Rotary File and Machine Company in Brooklyn, New York. Yung seems to have made this new proposal because he realized he was out of touch with the situation in China. He had not been there for eight years and knew of conditions only through occasional correspondence and visits by acquaintances. He had never commanded a large personal following among the various political groups, nor did he know their leaders aside from K'ang and Sun. Allen had requested him to provide "a list of people, officers, offices & c. of the various societies with the location of their headquarters and general objects [sic] which they propose to follow."[33] Yung was unable to comply, but he considered that "of no consequence, as their names could not subserve [sic] any practical purpose."[34]

Lea and Boothe apparently recognized Yung's inability to supply Allen with the information necessary for enlisting the support of U.S. financiers. In modification of Yung's revised plan, Boothe proposed to Allen to accompany the son on the mission to China and to thus obtain personally any assurances required by financial groups.[35] But before Allen could react, events in Peking drew the attention of the conspirators.

On November 15, 1908, the Court in Peking announced the death of the Empress Dowager T'zu-hsi and, simultaneously, that of the

Kuang-hsü Emperor, who was said to have expired the day before her demise. The removal from the scene of the two figures was bound to affect the conspiracy, although Boothe assured Allen, probably on the advice of Lea with whom he discussed his correspondence with Allen and Yung Wing, that the deaths would leave matters essentially unchanged, "making it only necessary to approach the subject perhaps a trifle differently."[36]

As to the deaths themselves, it was and still is widely suspected that T'zu-hsi, knowing that her days were numbered, had the Emperor poisoned. The possibility cannot be excluded, however, that the Emperor died *after* his aunt, either by orders she gave before her death or at the hand of members of her circle who feared the loss of their power if he should survive her. Perhaps it was no coincidence that a day before the Emperor's demise the Empress Dowager had already taken steps to arrange for the succession to the throne by appointing his eventual successor, a minor, to the Imperial Palace School. And on the very day of the death, that minor succeeded him through her edict.[37]

It has also been speculated that Yuan Shih-k'ai, a crafty and powerful general from the north, had the Emperor murdered either before or after the death of the Empress Dowager. Yuan had betrayed the Emperor during the Empress Dowager's coup in 1898 and, with her gone, may have feared the Emperor's revenge.

The death of the Kuang-hsü Emperor was a severe blow to K'ang because, with the Emperor dead, his cause was gone, too. At first he refused to accept the announcement as true but interpreted it as part of a scheme by Yuan Shih-k'ai to have the Emperor murdered. To forestall that eventuality he sent three telegrams to President Roosevelt on November 15 asking him to intervene and prevent the murder. Aside from making inquiries about Yuan and K'ang, the U.S. Government could do nothing since the Emperor had, in fact, died. These inquiries revealed a decided partiality of the U.S. diplomats in Peking toward Yuan and their low opinion of K'ang, who was reported as having no following in China and having collected large sums from his followers abroad under false promises.[38] K'ang also wrote to the new Regent, Prince Ch'un, warning against Yuan and his lust for power. Whether or not K'ang's diatribe played a part in the Regent's decision to dismiss Yuan cannot be ascertained. The dismissal occurred on January 2, 1909, and only two days later Yung Wing told Boothe that the removal from the seat of power of "the strongest man in China during her transitional period . . . will necessitate a material change in the program of our procedure." At the same time he insisted "that we must eliminate Kang Yu Wei in our reckoning. I shall have nothing to do with him. He is not a safe man to be associated with in a big enterprise."[39]

It was a sudden and surprising turnaround on the part of Yung Wing. Until then K'ang had figured prominently in his plans. The whole scheme had been based upon K'ang as the leading Chinese figure, who, aside from Sun Yat-sen, was the only leader whom he could name in the conversations with Allen. Now that K'ang, with the death of the Kuang-hsü Emperor, had lost his chance of ascendancy in Peking, he was ready "to discard and throw overboard" K'ang as "impractical, fantastic, and a paper reformer."[40] It was now that he accused K'ang of having "raised about $800,000 from laundrymen and others" and used the money for his own purposes.[41] Moreover, he proposed "to lope [sic] off all useless, and harmful factors & elements that are calculated to give us a bad name, & not acceptable to the people of China, nor to the whole civilized world." Among those elements he counted "those whose whole career have [sic] been given up to brigandage, pilage [sic], and plunder as the Triads, The White Lily, & The Broad Sword" societies. Convinced the time had come for "mastering an Empire, instead of gaining a petty Republic,"[42] Yung Wing was ready to ignore also the republican cause of Sun Yat-sen and the secret societies, which were one of Sun's bases of strength. In a complete change of the Red Dragon plan, he advocated that the conspirators stake everything on Yuan Shih-k'ai, a warlord with a strong army, who, on account of his dismissal by Peking, would prove to be a powerful ally. He saw it as an additional advantage that Yuan was greatly esteemed by the Western powers, including U.S. officials and business interests who considered him the champion of law and order.[43] Yung Wing no longer wanted a revolution with the help of the rabble such as the secret societies but a coup d'etat with Yuan's support. "Now that Yuan Shih-k'ai is divested of all his political power . . . & dismissed summarily, I am seriously thinking of winning him over to our cause. . . . He is worth a thousand Kang Yu Weis. He has gained the respect, & the good opinion of all the foreign representatives in Peking. If he embraces our cause, our battle for the Empire of China is already fought, & won."[44] At that time, the Chinese Foreign Minister, known as a close friend of Yuan, was staying in Hartford with neighbors of Yung, who saw this as an opportunity to approach Yuan through this official. But the Minister avoided any contact with him and slipped quietly away. Yung then proposed to induce Yuan to come to the United States under the pretext of enrolling his children in an American school.[45] But nothing came of that plan.

Lea and Boothe accepted Yung's sudden abandonment of K'ang and his newly found enthusiasm for Yuan Shih-k'ai with a measure of caution. While inclined to agree with him on his criticism of K'ang who had been "impulsive, unwise and untactful in some matters," they intended to "hedge a little" in replying to Yung Wing. But they conceded, "in view of the change in the situation . . . that an alliance can now be made in another direction with quite as good effect."[46]

During all these months of furious correspondence, the four plotters never met face to face. Several months passed by before even the two men in the east, Allen in New York and Yung Wing in Hartford, managed to see each other. A first meeting between them was scheduled in the first week of January 1909, but Yung Wing, who was trying to see the Chinese Foreign Minister, sent his son to Allen with an outline of his ideas under the heading "Wants of China."[47] The memorandum appears to have been formulated before Yung Wing decided to stake everything on Yuan. It still followed the Red Dragon plan of a revolution in Kwangtung province and the conquest of neighboring Kwangsi. But after the success of the revolution, he proposed to establish a constitutional monarchy as the form of government best suited for China, which he considered a compromise between the reigning autocracy and the opposing popular democratic tendencies. He did not explain who should function as constitutional monarch, but Allen had his suspicions: "Our Hartford friend suspects himself to be a shining mark for the imperial lightning and he is not disposed to put up any apparatus to dissipate it. In other words, 'The imperial Bee is buzzing in his bonnet.' "[48]

In the meantime, however, there was no choice but to proceed with the original plan. Again Yung Wing proposed that his son go to China to present "to ten or more of the revolutionary leaders in South China" a proposal for the organization of "a skeleton republic modelled and copied after the republic of Panama with themselves as officers." To that effect the son was to take along "the constitution and by-laws of the republic of Panama translated into Chinese." Once convinced of the scheme, the leading and as yet unknown revolutionaries were to place a certain amount of money in the treasury of the new Kwangtung Republic, "adopt a plan of operations as outlined" for them, and establish a stable government "following a systematic and orderly military occupation of the province." The U.S. syndicate would then loan a certain sum to the Republic of Kwangtung "upon its bonds and notes same being a first lien on the proceeds of the maritime customs duties of the Port of Canton," and repayment with interest would begin immediately upon the capture of Canton. The new Kwangtung government should also guarantee to the syndicate, for a certain number of years, exclusive banking, railway, and mining rights in the territory under its control. To accomplish all this, Allen should meet the revolutionary leaders on Chinese soil once the son had reached an agreement in principle.[49]

In his naive optimism Yung Wing expected that the conquest and "orderly occupation" of Kwangtung province could be effected by his son's brandishing a Chinese translation of the Panamanian constitution and Allen's promise of a loan. Taking the province of Kwangsi "from the handful of Imperial troops" he considered less difficult than establishing "a good lobby in Washington, London and Tokio." As an inducement for Allen, "a practical man of business," he pointed out "the vast opportunity for those who finance a successful attempt of this kind in China."[50] There was no mention of any contribution to the military effort by Lea, nor of any role for Boothe.

Allen and Yung Wing met for the first time in the second half of January 1909. The meeting was short and desultory but served for their getting acquainted. In a second meeting held shortly afterward, Yung Wing stressed again the uncertainties surrounding K'ang and the importance of Yuan, "a tower of strength," to the conspiratorial scheme. The two men disagreed on one point as long as the option of relying on Yuan could not be realized. Yung Wing stayed with the proposal that in that case the campaign start in Kwangtung. Allen thought the ground should be prepared in the whole of China and when the situation was ripe "the project should break out all over the country at a given hour and the work be done and completed between sunrise and sunset, or between sunset and sunrise." He feared that a protracted rebellion or civil war would frighten away the financiers who had the right to approve, if not to determine, the strategy.

Allen, too, preferred a monarchy, though not necessarily one headed by Yung Wing, to a republic, because he did not believe "that the Oriental mind, or training, will admit of a Republican form of government." He was also concerned about the unfavorable reaction of financial circles that would hesitate to support a government in which the secret societies and other revolutionary groups played a role.[51]

Boothe had introduced Yung Wing to Allen as "somewhat reticent in manner but a man of great ability, pronounced by Marquis Ito of Japan [a foremost Japanese statesman of the period] as unquestionably the greatest man of his nation and generation." He cautioned Allen, however, "to exercise some patience during his development of his plans, for while largely American in thought and in action, he still retains some of the hereditary instincts of his race."[52] This was to say that Yung Wing might be slow in coming to conclusions and in carrying out any plans agreed upon.

Although Allen characterized his conversation with Yung Wing as very instructive and satisfactory, he had reservations concerning him. In this he showed himself as a man of common sense and a shrewd observer. He correctly questioned what standing Yung Wing could have in China after an absence of eight years of rapid change and without having an organized system of communication with local political groups. He also questioned the strength of Yung's character in an emergency situation, but "speaking racially" he considered him honest, at least as much as Allen could say that about any person of his race. Assured by Yung Wing that he would safely handle any money placed into his hands, Allen was shocked by this "first introduction to the idea that an Oriental would ever be called upon to disburse the money of an Occidental." Moreover, he warned Lea and Boothe that Yung Wing possessed limited patriotism and was not fully committed to the cause. Again his racial prejudices came to the fore when he questioned whether such a thing as a complete and full commitment could exist in China where, he thought, everyone pursued his own personal interests,[53] thereby forgetting that financial gain was his own reason for taking part in the conspiracy.

Boothe, speaking also for Lea, defended Yung Wing as an extremely modest man. He attributed his reticence in speaking in concrete terms to "the Oriental mind," which "proceeds very, very cautiously to unfold its purposes," and to a desire to protect the sources of his information.[54] He maintained Yung Wing had remained in close touch with developments in China. In short, he considered him a man in whom all factions could unite.

The success of any attempt to overthrow the "Jingo" and to set up another regime, be it a republic or a constitutional monarchy, depended first on obtaining funds for the plotters. In his letter of invitation to the four associations, Yung Wing mentioned arbitrarily the sum of $1.5 million dollars, which would be successively turned over to the provisional government "and so on." He had not the slightest assurance that the money would be provided by whatever source. Allen did not even commit himself to furnishing an amount as small as $8–10,000, which Yung Wing considered necessary for his son's trip to China. Nevertheless, everybody spoke in terms of millions of dollars when it came to estimating the funds required for the undertaking. Yung Wing spoke to Allen of five million dollars, including the cost of 100,000 guns and 100 million cartridges for which he earmarked two million dollars, and of a substantial amount "to be used in a persuasive way." Allen found that estimate too low and thought of $9 million as a more realistic figure.[55] Lea, too, spoke of high figures. He "carefully planned out his campaign" and concluded that approximately 10,000 combatants and 5,000 noncombatants would supply him with all the force necessary to accomplish what he desired. "The cost of munitions, subsistence for from six to eight months accoutrements, transportation, and so forth will figure out about $2,500,000," plus $2 million as a contingency reserve.[56] Yung Wing, in "A plan to negotiate a Loan," eventually doubled his estimate of funds needed to $10 million "to be paid in five Instalments [sic] of $2,000,000 each, or as often as the exigencies of the case require." The Financial Syndicate was to grant that loan for a period of ten years at 15 percent interest. The loan was to be secured by having the "New Government" appoint members of the Financial Syndicate, that is, foreigners, as commissioners of customs in each of the Chinese provinces for 15 years. These commissioners were to levy customs on both imports and exports, thus guaranteeing the repayment of principal and interest. In addition, the Financial Syndicate would be granted a 15-year monopoly on the ramie trade, a vegetable fiber used in textile manufacture, on spruce wood pulp, the petroleum trade, and the telepost business. Finally, each province, beginning with Kwangtung and Kwangsi, would have to set aside a certain percentage of its revenue to liquidate the debt to the Syndicate.[57]

Allen made substantial revisions in the plan. He proposed setting up an "Outside Syndicate" consisting of U.S. financiers who were to raise 5 million dollars. An additional 4 million dollars were to be contributed by members of "approved societies or guilds" in China, who, together with the outsiders, would form a "Combined Syndicate." This would be given "the sole and absolute direction of the entire project from start to finish" and would command the "absolute and unqualified submission and obedience" of the approved leaders of the participating Chinese societies. The controlling power, however, would rest in the hands of the outsiders not only by their larger investment but also "by virtue of [their] origin, . . . experience and business training." The invested funds were to yield a 10 percent interest. Additional revenues, to be distributed proportionately among the members of the Combined Syndicate, were to come from a number of concessions, including a 99-year concession for the construction and operation of a railroad system in the whole of the national territory; a banking monopoly to include a central bank for a not yet specified period of years; a 25-year coinage concession; and mining rights for coal and precious and nonprecious metals for an unspecified term.[58]

Allen considered his plan a more businesslike approach because it required a substantial minority contribution from local interests who, he thought, "should realize that [the U.S. members of the Syndicate] are not grasping the last cent of profit but are willing to share proportionately with local contributors and so give them an opportunity to enjoy a measure of the harvest."[59] At the same time Allen's plan offered greater financial rewards to the U.S. capitalists. But neither Yung Wing nor Allen nor, for that matter, Lea and Boothe seem to have considered that their plans, if adopted and carried out after a successful overthrow of the existing Chinese government, would have submitted the country to foreign exploitation no less stringent and perhaps more pervasive than that prevailing under the Manchu regime. By this time, the original Red Dragon scheme, which entailed revolution through various societies and associations, had been abandoned because the plotters had found no way to enlist them. In their place, Lea intended to raise his own body of men, "ten thousand combatants and five thousand non-combatants," but it was not revealed where he expected to find and how he proposed to organize that force.[60]

In the event Allen took his plan to "a big man who," he emphasized, "shall be nameless, . . . *the One* of all others, whom I shall prefer to have behind me in a venture of the sort under consideration. He has the reputation of never turning back after he once 'put his hand to the plough.' When you learn the name," he wrote to Lea and Boothe, "you will be satisfied that I have the very best in sight."[61]

The "big man" to whom Allen stated his case was no other than J. Pierpont Morgan. But Morgan's answer, "concise and clear," was entirely negative: "I am ready to do business with any *established* government on earth but I cannot help to make a government to do business with."[62] Having failed to enlist Morgan's help, Allen tried to interest other capitalists in the venture, but with no more luck. He reported to have spoken to a man whom he described as "the salt of the earth" and as someone with "an extensive and successful experience in projects of this sort, and . . . in close touch with much, much money." This individual who remained nameless, also gave a negative answer after attempting "to develop the proposition in influential circles."[63]

An effort to interest the meat-packing industry in financing the project also came to naught. The Chinese boycott, which, in any case, was a thing of the past, had not harmed that industry; the meat packers were not even concerned with the Chinese market as they had their hands full in others such as South America and Australia. Whatever the specific reasons for his constant failure to obtain the support of U.S. financiers, Allen blamed the general vagueness of the planned undertaking. He had the feeling that he and his coconspirators were dealing in a political vacuum. Without contact to powerful groups and leading personalities in China, they had "in sight only an elderly gentleman [Yung Wing] who has continuously resided [in the United States] for eight years; who has been entirely outside the public eye for that time; who has maintained no organized correspondence from, or representation in, the sphere of action [China]; who controls only a few of the student class, or hopes to control; and who can give no binding assurances which may not be rendered valueless in a moment by those now occupying, or lately occupying, very much more prominent positions than he ever did." Matters would be different if a connection could be established to a man like Yuan Shih-k'ai, who "doubtless has his agents and followers in *medias res* at this moment and, above all, probably has supreme control over a certain group of men already trained in obedience." The enlistment of Yuan in the cause appeared "possibly. . . the only road to success."

In the meantime, however, Allen's appetite for business ventures was whetted by another project that, apparently, had been brought to his attention by Yung Wing in a letter that has not survived. Yung Wing had mentioned considerable silver deposits in Kwangsi province worth $3,000 per ton, which would render the capital necessary for the project. In the meantime, the local leaders would prepare the ground for the uprising, but Allen warned that they should not expect any financial returns from the funds accumulated by the mining operations until they had finished their preparations for the revolt. As Allen remarked, "He who would pay before work would be unwise indeed."[64]

The silver mining project did not originate with Yung Wing. It had been put forward by K'ang's group of reformers as a means to obtain funds. Lea knew of these plans and, on hearing that Ou Gai Gap, a vice-president of the Pao Huang Hui, was in Canada, suggested meeting him in Los Angeles for a discussion of the mining project. It is not known whether that meeting took place.

Yung Wing had heard from one of his two sons of the existence of a syndicate formed by members of K'ang's group for the exploitation of the silver veins in Kwangsi province. The son had been approached by the syndicate with the proposition to go to China and act as superintendent of the mines. Yung Wing favored the idea because his son could use the opportunity to find out the mood of the country and thereby assess the chances for the success of the conspiracy. He may also have thought that, with his son in charge of the mines, he and his associates could profit from the mining operations.

But he had a second money-making scheme in mind. As he told Boothe, "I am providing more than one string on my bow. In case our great enterprise should fail of being carried out, either from our inability to raise enough money, or from other causes, I hope to fall back on the Ramie Industry." Yung Wing had learned of a method to convert ramie into silk at an enormous potential profit. He proposed the idea to Allen and hoped for the backing of Lea and, particularly, of Boothe. To begin with, he suggested to Boothe to raise privately $100,000 so that he, Lea, Allen, and his other son could travel to Kwangsi and purchase the machinery necessary to get the project started. Two companies were to be set up, one in Canton and the other in Shanghai, and placed under the stewardship of his son. The trip should serve to evaluate the ramie project and also provide the opportunity to "find out the prevailing sentiment of the people of the provinces." He was so convinced of the feasibility and profitability of the project that he declared himself willing to sign promissory notes for the repayment of the $100,000 within two years, with the handsome interest of 100 percent. And without waiting for Boothe's answer, the 81-year-old man expressed his readiness to move to China where he would have access to local capitalists and gain the confidence of officials. With the expected immense profits, he would be in a position to influence public opinion in favor of reforms and the general welfare of the country. In this way "great political movements will not be wanting in material resources," but, he assured Boothe, "your personal share in the profits of the two Cos. will be determined and recognized."[65]

Boothe did not share Yung's enthusiasm about the mining and ramie projects, and, presumably, neither did Lea. Perhaps they tended to agree with Allen, who considered "enlightened self-interest" rather than political commitment to be Yung's motivating force.[66] Moreover, Boothe doubted the technical and commercial possibilities of converting ramie into silk, having once studied a similar proposal. In addition, he considered it difficult, if not impossible, to raise any money for it and, particularly, for establishing a factory in such a faraway locale as Kwangsi. Instead, he urged Yung to revert to the "first plans," the raising of money in the United States for the revolution in China so that headway could finally be made.[67]

But the chances for making headway seemed to have gone. Not only did the correspondence about silver and ramie come to an end, but the meetings between Allen and Yung stopped also. After a few months Yung took notice of the halt in the discussions about "the great project." He told Boothe that he had concluded upon further consideration that a peaceful resolution of the situation in China was preferable to a revolution that would plunge "the whole nation in the vortex of anarchy & chaos." The Manchu court had announced serious reform measures and, therefore, Yung felt it necessary to go to China to ascertain the true state of affairs before risking the lives of millions of people. In Yung's letter of resignation from the revolution, he said, "I wish General Lea could plan to go with me." After reading the letter, Lea had Boothe tell Yung that nothing would please him more than to accompany him to China.[68] But Lea concealed from Yung that he was trying hard to go to China on his own. At the time he was making his unsuccessful efforts to be appointed U.S. Minister to China.

—8—

Ally of Sun Yat-sen

Consistency was not one of Yung's strong points. Three months after he renounced violence as a means to change conditions in China, he criticized Lea for failure to take military action. "I suppose," he wrote to Boothe, "General Lea is still engaged in writing books which he may find more profitable than planning military campaigns in China. Just as soon as he get [*sic*] through with his literary work, & is ready to take on the role of a field marshal, he must let me know, for I can help him in a civil capacity."[1] Not only had he forgotten his own preference for a peaceful solution to the China question, but he also ignored that at the beginning of his letter he had excused his long silence with his own literary occupation, the writing of his autobiography.

Boothe apparently thought that Yung's criticism was based upon Lea's lack of readiness to travel with him to China. So he replied that Lea had no immediate travel plans in view of his father's recent death.[2] Yung Wing understood but referred again to Lea's important role in China's future: "I imagine," he wrote, "that the great stir he will make in our world, will not by his books but by his ability to demonstrate that he has . . . in him the capabilities of a great soldier. The day may not be very distant when he will be called upon to take to the field." Disregarding once more his earlier point of view he added, "I wish there was no need for another revolution in China, & that the transformation of an Old China into that of a new, may be brought about peaceably without her going through the ordeals of fire & sword, but that is an impossibility."[3] Boothe assured Yung that the General could be depended upon to act whenever the need for military action arose and emphasized that the literary work took second place to his political interests.

At the same time Boothe replied to a telegram from Yung that marked the opening of a new era in Lea's life, his association with Sun Yat-sen. The telegram had announced Sun's arrival in New York and invited Lea and Boothe to come to New York or Hartford for a conference with the famous revolutionary leader. Boothe answered that the trip was not convenient because Lea had been ill for several weeks. He suggested that Sun and Yung come to Los Angeles, adding that he did not know Sun's reasons for the proposed meeting.[4]

There is no evidence to show that Sun and Yung had been in contact before Sun's visit to the United States or that Yung had known of Sun's impending arrival. In retrospect, however, it appears possible that Yung's reconversion from a pacifist to a partisan of a revolutionary solution was brought about by such knowledge. In fact, very little is known about their relationship and nothing about the circumstances of their meeting in New York. They knew of each other at least since 1899 when a faction in Sun's group proposed Yung Wing as leader in place of Sun.[5] They never met personally before April 1900. At that time, a mutual friend of both in Hong Kong noted in his diary a statement by Yung, "I have not met Dr. Sun Yat-sen yet. What is his age? I don't think much of Sun as he is too rash." A few days later, their friend noted in his diary, "Dr. Yung Wing leaves for the United States by the s.s. 'Empress of China.' I write to Dr. Sun Yat-sen advising him to meet Dr. Yung Wing in Japan,"[6] where Sun was staying at the time. It is not known whether they actually met during Yung's stopover. There is a short reference to Sun in Yung's diary for 1902, but this does not necessarily indicate a personal acquaintanceship.[7]

According to Sun's official Chinese biography, Sun wrote to Lea directly after having read *The Valor of Ignorance*, probably while in London in 1909, asking him for a meeting in New York.[8] However, there is no record of such a letter. Had it been written, Boothe might not have been ignorant of the purpose of Sun's visit and would not have questioned the reason for the meeting. Under the circumstances it seems that, upon learning of Sun's coming or after his arrival, Yung Wing conceived the idea of reviving the conspiratorial project with the participation of Sun.

It was Sun's third trip to the United States, after the earlier visits in 1896 and 1904. By 1909 he had led or promoted eight revolutionary uprisings, all of which had failed. He now came to America to raise money for still another attempt at revolution. Since K'ang's decline, fund raising had become easier for him, as many overseas Chinese had transferred their loyalties from K'ang's Pao Huang Hui to Sun's T'ung Meng Hui or to the Chih Kung T'ang, which had moved closer to Sun's cause. While the funds from these organizations greatly improved Sun's situation,[9] he still needed the backing of Chinese and foreign capitalists. Now his contact with Yung Wing opened a new and, probably, unexpected avenue for obtaining substantial financial help from U.S. sources.

Already early in the year, in his first conversation with Allen, Yung Wing had mentioned Sun's name and spoken of him as being "considered the most reliable of all [Chinese leaders]. . . . He is considered a tower of strength in the Canton province and a man that can be relied upon, although probably somewhat too mercurial and liable to act in advance of the right moment."[10] At that time Yung Wing had his sights set upon Yuan Shih-k'ai. In alluding to Sun, he did not intend to convey to Allen that he preferred Sun to Yuan through whom, at the time, he thought one could control the whole of China. He rather wanted Allen to understand that Sun was more active and decisive than other opponents of the regime, particularly K'ang.

In any event, Yung Wing introduced Sun to Allen. The details of their conversation have not become known, but they concerned, as was natural, Sun's plans to overthrow the Manchu regime and the funds required for that purpose. Allen seemed to have been noncommittal and, a month or two later, suggested to Boothe that he not make a financial commitment either. Although he said he liked Sun as a person, he considered him naive and lacking the required circumspection. He expressed strong reservations regarding Sun's ideas, which he called utopian. Allen found his leadership wanting, his organization diffuse and poor in discipline, and his attempts at revolution badly planned and ineffectual. For these reasons "it would be an insult to the intelligence of any capitalist to ask him to risk his money in [Sun's] project, and the man who would propose it would be damned for all time." Just at the time of his talk with Allen, Sun's followers in Canton made their ninth revolutionary attempt. Allen saw it as a sign of Sun's lack of leadership qualities that he remained in the United States instead of taking charge of the action in China. Allen's criticism was unjustified but explainable because of his ignorance of Sun's role. As the leader of the republican revolutionaries, Sun was an untiring agitator and propagandist, and, with close associates, planner and unceasing promoter of revolts and uprisings. But his forte was that of spokesman for the revolution, its representative among foreigners, both governments and interested private parties, and, particularly, that of a fund-raiser.[12] When less than two years later, the revolution that did overthrow the Ch'ing dynasty broke out, Sun was again in the United States. Even then he did not rush to the theater of action but, slowly and deliberately, he proceeded from Denver via Washington to London and then from Paris to Marseilles, where he took a boat through the Mediterranean to the East, arriving in Shanghai after victory seemed certain.

Yung Wing used the opportunity of Sun's visit to put before Sun his own thoughts and plans for a successful revolution. Although there is no direct record of these talks, after Sun's departure Yung wrote to Sun in San Francisco to confirm what he believed were the prerequisites for succeeding: a credit in the bank of at least $1 million plus $2 million for emergencies; a provisional government to administer conquered territories; a competent military leader; and the rudiments of a naval force. More importantly, however, he arranged for Sun to meet Lea and Boothe in Los Angeles.[13]

Lea, too, wrote to Sun in San Francisco, asking him to come to Los Angeles for discussions with himself and Boothe. That Lea's letter has not been preserved raises again some tantalizing questions. Did it indicate that they had met before, or was this to be their first meeting? Or, if they had not met, had they been in correspondence in the past and when? Would Sun have wanted to see Lea even if Yung Wing would not have acted as their intermediary? The answers to these questions would greatly elucidate Lea's stand in Chinese political affairs and help to understand some of his past actions. As it is, we only know from Sun's answer to Lea that, in his letter, Lea voiced his sympathies with Sun's movement. Curiously, Sun's answer was couched in words similar to those that K'ang had used in 1904 when he heard from Lea before coming to the United States: "Many thanks for your noble feeling toward our cause," replied Sun.[14] Thus began a new chapter in Lea's and his associates' efforts to advance the cause of the Chinese Revolution. They had first pinned their hopes on K'ang Yu-wei but had given up on him after the death of the young Emperor and the decline of the Pao Huang Hui. Their attempt to enlist Yuan Shih-k'ai as the leader of the undertaking had been stillborn. Now they were prepared to rely on Sun Yat-sen and his revolutionary allies.

Sun arrived in Los Angeles toward the end of February 1910. By March 4 Yung Wing had learned from Sun of two meetings with Lea and Boothe and of a third conference between the three a few days later. It is possible, though, that they met more often as no records of the discussions were kept by any of the participants and Yung Wing was not informed of any details. Sun continued to correspond with Yung Wing but divulged no information. As a result, Yung Wing concluded, no definite decisions or agreements had been reached, and, therefore, he submitted to Boothe and Lea after Sun's departure another plan of his own, which also has not survived.[15] Apparently, one decision taken was the elimination of Yung Wing from any plans and projects because neither Lea nor Boothe ever answered his several requests for information. A few weeks after the meetings, Sun told Boothe "in regard to Dr. Y. I did informed [*sic*] him of our conference but did not tell him anything particular. . . . I leave the matter entirely to your decision."[16] Still, Yung Wing continued to inquire about the progress of the matter and even offered to come to Los Angeles together with one of his sons for a meeting with Sun, Lea, and Boothe.[17] Again, there is no indication of an answer. Yung found a chance for a final letter later in the year when offering congratulations on the marriage of a daughter of Boothe, but he made no reference to Sun.

He did, however, revert to his stance of the previous year when the Red Dragon scheme had come to an end. He rejected a solution "which may plunge the nation into a chaotic revolution like that in France in 1788 & 1789." Instead he opted for a "limited monarchy modified by certain well defined reforms."[18] It sounded like a case of sour grapes.

A few months afterward, in the spring of 1911, Yung suffered a stroke, but he still continued to watch affairs in China. In December of that year, a few days before Sun's inauguration as Provisional President of China, he sent him greetings and congratulations and expressed the hope that he could "have a sight of the New Republic."[19] Sun graciously invited the old man to come and help in the reconstruction of the country. The invitation arrived a few days before Yung's death in April 1912.[20]

Lea's choice of Yung as a member of the conspiratorial quadrumvirate had not been a fortunate one. He had been misled by the aura of elder statesman that clung to Yung's name and apparently been unaware of his estrangement from his native land, his lack of political connections among Chinese at home and abroad, and the absence of firm political principles due to, perhaps, what Allen had called "enlightened self-interest" of the garrulous old man. Evidently, Lea's misjudgment of Yung Wing reflected his own marginal and ineffectual participation in Chinese revolutionary politics. He had been close to the scene of action during his trip to China in 1900, and, although he may not have exerted any influence, he was involved in or, at least, tried to affect important decisions such as the potential cooperation between K'ang's and Sun's groups. He may also have seen military action in the field. After his return he remained an ally of the reformers and a member of their organization in the United States. But his role on the occasions of Liang's and K'ang's visits had been essentially a ceremonial one, and personally he was never close to either man. Nor is there any indication that his voice counted in the councils of the reformers or that his opinion in political or military matters was ever sought by them. It is true that he helped them to organize the Chinese Imperial Reform Army and served as its head, and thus he may have advanced their political fortune in the United States as well as their financial situation. But the military companies were a shadow army far away from the field of action. Their weight and that of their chief were not felt where it counted. Nor did the Red Dragon scheme and the discussions among its four protagonists, which were held in a vacuum, so to speak, without the concurrence of the Chinese political opposition, alter Lea's situation on the margin of the Chinese political situation.

All that seemed to have been changed by Sun's visit in California. An association with Sun heralded active participation in the revolutionary movement through one of its foremost and best-known leaders. Lea finally saw a chance for leaving the sidelines for the center of the action to assume the role that had eluded him during so many years. As for Sun, he saw in Lea an ally who would not only contribute his military expertise to the struggle but also, with Boothe's help, open the door to U.S. financial backers. To begin with, the two men almost immediately established a close personal bond, if not a friendship. From the first day on, they remained in constant communication with each other by letters and telegrams when they were not together. It was a mark of the strength of their bond that after Lea's demise Sun remained in contact with Lea's widow during most of the rest of his own life.[21] Several factors may have been responsible for the attachment. Sun, no intellectual in either the Confucian or the Western sense, greatly admired Lea, the author of *The Valor of Ignorance*, as a military expert or, as he said in the eulogy on Lea's death, as "a great military philosopher, well poise [*sic*] in high military problems."[22] He found that Lea shared his outlook on life. Already as a young man Sun had been attracted by Darwinism,[23] and thus he agreed with Lea's social Darwinism as represented in his book. Finally, both men shared certain personal qualities, which may have contributed to their mutual compatibility. Both pursued their objectives with a persistence that could be seen as naive, and though their efforts were often thwarted, they renewed them time and again. Sun's "audacity and optimism, resilience, and above all, monumental self-confidence,"[24] were also character traits of Lea. Moreover, both were essentially self-made men. Lea, with his incomplete education, embarked upon a military career and became known as an amateur, though acknowledged, strategist. Sun, who lacked the classical education expected of a Chinese leader and who, despite his Western training, had serious gaps in his general knowledge, was recognized as the chief opponent of the rulers of a great empire.[25] In a sense, both of them were upstarts and outsiders when they joined hands in March 1910. Sun was a marginal man,[26] as unquestionably was Lea. This situation forced both of them to dissimulate and improvise. Of course, the comparison with Lea does not diminish the greater stature that contemporaries and posterity accorded to Sun Yat-sen. In 1904 Sun had expressed the hope that he would find many Lafayettes in America.[27] Had he lived longer, Lea might indeed have become Sun's "Lafayette," but, of course, Lafayette was also outranked by George Washington.

The discussions in Los Angeles between Sun Yat-sen, Homer Lea, and Charles Boothe lasted about two weeks, ending on March 14, 1910. Sun appears to have left immediately thereafter for Bakersfield, Hanford, and Fresno. He arrived in San Francisco on March 21 and sailed the next day for Hawaii on the S.S. *Korea*.[28]

The details of these discussions can be pieced together from the various documents and handwritten notes that were preserved and from later correspondence of the three men. They arrived at a complete understanding about their future course of action and the role of each of them. In particular, it was agreed that preparations were to be made for a revolution in the whole of China under Sun's leadership, who assumed the title of "President" of the undertaking. Lea was to be the "Commanding General" of the movement and Boothe its "Financial Agent." Just as in the previous projects, finances were considered crucial to the success of the venture, with the required funds expected to come from U.S. sources. For the benefit of potential financiers, a document was drafted that listed the basic strengths of the revolutionary movement and proposed terms of the eventual loans.[29]

As the "first basis of strength," the document named the Triads and Sun's organization. The Triads appeared in the document under the name of Tien Ti Whui (T'ien Ti Hui, or Heaven and Earth Society), with its five regional subdivisions: the Society of Elder Brothers (Ko Lao Hui) in the Yangtse Valley; the White Lotus Society (Pai Lien Hui) in Fukien and Chekiang; the Triads of southern China; and the Big Sword Society (Hsiao Tao Hui) in the north of China. The membership of these secret societies was given as 10 million or more. Added to these millions was Sun's Chinese Alliance (T'ung Meng Hui), which in the document was listed as Kah Ming (Kê Ming, or Revolutionary Alliance) to stress its revolutionary character. It was said to be "composed of thirty thousand of the most intellectual men, students in China and Chinese students graduated from [schools in] foreign countries." Sun as president of the Chinese Alliance was also referred to as president of the secret societies, thus extending his writ "from Manchuria to the Southern Provinces of Kwangtung, Kwangsi and Yunnan, from the Eastern Provinces bordering on the China Sea to Turkestan on the west."

Sun had strong connections to the secret societies. He did not exercise control over them, though he may have wielded considerable influence among some local and regional groups. Moreover, their membership was diffused and unorganized and could not be reckoned in numbers. The numerical strength of Sun's own group, the Revolutionary Alliance, was also exaggerated. It had probably no more than 10,000 members of whom only a few hundred constituted the active core.[30]

As his "second basis of strength," Sun mentioned the military, but he exaggerated the revolutionaries' influence in the Manchu army, too, in order to impress prospective financial backers. For instance, he claimed control of a "division of modern drilled troops in Manchuria, twelve thousand men, twenty thousand irregular Cavalry in Manchuria, known as the HUNG HU TEE." Sun's information on military matters in China came from his comrades and lieutenants in the field, notably from Huang Hsing who, two months later, gave a more modest estimate of revolutionary strength in Manchuria. Huang mentioned contact with "some Manchurian 'mounted bandits' " who, "given financial aid could organize an uprising that could at least hamper troop movements in the North."[31] He did not mention any contacts within regular army units in Manchuria. The "bandits" probably belonged to a secret society, the Red Beards (Hung Hu Tzu), also known as the Horse Thieves, whose main activity was brigandage.[32]

Furthermore, Sun listed as loyal to his movement "four Divisions in the Valley of the Yangtse of modern drilled troops." Also, 2 divisions in Kwangsi, 2 in Yunnan, and 2 uncompleted units in Szechuan were cited as being loyal to Sun. In fact, once understrength divisions had been brought up to normal size, he expected to control all 13 "modern" divisions, in addition to 70,000 troops in the "old" army.

What Sun called "modern drilled troops" were units of the so-called New Armies established by the Peking government after 1903 under a military reform program. Recruits came from settled peasant families. Their education, training, and discipline were far superior to the traditional "old" armies. Even intellectuals and students enrolled in the "New Armies," which thus became foci of revolutionary activity.[33] But the inroads Sun's organization had made, not to speak of the old army divisions, were by no means as spectacular as he claimed. Huang's estimates were again much more moderate. In Kwangtung any success depended on the conversion of the army. On February 12, 1910, when the ninth revolutionary attempt was made by Sun's people in Canton, three regiments and some other units were strongly infiltrated by the revolutionaries, and many of the 3,000 soldiers in the Provincial Reserve Forces were sympathetic and could be counted upon. As to other provinces, Huang spoke merely of several scores of revolutionists among officers of the Kwangsi army and of many among the officers in the armies of half a dozen other provinces. In Yunnan he reported the revolutionary situation within the army very acute, while the secret societies in the Yangtse Valley, especially those in Chekiang province, could be useful as auxiliary forces.[34]

So much for Sun's "second basis of strength." As to his third, he threw in, for good measure, the total population of Kwangsi, Kwangtung, and Yunnan, amounting to 70 million people, and "all the more intelligent portion of the population (about fifty per cent) in the other Provinces," who, he claimed, were sympathetic to the movement.

Sun showed himself more circumspect when outlining the terms for the financial support of the campaign. Any loans granted would earn interest at the legal rate but were to be paid back threefold in view of the great risk involved. A syndicate formed by the lenders would have first option for any loans to the new government when established. No railroad concessions would be granted to foreign interests, and mining concessions would be approved only under just and proper conditions at the option of the government. For an unspecified period of years, all military supplies were to be procured through a representative of the syndicate. The funds needed for the campaign were to be paid over by the syndicate to the financial agent within 2, 8, 14, or 17 months after the conclusion of a formal agreement.

A second document listed the total financial requirements for the campaign of $3.5 million.[35] The sum was divided into numerous items that generally could be disbursed by the financial agent only upon requisition of the president or the commanding general. The money to be spent by Sun was to be used mostly for political and organizational purposes, while the larger part was reserved for Lea's disbursements for the military payroll, equipment, and supplies. These military items were based upon handwritten notes made by Lea.[36] These were quite detailed and included costs of items such as numbers of various types of ammunition for infantry and artillery, specific weapons, uniforms, and so forth. After the first two months, Lea could request the pay for 5,000 troops and officers; after another six months for 5,000 additional troops and 5,000 coolies. And, finally, there was a surprising provision for the "pay of American Officers for three months—$50,000.00." From Lea's handwritten notes, it appears that he had in mind to transport 500 men from the United States to China to serve as officers, presumably members of his military companies. After almost five years during which Lea's army in the United States had not been mentioned by anybody, it was expected to play an active role in Chinese affairs and, at that, on Chinese soil.

On the conclusion of the discussions on March 14, 1910, Sun, as president of his Chinese Alliance or Federal Association of China (T'ung Meng Hui), signed a formal document appointing Boothe sole Financial Agent of the Alliance. He was given power of attorney to act in the name of the Alliance when negotiating loans, to receive and disburse sums of money as authorized by the president, and to enter into agreements as directed by Sun. Such agreements were to bind the Alliance as though they had been signed by its president or council.[37]

It was further agreed that a Chinese translation of Boothe's letter of appointment should be signed and sealed by the president and the 17 provincial heads of his political group. In this way the financial backers of the enterprise were to be shown that Sun, indeed, enjoyed the support of the other leading members of the T'ung Meng Hui and spoke for the organization as a whole. Such a formal document was received by Boothe on July 18. Lea examined it and confirmed its authenticity, since he was familiar with some of the signatures. Huang Hsing had signed for Hunan province.[38]

None of the documents prepared by Sun, Lea, and Boothe expressly stated that the operation would encompass the whole of China, but this objective follows from their texts. For example, funds were allocated for military activities in central and northern China, for military forces along the Tonking border, and for gaining control of five divisions near Peking and four cruisers constituting the Chinese navy. Moreover, half a year later when it became doubtful whether sufficient funds could be secured, Sun confirmed the existence of a plan to start the revolution in the whole of China. However, due to the lack of funds, he proposed a more limited operation. "We can start a movement with [sic] a much easier and quicker way than that as we have arranged in the Long Beach Hotel, and with much less expenses. I feel sure that Canton city can be captured from the outset. . . . In possession of that city we possess at least a hundred thousand of modern rifles and sufficient quantity of ammunition, and many hundred pieces of modern artilleries, and rifle and cartilage [sic] factories, and besides plenty of ready money and vast sums of material supplies. Most of the [other] leaders are very reluctant to do anything other than capture that city from the very start. I think also that that city is the main object from the beginning. . . . The money use [sic] for this purpose will [be] much less than the other scheme which we worked out in America."[39]

The plan to start in Canton was that of Huang Hsing, who had outlined it to Sun in answer to Sun's letter of March 28, which has not survived. Sun probably told Huang of the decisions taken in the conferences with Lea and Boothe, to judge from Huang's reply of May 13. Huang took the position, which was proven correct by later events, "that the best force for overthrowing the Manchu government was its own army." Canton's capture, where the revolutionaries had a relatively strong organization within the army units, would be followed by the seizure of Kwangtung province. This was the strategy that Huang had followed in February just before Sun arrived in California and that he would employ, again unsuccessfully, in April 1911, but it was proven correct in the successful uprising of October 1911. Whether Sun accepted Huang's strategy because of the difficulties of obtaining funds for the larger project or because he agreed with Huang in principle can probably not be determined.

Furthermore, Huang disagreed with Lea's plan to station the 500 American officers in Kwangchowan, a French-leased peninsula in southern Kwangtung province, where Lea wanted them to train Chinese soldiers. Sun seemed to have considered that option in his March 28 letter to Huang. The latter "politely rejected the 'army man's' idea of inviting

foreign army officers and technicians to train troops in Kwangchowan,''
because ''it would be difficult to find a place where training could be
carried on and that even if a place could be found . . . the activities . . .
would inevitably arouse the attention of the Manchu government.''
Huang added, however, that he would welcome the help of foreign sympathizers *after* the outbreak of the revolution.[40]

It may be presumed that Sun informed Lea of Huang's negative
reply to the proposal to station 500 men in Kwangchowan although no
specific reference to the refusal appears in any of Sun's letters to Lea. He
did mention, however, having received information from Huang that the
latter, independently from Sun and Lea, had set up a base for men and
arms in the sanctuary of the French concession ''before they know [*sic*]
anything of our proposition out here.'' Huang brought his soldiers into
the territory disguised as farmers to whom the French authorities granted
permission to settle.[41]

There is no indication of Lea's reaction to the change of plans. If he
felt any disappointment or resentment, he may have kept quiet because
the funds upon which the decisions in California had been based had not
arrived, and, therefore, the corresponding plans could not be carried
out. In any case, his replies to Sun's letters were not preserved, and those
of Sun that are available do not contain any further reference to the stationing of Americans in Kwangchowan. Sun himself seems to have accepted Huang's views without any objections. At that stage, he left military matters mostly to Huang with whom he had a harmonious
relationship.[42] Nor is there any indication that he tried to use Lea in order
to gain greater influence on decisions of a military nature or that he ever
attempted to play one man against the other. A year later he seems to
have considered bringing the two together, perhaps to define their mutual responsibilities and positions or to coordinate their military plans.
That meeting, however, did not take place. Lea was at the time in Europe, and, as Sun wrote to him, ''General Hwang had [*sic*] not been
ordered to Europe yet as he has much to do in China.''[43] In the meantime, Sun continued to supply Lea with information on military developments.

It was part of the original plan that Lea would go to China and,
presumably, establish his military headquarters for which the sum of
$10,000 had been budgeted.[44] While still in Hawaii on the way to Japan
and the Asian continent, Sun asked Lea, ''When you start for the
East?''[45] He brought up the question a few weeks later in another letter
from Honolulu. There was a possibility of buying arms from a firm in
Hong Kong and having them delivered to any place on the coast of
Kwangtung. ''I should like you to see this Hong Kong firm first before
we enter into contract with any others.''[46] At the time Sun had probably

not yet learned of Huang's scheme, nor were the funds available for Lea's departure to the East and the purchase of arms. In any case, Lea's trip was never brought up again.

Sun left Los Angeles in the conviction that his financial worries were coming to an end. Within a week after the conclusion of his talks with Lea and Boothe, he wrote to the latter, "I hope to have good news from you soon."[47] A few weeks later he asked Lea, "How is our scheme getting along? When can Mr. B. let us know anything definite?"[48]

Boothe did not lose any time in working on the financial problem. He succeeded in dispelling Allen's doubts about the leadership and prospects of Sun. This seems to have occurred during a trip to New York immediately after Sun's departure because there is a gap in his correspondence with Allen from March 14 to April 4. On the latter date Allen spoke already of the raising of money for the project,[49] and within another few weeks he travelled to Los Angeles for more discussions on the matter.[50] In the meantime, Sun kept pressuring Boothe who, in answer to a lost letter from Sun, assured him of his steady efforts. "While I am not yet able to advise you of the final results, . . . so far I have received very satisfactory encouragement. I have had frequent conferences with the General and . . . our New York friend A," who will "lay the ground work for arrangements, which I will go East to conclude."[51]

For Allen and the financial circles he was trying to interest in the project, it appeared essential that they were dealing with a well-organized and -coordinated political movement under firm and responsible leadership. A revolution should not be a protracted affair but, as Allen had expressed it a year earlier, be accomplished "between sunrise and sunset, or between sunset or sunrise," to avoid prolonged instability. Law and order would have to be maintained if the unlikely marriage between the Chinese revolutionaries and Wall Street bankers was to take place. Just when Allen had been won to Sun's cause, in early April 1910, newspapers reported that a bomb had been found in the Prince Regent's home in Peking. Nothing indicated that Sun or his followers were involved in the incident, but Allen feared that such terroristic acts might interfere with his fund-raising activities. "I understand perfectly well that all this about the bomb may be false," he wrote to Boothe. "Also I understand that it was probably not set there by any of S-'s people but, — Anything of the sort which can in any way be laid to S-'s people will kill all hope of raising money here as 'dead as a mackerel.' It is of prime importance that he is so informed and made [to] understand that he must take every possible precaution against such things and must issue the most stringent orders to that effect."[52] Boothe accordingly advised Sun to have his people withhold any action until a well-planned and perfectly concerted effort could be made.[53]

A report of disturbances in the Yangtse Valley alarmed Allen again. When he informed Lea of his concerns, Lea explained that these had happened while Sun was travelling from Hawaii to Japan. In the meantime, however, things had quieted down, and Sun appeared in complete control and would maintain it as long as he expected Allen to succeed in the financial matters.[54] Sun took the requested action and asked his people to halt all premature movements. "I think all such kind of movements can be stopped up to the Winter of this year. So we still have many peaceful months" to get the promised funds.[55]

In regard to the progress on the financial front, Boothe assured Sun again that things looked favorable in New York, where he spent some time in the latter part of June. Allen, too, continued to be active in the matter. He reported to have approached an executive from the important engineering firm J. G. White & Co., which, at the time, was also engaged in the financial business. Apparently he had talked to him once before without any results. Now he intended to broach the subject again "over the coffee and cigars," although "I still contend and believe that John [P. Morgan] is the one and only man on earth for us."[56] There is no information, however, that he discussed the matter again with Morgan. He did speak repeatedly to someone identified as Schmidt who was trying to interest an unnamed financier then traveling in Europe. Schmidt had returned without any results, and so Allen concluded, "evidently a trip across the water will be necessary before the proper position can be secured here."[57] But nothing developed, and, although there were references to the syndicate, its members remained unknown if, in fact, it ever existed.

As the summer passed without word from Boothe that he had succeeded in obtaining funds, Sun's tone became petulant if not desperate: "Everything must have been settled by this time. What is the final result now? Is it succeed or fail [sic], in any case I should like to know the result as soon as possible, so that I may take independent measure in the future." Sun was in a quandary. On the one hand, he did not want to foreclose the possibility of getting a large war chest through Boothe and Allen and, therefore, had asked his associates to withhold any action until the winter, as he assured Boothe again. On the other, he agreed with his comrades that the decision to proceed with the revolution in Canton had to be taken before long. For that smaller project money was needed, too, and so he asked Boothe whether he could not advance on his own the small sum of $50,000 for what he called "preparatory work."[58] In a letter to Lea, he was more explicit regarding the purpose of that money. "Now if Mr. B's New York project failed I want you [to] try some other way to get me half a million dollar[s] (gold), for the Canton scheme only, put the others aside for a while, until we achieve our first object. Can you succeed in raising that amount of money in the shortest possible time? If not try to get as much as you can, but in any case send fifty thousand at once for preparatory work. Since I stopped the movement this summer . . . all our hopes are concentrated in the American project.''[59] A few weeks later he repeated his request to Lea for money, but this time he thought "a quarter million of gold dollars will be quite enough for the whole thing, even less than that may enable us to do some wonderful work." Having restrained his comrades from action with the promise of funds from the United States, his leadership position was endangered. "It will be a great blow to my influence," he pleaded, almost begging Lea to save him from "discredit." He also spoke of a recall of Boothe's power of attorney.[60] Lea responded by offering Sun the royalties of the Japanese and Chinese editions of *The Valor of Ignorance*. Sun immediately arranged for the Japanese translation and may indeed have received some money from the sale of the book, but he was less hopeful of any gain from a sale of a Chinese edition. It was November by that time, and Sun again entreated Lea and Boothe for money even if it was only one-tenth of the sum originally projected.[61] On his part, Boothe had gone to New York toward the end of October "for a very important appointment there, which ought to determine something decisive."[62] On that trip, he seems to have met with C. B. Hill, a member of a New York law office, whose name had been given to him by Lea on his first visit to New York in September 1908. Hill was associated with commercial interests that, according to Lea, would benefit from the end of the Chinese boycott.[63] Hill took some vague interest in the matter, and, although Boothe pointed out to him the great advantages that would accrue to the United States if Sun would gain certain victory with American help, this approach also remained fruitless.[64]

By the middle of November, Sun's group decided not to wait any longer for funds from U.S. financiers. Huang Hsing and a number of other leaders met with Sun in Penang, where he had been staying for some months. The decision was reached to make another, determined effort in April 1911 to capture Canton as the first step in the revolution. The money was to come from overseas Chinese. It fell to Sun to raise funds in North America. He left Singapore within a few weeks after the conference and arrived early in the year in New York.[65]

Even before the meeting, Sun had expected the uprising to occur in the spring. He had written to Boothe that if money could be obtained "within three months from date" (November 8) it would be available "just in time for our purpose."[66] Even after the decision was made to collect the required funds from Chinese communities abroad, he did not count out Boothe entirely. While on his way to the United States via Europe, he told Boothe again that a contribution of "a few hundred thousand" would be of help, and if Boothe could make it available he would come straight to Los Angeles. "But at [sic] any case whether we have [that] money or not, I am sure of our success in the next move."[67] Boothe then tried to set up a meeting between Sun and Hill on Sun's arrival in New York, but they did not see each other.[68]

From New York Sun traveled to Chicago, where he sought and obtained money from Chinese groups, and then continued to San Francisco. He did not visit Los Angeles but proceeded north to Vancouver from where he asked Boothe for the last time whether there was "any hope of doing something in a smaller scale than our original plan." He claimed to have already raised more than half the money needed and expected to obtain the rest on his way eastward through Canada and to be again in New York in about a month, by the middle of April. In case Boothe could not procure any money, he should return to Sun the power of attorney because Sun had promised his "comrades to return their signatures in case of failure of raising the intending [sic] funds."[69] Boothe responded by proposing again a meeting with Hill in New York. "There have been obstacles in the way of accomplishing what we wanted to accomplish, which it has been impossible so far to overcome. Whether they can be overcome depends very much upon the result of your interview with Mr. Hill." It is not known whether that interview took place. In any case, Hill had been anything but optimistic about the project. As for the document conferring power of attorney, it had been placed in a safe and would be returned as soon as a secure way could be found.[70] It is not known whether it was ever given back to Sun.

Thus ended the contact between Sun and Boothe and with it another attempt to get U.S. funding for a revolution in China. Ironically, there existed at the time a considerable interest in China on the part of American capitalists. Ever since the Russo-Japanese War, they had been trying to promote and finance the construction of railroads in Manchuria, rivaling the efforts of the Japanese and Russians. Around the middle of 1909, U.S. interests saw a chance to participate in railroad construction in Szechuan province. They obtained the backing of the administration in Washington and had President Taft cable the Prince Regent in Peking in July 1909, virtually forcing American capital upon China: "I have an intense personal interest in making the use of American capital in the development of China an instrument for the promotion of the welfare of China, and an increase in her material prosperity." Thus backed by their government, U.S. financiers became partners in an international consortium that, just at the time when Boothe put his power of attorney at Sun's disposal, obtained the agreement of the Chinese government for a large loan.[71] Wall Street's readiness to do business with an established government, while unwilling to create a government to do business with, effectively ruled out a revolutionary like Sun Yat-sen as a proper business partner.

As for Lea, Boothe's failure to raise the funds was just another, temporary setback. He continued to believe in the cause of the Chinese Revolution and in Sun as its leader, just as Sun remained convinced of the contribution that Lea could make to his work. Half a year earlier, when Sun had accepted the plan of starting the revolution in Canton, he had proposed to Lea that before the uprising they meet in London. "It is of vital importance for us to secure a perfect understanding of the English Government. To do this you and I must go to London and work together. If the project of getting money in America is succeeded [sic] and the 50,000 duly sent to me I will . . . go to London immediately and meet you there."[72] Alas, not even the $50,000 were forthcoming, and as long as Sun was not certain of receiving the money, there was no point of talking with the British Government. Under the circumstances Sun went to the United States without meeting Lea in London. It has not become known whether he saw Lea during his sojourn in North America. Their later correspondence, however, leaves no doubt that they remained in close touch with each other during that period, while there is no sign that Lea had any further contact with Boothe.

Meanwhile Sun succeeded in raising a fair amount of money. Although he collected only HK$14,000 in the United States, his Canadian tour netted four times as much. Chinese in Malaya, Siam, Indochina, and the Dutch East Indies contributed more than HK$100,000 to the war chest. The total sum available to the revolutionaries seemed sufficient to start the uprising in Canton by the middle of April, but the date had to be postponed several times, as men and supplies were arriving with delays. Finally, because the Manchu authorities learned of the impending revolt, Huang was forced to act on April 27 although not all men and weapons were in place. Nor was there sufficient time for regiments that supported the revolution to join in the fight. As a result, Sun's tenth attempt at revolution also ended in disaster. It did, however, greatly contribute to China's increasing instability and agitation among its armed forces.

At the same time, Lea also suffered a setback. He had completed *The Valor of Ignorance* early in 1909. In June of that year he attempted a dramatization of *The Vermilion Pencil* under the title *The Vermilion Spider*. He also began work on *The Day of the Saxon*, but the work progressed slowly. A year later the book was not yet completed, although he expected to finish it in a short time.[73] He was too optimistic, however, as various circumstances slowed down his work. His house was broken into several times by "unknown parties," presumably agents of the Chinese government, which prompted him to move his papers to Boothe's residence. Lea moved about considerably during the latter part of 1910.[74] Moreover, to enhance his stature as a military expert, he published a lengthy article on a novel military subject, "The Aeroplane in War,"[75] and also took a prominent part in the Pacific Slope Congress, which was held in San Francisco in November 1910.[76] By April 1911 his worsening eyesight brought his work on the new book to a standstill. He mentioned his predicament to an English friend, Sir Tollemache Sinclair, to whom he had given the rights for the French translation and publication of *The Valor of Ignorance*. The news perturbed Sinclair who, in cables and a letter, insisted that Lea consult a world-famous oculist, Dr. Pagenstreicher in Wiesbaden, Germany, to avoid total blindness. Once in Europe, Lea should come to London for the coronation of King George V. "Lord Roberts, Lord Charles Beresford and others would show you the greatest attention. . . . I might be able to have you made an honorary member of the Travellers Club. . . . In fact, you would be the chief lion of the season."[77]

Lea was persuaded to make the trip not only for medical reasons but also for the opportunities it afforded to advance Sun's cause through his connections in the United States and England. He decided to intercede for Sun in Washington and to proceed from Germany to London just as soon as the condition of his eyes permitted an interruption of the cure.[78] Ethel was to accompany him, and so they thought it proper to get married. Less than two weeks later, the pair were in Washington where they obtained a passport. Having failed to enlist the financial support of private interests, Lea now conceived the plan to ask the U.S. Government for political, military, and financial assistance to Sun Yat-sen's revolutionary movement.

Lea started with the premise that China had entered a period of revolutionary instability that could no longer be controlled by the Manchu regime. U.S. support of the present Chinese government would, in the end, harm American interests as it would make the United States an enemy in the eyes of the Chinese people. Moreover, continued unrest would play into the hands of the Japanese and the Russians. For these reasons, the United States should work toward a stable regime that could guarantee the preservation of American commercial and political objectives. Increasing revolutionary upheaval and political instability could be avoided only by Sun and his people. That nationwide movement of which Sun was the firm and undisputed leader enjoyed not only popular support, but had many sympathizers also in the armies of the Manchu regime. Rather than have revolutionary unrest fester for an extended time until Sun would emerge as the inevitable victor, Lea proposed that Washington support Sun financially and politically from the outset. Money was needed "to secure perfect cohesion and unity amongst [the] forces scattered over so vast an area as China" so that the revolution could be accomplished without bloodshed. Apparently, he expected the government in Peking to abdicate, once its troops rallied to a national government headed by Sun and supported by the United States.[79]

Lea tried to present his views to Secretary of State Philander Knox, who, however, declined to see him "for official reasons."[80] Presumably, the U.S. Government did not agree to support a revolution against a government with which it had friendly relations. However, Lea did explain his views to Senator Root and several other prominent men and was "made much of during his visit to Washington."[81] Apparently, he came away with the conviction that his proposals had been received favorably by Senator Root and other politicians. He informed Sun Yat-sen of his presumed success in Washington and asked him to increase the influence of his Chinese Alliance among the Manchu divisions and to firmly buttress his position as the sole and recognized leader of the movement. Sun confirmed "that more than ten divisions of the new army outside of Peking are sure, and all the Chinese divisions in the Capitol [sic] are very promising." One of his men had recently been given command of a division in Peking, and Sun could count on many officers in other divisions. Moreover, he replied, "there are none who would divide power with me at present, all leaders of different provinces are only too welcome for me to take up general command, in fact they [sic] only fear is that I would not accept that position."[82]

Notwithstanding Lea's optimism about the success of his mission in Washington, Senator Root's eventual answer was disappointing: "I wish I had something cheerful to say on the subject concerning which you talked with me in Washington. I find, however, that it is quite impracticable to secure any such assistance as you require to carry out your plan. I see that there is a good deal of disturbance now in China, which I suppose very likely has a definite relation to the conditions which you described to me."[83]

Sun came independently to the conclusion that he could not count on the U.S. Government for help. Not yet informed of Senator Root's negative answer, he told Lea, "In regard to how and when and where to obtain the necessary funds, I really cannot form an [sic] decision. I only hoping [sic] to get it as soon as possible. . . . I will try to come over to Europe to see what could be done with France and England."[84]

—9—

Chief of Staff

Lea and his wife arrived in Wiesbaden in the latter part of July 1911. For reasons unknown it was not Dr. Pagenstreicher who treated him, but a Dr. Meurer. By August 10 Sun in San Francisco already had a letter from Lea in which he said his eyes were rapidly improving.[1] The progress continued, according to a letter to a friend of August 18: "I am doing a little work every day now, so you know that my eyes have improved a great deal."[2] Ethel noted the improvement in a handwritten note to her sister Agnes[3] and also to her son Joshua on September 3. By that time Lea was working about three hours a day. "Finally [he] has the last chapter of the first half [of *The Day of the Saxon*] finished . . . and he is now at work on the second part . . . and we are hoping it will be completed by November. We intend leaving as soon as Dr. Meurer says it is safe."[4] Plans called for visits to Nuremberg, Munich, and Berlin and a sojourn in Paris during the winter, with a few weeks in London in between.

The trip also provided a welcome opportunity to get to know Germany, a country that played an important part in *The Day of the Saxon*. Germany's military and political circumstances interested him greatly. He saw Germany as a politically conscious nation, ready at any moment for expansion and dominion. Other nations would act only when conditions made them aware of opportunities that could be exploited for their benefit. "The German nation," however, "waits only as Bismarck waited for conditions to shape themselves. . . . [His] heavy spirit has settled upon it. It wears his scowl. It has adopted his brutality, as it has his greatness. It has taken his criterion of truth, which is Germanic; his indifference to justice, which is savage; and his conception of a state, which is sublime."[5] Whereas other Americans of his and preceding generations had gone to Germany to study its cultural life and its institutions, Lea's interest focused exclusively on the military establishment and the military strength of that nation.

In Washington, while on the way to Europe, he had already written to the U.S. military attaché in Berlin and asked him to obtain permission for his attendance at the imperial maneuvers.[6] Not having had a reply on his arrival at Wiesbaden, Lea repeated his request and also asked for an official introduction for viewing a military parade before the German Emperor, which was to be held in nearby Mainz.

Lea got to see the parade of 26,000 soldiers with the Emperor in the reviewing stand "and enjoyed it immensely. Billy [Wilhelm II] is a little man but is certainly a soldier"—a curious and revealing remark by a military man even shorter than the Emperor—"and he had a fine bunch of men pass in front of him and show off their paces."[7] As to the attendance at the imperial maneuvers, the attaché was unable to be of help because only foreigners especially invited by the Emperor could be present. He held out hope, however, of arranging for Lea to attend some less important brigade, division, or army corps maneuvers.[8] There is no evidence that he saw any of these, but among his remaining papers there is a map of the maneuvers of the XVIII Army Corps held in 1911 in the immediate neighborhood of Wiesbaden.[9] It is possible that he attended this, particularly because he got to know several young army officers in Wiesbaden, in whose company he occasionally had some drinks.[10]

Lea's attendance at the maneuvers has become of some significance for the legends that grew around them. It has been said that the Emperor had read *The Valor of Ignorance* and arranged for its distribution among his officers. It has also become part of the legends, but not of history, that Lea received "a personal invitation from Kaiser Wilhelm II, to witness the German war maneuvers of that year" and that "in full dress uniform (probably of his own imaginative designing) he witnessed the German maneuvers from a carriage with high cushions, which the Kaiser (himself a cripple, with his shriveled arm) had especially ordered." It belongs in the same category of tales claiming that "all political and military doors in Germany were automatically opened to the 'General.' "[11] Of course, Lea would not have been one to refuse such honors, had they been offered, but there is no indication that they were.

While waiting for his complete recovery, which he expected by the first of November, and unable to devote more than a few hours to his book in progress, Lea partook of the entertainments that the spa of Wiesbaden had to offer. He looked forward to the horse-racing season in September and, in the meantime, attended one of three concerts that were given daily on the grounds of the spa. "They occasionally vary the programme with a military band, and it is then very fine. Every few days they have fireworks. . . . We went once and I was laid up for two days with my eyes from the lights, then I decided to stay away from such occasions.''[12] But after a few weeks he grew restless. A trip to Switzerland in mid-August provided diversion, especially a drive across the Simplon Pass, which evoked pictures of Napoleon's army crossing into Italy. The desultory correspondence with Sun Yat-sen, friends and family back home, and acquaintances in England along with the limited time he could spend on his book did not fill his days. He looked forward to a meeting with Sun who was thinking of establishing his headquarters in Paris or London. Lea also eagerly anticipated attending a conference with Huang, but this never materialized. It was feared Chinese army units friendly to the revolutionaries might launch an uprising before preparations had been completed, and it fell to Huang to keep the situation under control until everything was ready. But suddenly events took an unexpected turn, prompting Lea to leave the somnolent atmosphere of Wiesbaden and rush to London.

By October 1911 revolutionary agitation and unrest, especially among New Army units in the Yangtse river region, had reached a high point. Huang Hsing found himself in a dilemma. On the one hand, he wanted to delay any new attempt at revolution until it was well prepared and he had new funds available for it, so as to avoid the risk of another failure. On the other, he feared that he could no longer remain in control of events due to the explosive mood among his comrades, particularly his partisans in the army, and so he decided to strike at the end of the month. In the meantime, he hoped to obtain the needed funds. At about the time when Sun Yat-sen wrote to Lea that Huang's trip to Europe had been postponed, he received a coded cable from Huang. Sun was then in Idaho on the way to Denver where he arrived on October 10. In his autobiography, Sun recounted his side of the story:

> About a fortnight before, I had received a telegram from [Huang Hsing] in Hong Kong. Because my secret code book was in my trunk, which had already gone to Denver, I had no way of translating it on the way. That night, on arriving in Denver, I took out the secret code and decoded the telegram from [Huang], which read: "representative . . . arrived at Hong Kong from Wuchang, reporting sympathizers in the New Army are determined to move. Please remit funds at once," etc.
>
> I was then in Denver, and I could think of no way to get funds. I was thinking of wiring an answer, "Do not move," but it was late at night, and I was extremely tired from the day's tedious traveling, and I was confused in my thoughts. I thought I would have a good night's rest first, and then would answer him next day after giving

the matter some more thought. However, I slept until eleven o'clock
the next morning. When I got up, I was hungry. I went to a cafeteria
to get my breakfast. On passing a newsstand in the lobby, I bought a
newspaper which opened with the news, "Wuchang occupied by the
revolutionists." All the difficulties in answering Huang's telegram
were completely removed. Consequently, I sent a telegram to him,
explaining how my reply was delayed and telling him my plan.
I immediately left for the eastern part of the United States.[13]

The Wuchang Revolution of October 10, 1911, was the eleventh
and, finally, successful attempt of Sun Yat-sen's movement at the overthrow of the Manchu regime, not to count six other, independent uprisings. It came as a surprise not only to Sun. A bomb that accidentally
exploded in the morning of that day in the Hankow revolutionary headquarters caused the Manchu authorities to take action against the rebels,
and this, in turn, forced their sympathizers in the army to attack for fear
of being discovered. Virtually leaderless, the T'ung Meng Hui people
and the rebellious soldiers attained some initial successes and proclaimed
a revolutionary military government. But they needed a head for it, and
so they practically forced a reluctant commander of a brigade named Li
Yüan-hung to assume the leadership. It was the beginning of an important political career for the hapless Li Yüan-hung. On October 28 Huang
Hsing arrived at the scene, took command, and became the central figure
of the revolution. The movement suffered some initial reverses but tri-
umphed after several other provincial centers joined it. When the Manchu court came to doubt the loyalty of its forces, it called on Yuan Shih-
k'ai, then living in retirement, who enjoyed the support of the northern
armies. Yuan hemmed and hawed until he had been put in command of
all the imperial armies and, finally, the regime, in its desperation, appointed him premier of the central government. Thus he came to represent the Manchus in the ensuing negotiations with the rebels. In these
negotiations, which began early in December, Yuan's deputy, T'ang
Shao-i, adopted a conciliatory attitude and hinted at Yuan's leaning toward the republican side. In hindsight it appears that Yuan was interested in neither side but his own. The negotiator for the rebels was Wu
T'ing Fang, who had been the Chinese Imperial Minister to Washington
during Lea's first trip to China and again from 1908 to 1909 and since
then had openly converted to the republican cause.
    In the meantime, the rebels had formed a Representative Provincial
Council with delegates from the provinces involved in the rebellion. A
tug of war ensued between elements of the T'ung Meng Hui, who favored Huang Hsing as leader, and military men and members of the gentry who had joined the rebellion and who preferred Li Yüan-hung, one

of their own. In the interest of unity, Huang Hsing granted Li precedence and declared himself satisfied with the position as Li's deputy. The Council called a meeting of all provincial delegates, to be held at Nanking at the middle of December, to elect a provisional president, but the delegates in assembly on December 15 postponed the election due to a split in their ranks. The military and the gentry preferred Li, while the T'ung Meng Hui people wanted one of their own in that position.

When he learned of the Wuchang Revolution in Denver, Sun Yat-sen decided against returning to China, not because he thought that it would again end unsuccessfully, but because he felt he could be more useful abroad. As in the past, he was convinced that his "contribution to the revolutionary work was not in the battlefield but in diplomatic circles."[14] In his opinion, the revolution needed for its ultimate success the recognition of the revolutionary regime by the Western powers or, at least, their neutrality; and, of course, the matter of financial support of the revolution and, if successful, of the emerging republican government was very much on his mind. Accordingly, he resolved to make his way to China via Washington, London, and Paris.

Sun left Denver for Washington by way of St. Louis and Chicago where he was reported to have collected $10,000 from local Chinese. On October 18 he was in Washington and tried to see Secretary of State Knox, but there is no evidence that he managed to talk to him.[15] Nor is it known whether he met with other members of the administration or politicians as, for instance, Senator Root. At about the same time, he cabled Lea in Wiesbaden, asking him to proceed to London and mobilize his friends and acquaintances so that, on Sun's arrival, negotiations could begin about a loan to the revolutionary government.[16] Lea travelled to London on October 19, immediately after receiving the cable. Ethel stayed behind, thinking "he would accomplish more without having me to think about." She expected him back within a matter of days to settle affairs in Wiesbaden and then to return to London to meet Sun, but Lea decided to stay in England. To Ethel it seemed "that the big act is about due and we are merely waiting for our cue to put in an appearance. Homer may be said to have received his already."[17]

Lea arrived in London extremely fatigued. He suffered from a severe headache, which started in the train that took him from Wiesbaden and continued throughout his first day in London. For that reason he did not write to Ethel on the night of his arrival.[18] He did write a letter to Lord Roberts, however, but his handwriting was so erratic that the fatigue seemed to have affected his eyesight. From the letter it appears that he had contacted his friend, Sir Tollemache Sinclair, before or upon his arrival, who, in turn, had approached Lord Roberts and ascertained that Roberts could see Lea the following Monday, October 24.[19]

Lord Earl Roberts, Field Marshal and former Commander in Chief of the British army, had corresponded with Lea since he read *The Valor of Ignorance*. Lea's call for a professional army and other theses of his book agreed with Lord Roberts's points of view. Roberts had bought all six copies of the book available at Harper's in London and asked the manager to cable for more, which were sold as soon as they arrived, leaving additional requests unfilled.[20] Lea had been flattered by the great man's laudatory words and had confided to him that he was planning another book, which would deal with the British Empire and the survival of the Anglo-Saxon race on both continents.[21] Now, on his arrival in London, he sent Lord Roberts the first chapters of the new book and suggested that he read them over the weekend. "I have some very important matters concerning our race in the Orient that I will speak to you about in relation to some of these chapters," he wrote with unsteady hand.[22] Apparently, to gain Lord Roberts's backing for his mission, Lea was not prepared to put on paper the reason that had prompted him to go to London and seek an appointment, but relied on their common outlook on military and political questions as developed in his new book.

An attempt to establish immediate contact with Lord Charles Beresford, doubtless for the same reason, was in vain because Beresford was out of town. Lord Beresford, a former Lord Commissioner of the Admiralty and an author on China, had been in that country shortly before Lea's first trip. He had become a friend of Yuan Shih-k'ai and was also close to K'ang Yu-wei, who, when in London in 1899, had stayed at his house. He would have been another useful contact for Lea, had he been in London. It is not known how and when Lea became acquainted with Lord Beresford. It was perhaps at his suggestion that Lea was offered honorary membership in the Imperial Maritime League in which he was active. He may also have arranged for Lea to speak at a conference of the League on November 10. As it was, Lea was busily engaged in negotiations for a loan and had to send his regrets at not being able to be present. He did, however, forward a letter that was read at the meeting.[23] Finally, there is proof of their acquaintanceship in the form of a letter that Lord Beresford addressed four months later to Lea in China in response to one from Lea.[24]

With Beresford away and Roberts unable to see him until the following week, Lea faced a long weekend that tested his patience. The horrible weather was another aggravation. He stayed "in the hotel all day, but," as Ethel put it, "he neglects to say what he does at night," except for Friday evening, when the 87-year-old Sir Tollemache Sinclair took him to dinner and a music hall until well after midnight.[25] Realizing that he could not return to Wiesbaden within a few days, he decided to have

Ethel join him in London. He sent her money for the trip and a small amount still owed to Dr. Meurer. Ethel wondered what it all meant. Her guess was: China.[26]

On Monday, October 24, in his first meeting with Lord Roberts, Lea learned that Roberts liked what he had read of the new book. More importantly at the moment, however, Roberts was willing to help Lea in obtaining a loan and approaching the British Government for political and diplomatic support for the revolutionary regime. But it seems that he believed that Sun's presence in London was necessary before anything could be accomplished. And so the week dragged on without any progress whatsoever. The day after the meeting with Lord Roberts, however, Lea signed a publishing contract with Harper's London office for his new book, *The Day of the Saxon*, and received a welcome and needed advance on royalties.[27]

On October 28 the *Times* of London published a dispatch from Peking that Li Yüan-hung had informed the consuls at Hankow that he had been proclaimed President of the Chinese Republic.[28] Although this was followed by a report that the Foreign Office had no news of the proclamation, the dispatch must have disturbed Lea greatly. If the news were true, it would mean the end of his mission in England. It would doom Sun's attempts for political and financial backing and, possibly, terminate Sun's influence on events in China and his prospects of leading the revolutionary movement and its nascent regime. It would also dash any hopes of Lea for a role in the new China. The danger was so much greater because Li Yüan-hung had been a late and, at that, forced convert to the revolution. As head of the provisional government, he might betray the cause and revert to his old masters, the Manchus. Even if the news were untrue, Sun's chances to succeed with the British Government and financial circles would be made that much more difficult, if not impossible, as long as he could not present himself as the undisputable leader of the revolution.

In a cable that has not been preserved, Lea informed Sun of the dispatch and asked for his explanation and assurance. This was provided by Sun in his immediate cable reply dated October 31:

HOMER LEA SAVOY LONDON
LIYUEN PRO[CLAMATION] INEXPLICABLE, PERHAPS AMBITION CARRY BY SUDDEN SUCCESS BUT HIS LACKING OF GENERALSHIP CANNOT HOLD HIS OWN ANY LONGER. ORGANIZATION EVERYWHERE EXCELLENT. ALL LOOKING FOR ME TO LEAD. IF FINANCIALLY SUPPORTED I COULD CONTROL SITUATION ABSOLUTELY. NO STRONG GOVERN-

MENT COULD BE FORMED UNTIL WE GET THERE, THERE-
FORE LOAN IS NECESSARY. YOU ARE GIVEN FULL POWER TO
NEGOTIATE SUCH.[29]

While he found Li's statement inexplicable, Sun saw it, if at all
true, as a desperate move in the power struggle going on in the revolutionary forces, with his group rallying behind Huang Hsing and local
officials and army people supporting Li Yüang-hung. In view of the impending negotiations in London, Sun stressed his own leadership position and pointed out that he alone could form a strong government. A
loan was a guarantee of political stability, which, he assumed, the British
Government desired.

To assure Lea further and, through him, the British Government,
Sun dispatched the next day another cable reporting that Huang Hsing
had arrived in Hankow and taken things in hand and that "Things [had]
much improved"[30] from the point of view of the T'ung Meng Hui and its
leader, Sun. As Huang Hsing did not arrive in Hankow until October 28,
Sun's cable showed to Lea, and hopefully also to the people with whom
he may have been engaged in negotiations, that Sun kept in close touch
with events in China. The cable also brought Lea the welcome news that
Sun expected to embark a day later for England.

On receipt of the second cable, Lea wrote to Lord Roberts telling
him of the improved situation in China.[31] Apparently, Roberts had also
been concerned about the report of Li's ascendancy and reverses suffered
by the revolutionaries. Lea told him in his letter that Huang Hsing had
superseded Li "whose dilatory tactics has caused us much trouble and
annoyance," a criticism of his own invention. Although Lea had never
met Huang, as far as is known, he added that he had more confidence in
Huang than in any other general in the field. The important thing, he
stressed, was to obtain a loan without which the revolutionary regime
would disintegrate and China would fall into chaos. "Do you not think it
would be possible for us to at least formulate a plan whereby we can proceed to secure the loan immediately," he asked impatiently. At the same
time he told Lord Roberts that he was writing to Senator Root again "to
make an effort in that direction" and explain to the President and to
Secretary Knox the new developments, presumably so that by the following week, when Sun was due to arrive, concerted action could be taken by
the United States and Great Britain.

In his letter to Senator Root, Lea emphasized the danger of prolonged civil war in China and the possible disintegration of the empire.
This could be avoided only by Sun, who alone was capable of establishing
a strong, central government. "Because of this lack of money . . . Dr.
Sun and myself have not at once gone to Hankow and formed this gov-

ernment," which, he said, was in the interest of the United States and Great Britain as much as in the interest of China. Even though he was in contact with "great and powerful men" in England who viewed the situation in exactly the same light as he, the British Government had not taken action, being dependent on Japan, an allusion to the Anglo-Japanese Alliance of 1902. "If our country would address a secret note here . . . it would turn the scale and by a secret acquiescence I would be able to secure money. In this way I could bring about I believe a tacit amalgamation of the Anglo-Saxon race in the Orient," or rather their policies. "I will therefore ask if you will not at once see the President and Mr. Knox explaining all that I told you [and] arrange with the government to permit one of our vessels to meet me at Hong Kong for transportation to Hankow. . . . This letter should reach you on the 8th. Will you not at once cable me using Western Union code Universal Edition. Address 'Homerlea Savoy London.' Should the President or Mr. Knox desire fuller and more complete information I will be glad to communicate it to our Ambassador here."[32] There is no record of any reply. In any event, the U.S. government did not order any of its gunboats to take Lea to Hankow.

Lord Roberts seems to have been impressed by Sun's cables and Lea's arguments, for he forwarded a letter from Lea to the Foreign Secretary, Sir Edward Grey, inquiring whether the Secretary would be prepared to see Lea during his stay in England. But the Foreign Secretary let it be known that he had too many parliamentary and official engagements that took all of his time.[33] Under the circumstances Lord Roberts abstained from approaching Prime Minister Asquith with the same request because he was sure the answer would be a similar one. He did invite Lea and Sun, after the latter's arrival, to his house in the country the following Sunday afternoon, "and of course your [Lea's] wife if she will come too."[34] There is no record of such a meeting and any further discussions about Lord Roberts's assistance in the matter of China. It has been said that the visit took place, but that Ethel did not join because she felt uncomfortable without her new clothes, which had not yet been delivered.[35]

After Sun's arrival on November 10, he and Lea used a new strategy to gain the attention of the Foreign Secretary. Since the appearance of *The Valor of Ignorance*, Lea was reported to have had correspondence with the well-known author and inventor of smokeless gunpowder, Hudson Maxim. There is no record of the exchange of letters, but a few years after Lea's death Maxim published a book of his own on the problems dealt with in Lea's work. In his book, *Defenseless America*, Maxim quoted Lea repeatedly and acknowledged his indebtedness to him. It has also been affirmed that, before he embarked for Europe, Lea visited

Maxim at Lake Hopatcong, New Jersey.[36] If this is correct, it is likely that he gave Lea an introduction to his brother in London, Sir Hiram S. Maxim, a British subject and the famous inventor of the automatic machine gun. Hiram Maxim was also a member of the British arms firm, Vickers Sons & Maxim, and, therefore, was for Lea a particularly good contact. By coincidence, Hiram Maxim sympathized with the revolutionary movement, which Lea may have known. Only half a year earlier, Hiram Maxim had offered the revolutionaries an improved rifle and had also called their attention to the military value of airplanes.[37] Under these circumstances it is understandable that members of Vickers Sons & Maxim were willing to assist Sun and Lea in their dealings in London, quite apart from the prospect of selling arms to a new Chinese government. At any rate, a member of the firm, Sir Trevor Dawson, who knew Sir Edward Grey, was determined to speak to him about the concerns that had brought Sun and Lea to London.

Sir Trevor Dawson saw the Foreign Secretary on November 24.[38] On the previous day, Dawson had transmitted to Grey a long statement by Sun and Lea that requested the British Government's support of the revolutionary regime in return for important political and military concessions after a new Chinese government under Sun Yat-sen as president had come into being:

Dr. Sun Yat Sen.
General Homer Lea.

Sun Yat Sen's party wish to make an Anglo-Saxon Alliance with Great Britain and the United States of America. They are in close touch with the United States of America through Senators Root and Knox.

General Homer Lea is chief of staff and responsible only to Sun Yat Sen.

There are 21 trained divisions of soldiers in China; 12 of these are controlled by Sun Yat Sen, 3 are enemies, and 6 are neutral.

Between 30,000 and 40,000 of the best educated students of China are sworn under a blood oath to the service of Sun Yat Sen, and several secret associations, consisting in all of about 35,000,000 people, are also sworn to the reactionary [sic] party, and to place Sun Yat Sen as President.

Sun Yat Sen requires the friendship and support of the British Government and will act under the advice of the British Government, and would accept the appointment of a [British] Political Officer on his Staff for this purpose.

He will agree, in the event of his party coming into power and his becoming President—which he believes now to be a certainty—

to make an agreement with the British Government and with the United States of America by which they shall have favoured nation terms over all other countries.

He will further place the new Navy under the command of British Officers, subject to his orders.

In regard to any agreement China may make with Japan they would act under advice of the British Government.[39]

With its reference to an "Anglo-Saxon Alliance" and the dubious assertion of close contact with Root and Knox, the memorandum bears the unquestionable stamp of Lea's coauthorship. It has been called "a desperate bluff,"[40] but, more than that, it was also a desperate gamble with the sovereignty of a republican China, which might have cost Sun's political reputation and position dearly, had the British Government accepted the proposals. As a gamble it is reminiscent of Lenin's agreement with the German High Command five years later, but posterity has not been permitted to judge whether Sun Yat-sen could have mustered the same political will and tenacity that enabled Lenin to overcome his critics. As it turned out, Sun's and Lea's memorandum did not move the Foreign Secretary, nor did the statement by Sun, "that he would be able to obtain a loan of 1,000,000 £ from private sources if the British Government agreed to it; and that he was quite willing that [Sir Edward Grey] should make inquiries in Washington to confirm what he had said as to his relations with Senators Root and Knox."[41] The British Government decided to stay neutral but was prepared to recognize any strong government that would ultimately evolve. The Foreign Secretary, however, preferred that "one good man," Yuan Shih-k'ai rather than Sun Yat-sen, be the head of the new government.[42]

Sir Trevor Dawson had success in one, though less important, respect. Early in his revolutionary career, Sun had been banned by the British Governor from staying in Hong Kong. That order was now withdrawn.

As to the conditional offer of a loan to a revolutionary government headed by Sun, Lea had established contact with the Four-Power Consortium, which had been formed by British, French, German, and United States' banking interests to provide loans to the government in Peking.[43] In his memoirs, Sun stated, "On my arrival in England, I entered through my English friend into negotiations with the Banking Consortium of the Four Powers."[44] He did not divulge the name of the English friend, but the original, Chinese version omitted the term "English friend" and identified him as Homer Lea.[45] Just then a new loan for railroad construction was ready to be paid out, and another was being processed by the Consortium. Sun and Lea pleaded with this body to stop all loans to the Imperial Government and to grant instead a loan to a new government to be headed by Sun.

The first request was redundant because in its meeting in Paris on November 10 the Consortium had already decided to withhold any further payments until the political situation in China had been stabilized.[46] Nevertheless, Sun claimed the credit for having stopped the payments: "Having received a favorable settlement [of this issue], I then turned to the Banking Consortium to secure a loan for the revolutionary Government." The answer was, however, negative. Loans would be granted only to a firmly established and recognized government, but the Consortium agreed to have a representative accompany Sun on his return to China so that on fulfillment of the two conditions negotiations for a loan could begin.[47]

Lea made another approach for financial help to the London branch of the Hongkong and Shanghai Bank, but given the existing circumstances no action was taken.[48] Nor was Morgan, Greenfell & Co., the Morgan bank in London, willing to respond to a request for a loan. Lea represented to them that in interviews with Secretary Knox, Senator Root, and others he had been promised the support of the U.S. Government if and when the revolution were successful. Bank officials took the precaution of inquiring with the State Department through the Morgan bank in New York. Of course, they were informed that Secretary Knox had declined to see Lea and that no such promises had been given.[49] This ended the search for money in London. The failure may have meant also a small, personal disappointment for Ethel. "Homer is on the trail of 5 million and I hardly see him," she had written to her sister. "I hope he gets it and that Sun is grateful enough to hand me over a little lunch at least." Perhaps she got her little lunch after all, in spite of the adverse outcome of Homer's labors, because Sun may have recognized that "he's worked awfully hard and his work has probably only begun."[50]

Indeed, Lea had been hard at work aside from the negotiations for money and support. Among other things, he was compiling a manual of tactics and drill for the new republican army, in which he expected to take a high position. He may have started on the manual before going to London, but now he discussed it with a well-known British military writer, Colonel F. N. Mande. The latter made several suggestions, including, in all earnestness, adding "a short introduction which should combine the straightforward simplicity of Suvaroff & Sir Charles Napier adapted to the ordinary Chinaman's phraseology." There were also more immediate, practical questions on which Lea sought Mande's advice. As he expected to lead the revolutionary troops against the armies of the Manchu regime, Lea pondered the best strategy. Mande suggested, just as earnestly, the use of the Napoleonic square when marching big masses of men across the country. This would provide a decisive advantage over the mostly German-trained officers of the enemy, because Germans were not acquainted with that formation. Finally, Lea discussed a plan for a British organization paralleling the, by now, defunct Chinese Imperial Reform Army in the United States. At the proper time he would instruct Mande by cable "to carry on." On receipt of the order, Mande would start to recruit a "considerable body of N.C.O.s etc," whom he would eventually send to China to serve as officers in Lea's forces. But, of course, there was the disagreeable matter of money, which the two had not, or not sufficiently, discussed before Lea departed from London. And so Mande dealt in a letter with several financial questions. Where was the money for office expenditures to come from? A quiet room in some friend's office might not cost anything, but a typist and a secretary might be needed or some other staff members. On the other hand, the prestige of the new republican government might require a more elaborate and costly setup, a decision that Mande left to Lea. The latter had decided that the men to be recruited by Mande were to be paid in accordance with the U.S. Army scale, but he had said nothing about the fare to Shanghai, an outfit allowance, and an additional month's pay prior to embarkation. As for himself, Mande was satisfied with Lea's offer of compensation, which was not specified in the letter, but here again some details had been overlooked. And so Mande stated, "I shall have to raise money somehow to pay for my fare out & buy my kit—so any help the Gvt can give me will be welcome & expedite matters."[51] There is no record of Lea's reply to Mande's letter, and, given the later course of events, the command to "carry on" was never transmitted.

There were other British officers whom Lea tried to enlist, among them Lord Stanhope who had seen service in the Boer War and in later life was to be First Lord of the Admiralty (1938–39) and Lord President of Council (1939–40). The Lord "was sorely tempted (albeit startled)" at Lea's offer to take him on his staff, but he declined politely because he felt he would be of little use, not knowing the Chinese language nor the people. He promised, however, to help: "I shall be proud in my humble way to back up your efforts. . . . If you or Dr Sun desire British policy with regard to China elucidated by questions in the House of Lords I will endeavour to extract the information."[52] Lea wrote to Lord Stanhope not long after he got to China,[53] but that letter has not been preserved.

On November 16, the day before his thirty-fifth birthday, a new uniform was delivered to Lea, which was made for him in London according to his own specifications. Unfortunately, these have not survived, but the outfit was probably just as splendid as the one he had designed for himself as commander in chief of the Chinese Imperial Reform Army. Of course, as a general and commander of the republican forces, he could not have worn the old uniform of the monarchy. Whatever the details of the new one, Ethel found, "he looked so nice" in it. Her pleasure was increased by Sun's birthday present: "Sun is going to make him Chief of Staff & he is wild with delight."[54]

The Leas departed from London to Paris together with Sun Yat-sen on November 20. Sun paid for the "tickets etc.,"[55] which probably meant that he paid also for the expenses in London as well as for hotel and incidental expenses of the trip to China.

From November 21 to 24 Sun held discussions with Chinese friends in Paris and with various politicians, among them former Prime Minister Clemenceau. He also approached French banking interests about a loan to the republican regime, but he was no more successful than in London. The French Government took the same "wait-and-see" attitude.[56] Lea was not involved in these talks, and so he and Ethel could do some sight-seeing despite the rainy weather.[57] On November 25 the party embarked in Marseilles on the S.S. *Malwa*,[58] and on arrival in Colombo, they transferred to the S.S. *Devanha*, which was to take them to Shanghai.

Little information is available on the first leg of the trip. Before the arrival in China, Lea tried to complete *The Day of the Saxon*, because he expected to be busy there with other matters. The leisurely voyage provided an ideal opportunity, but his eyesight had worsened and he could not use his eyes for any length of time. Ethel was "afraid he will have to dictate the last of it," which he probably did. Sun read the manuscript and liked it.[59] While traveling, Sun kept in touch with his organization by cable, and it may be presumed that he discussed developments with Lea. According to Ethel, all of Sun's cables were revised by Lea and in many cases written by him entirely,[60] which may or may not have been correct. As the S.S. *Devanha* neared China, however, Lea acted as spokes-man for Sun who was less inclined to meet reporters as long as he could not coordinate his statements with those of his associates in China. His chief of staff, who had no such qualms, aroused considerable interest wherever the boat stopped.

Indeed, Far Eastern newspapers had already speculated on Homer Lea's role in the campaign against the Manchu government when it became known that he was accompanying Sun Yat-sen. It was argued that, for the revolution to succeed, a military government was needed. "But over and above that there comes the remarkable statement that General HOMER LEA, formerly of the American army, now retired, has under-taken to direct that Military Government. At once there will occur to many the parallel between General GORDON, of the British Army, or-ganizing the forces of the Manchu Imperial Government and leading them to victory during the Taeping rebellion of half a century ago; and General HOMER LEA, late of the U.S. Army, aiding in the organising of the forces of the Chinese Revolution against the Manchu Imperial Government." But it was assumed that in joining the revolutionary forces Lea was motivated less by friendliness toward them and enmity toward the Manchu regime, but by a conviction that a militarily strong China, be it monarchical or republican, was the paramount interest of the United States. "HOMER LEA fears for the United States if the military and naval supremacy of Japan on the Pacific continue to be the monopoly it is at present. It is as a possible counterpoise, in future years, to Japan's power, that he earnestly desires to see a strong China. And it is therefore as an American officer that loves his country, and sees far more clearly than any of his fellow-countrymen what is needful for her security, that he has agreed to assist to organise the military Government that is, apparently before long, to displace the effete survival of the administration of Peking."[61]

A strong China was also the theme of his talk with reporters when the S.S. *Devanha* arrived in Penang on December 14. A strong China would not only be a counterweight against Japan but also put a stop to Russia's expansion, while representing a guarantee for continued U.S. trade under the Open-Door Policy. If China remained weak, its masses could be used by Russia for breaking down British power in the Pacific area and in India.[62] Standing on British colonial soil, Lea deemed it advisable to emphasize, too, the mutuality of British and U.S. interests. Two days later, as the ship docked in Singapore, it was reported that Sun refused a compromise with the Manchu regime and intended to establish a provisional government at Shanghai. "General Lea will unify the revolutionary army and it will march upon Peking."[63] Lea was also called "a first-class financial asset [of the revolutionaries], for his employment as a planner of the campaign, as in short the 'Von Moltke' of the Revolution, will have given to European, especially to American, financiers all the confidence necessary to back the Revolution with their credit on the money markets of the world. It will not encourage Peking to know that they have only Yuan Shih-Kai to put against the brain of Homer Lea. Then again it is true that Sun Yat Sen goes to Shanghai armed with the actual promise of monetary help from great banking houses in Europe and America, the sole condition being that he will agree to place himself at the head of the new Government."[64]

The information about prospective financial help from European and American banks, false as it was, may have come from Lea. It was not repeated, though, in the conversation that Lea had with U.S. Consul Anderson on the ship's next stop in Hong Kong on December 21. Anderson's report to the State Department did stress, however, the important role that Lea appeared to be playing in the events that were beginning to unfold. While considering Sun the moving spirit of the revolution, he saw Lea as his "Grey Eminence." "General Lea," he wrote in his dispatch, "has a great influence over [Sun Yat-sen],—almost a controlling influence in matters of relations with other powers."[65]

Upon arriving in Hong Kong, Lea had gone to see Anderson and, after giving him information on Sun's plans, arranged for a personal talk between Anderson and Sun on board the S.S. *Devanha*. As a result of that meeting and with the approval of Sun, Anderson and Lea drew up the text of a cable to the U.S. Department of State, that contained a statement of Sun's political plans and strategies:

> We propose on arrival at Shanghai to organize consolidated provisional government; Sun Yat Sen, President. A cabinet [and] governors [of] provinces will be appointed by him. Homer Lea, chief staff, will negotiate direct[ly with the] Manchus; will demand complete relinquishment [of] all power. Manchus will be allowed full enjoyment property; pension imperial clans. Provisional Government to establish peace, then call constitutional convention. We propose if necessary to request the President of the United States mediate with Manchus but offer no compromise or conditions but the above mentioned. We propose select[ing] the best provisional administrators independent [of] present officials. Provisional Government military; permanent Government strongly centralized Republican Government, [a] modified American plan. We propose employ[ing] eminent American jurists to assist framing constitution.[66]

In a letter confirming the cable, Anderson mentioned Secretary Knox and Senator Root as two constitutional lawyers whom Sun and his party would want to approach in connection with drafting a constitution of the Chinese Republic.

The idea that men like Senator Root should act as advisors to the revolutionary authorities had been in Lea's mind for some time. From Paris he had already written to Senator Root to that effect. Lea's letter is not preserved, but we know of it from Root's answer declining the offer. Although sympathizing with the Chinese struggle for self-government, he could not, as a member of the Senate and its Committee of Foreign Relations and, therefore, a constitutional advisor of the President, act in like capacity for a foreign governmental authority.[67]

Lea's desire for a strong relationship between the United States and the new China was also evident in an interview he gave in Hong Kong. He declared it to be his aim "to bring to China the same spirit that Lafayette brought to us in America. . . . I want America to take the lead in recognizing China, in assisting the movement, and to take the lead in bringing to this country the liberty that they in America enjoy. I want this in order that the Republic of China, and the Republic of America with the Pacific Ocean between them, will be able to conserve the rights and liberty of at least two-thirds of the human race."[68]

Finally, on Christmas Day 1911, the *Devanha* arrived in Shanghai harbor. It was a triumphant return for Sun. Four cruisers of the Chinese fleet, which had joined the revolution, went out to sea to meet the ship and accompany it to the dock. That they missed it did not dampen the enthusiasm of a large crowd of welcomers on the pier. A group of Sun's friends and associates came on board to greet him. A photograph was taken with Sun in the middle of a row of seated companions and another row of men standing behind them. And on the right of the first row, on the last chair, sat a lone Westerner, a young-looking man wearing a campaign hat and holding a cane: Homer Lea had also arrived to share in the glory of the moment.

A banquet was held in honor of Sun in the evening of December 25. It may be presumed that Lea took part in it, but nobody mentioned his presence. However, it did not take long for him to make his presence in Shanghai known. An interview with him was published on December 28.[69] His answers to a number of questions, not all of them truthful, characterized him as a clever politician and public relations man:

"What is your official capacity?"
"I am Chief of the General Staff."

. . .

"Then you will direct all the military operations of the Revolutionary Army, including those of General Li Yuan Hung. . . ?"
"No, I don't expect to interfere with General Li's operations. Of course, a chief of staff is simply the means of transmitting orders from the president to the army."
"Then you are assuming that Dr. Sun Yat Sen will be the president of the Chinese Republic?"
"To be sure. . . . We had a lot of trouble in London to prevent intervention, but the danger is all past now."
"Did you discuss the matter with Sir Edward Grey, and other European diplomats?"
"Yes, certainly."
"Then you had a diplomatic mission from the Revolutionary party?"
"No, they are my personal friends and came to call on me when I was in London. Lord Roberts called on me there. . . ."
"How can you act as a chief of staff of the revolutionary army when you are an American citizen?"
"That has been arranged. A number of American generals are coming out to help us."

"That is very surprising, that generals of the United States
Army should be allowed to come to China to take part in a fighting
like this."

"Then I suppose you will be surprised to know that English
generals are also coming to help us."

"When are they coming?"

"I can't divulge that, but they will be here. . . ."

"When did you get the title of General?"

"I was commander of four divisions, organized by myself for
the rescue of Emperor Kwang Su eleven years ago."

"Where was the army organized?"

"Chiefly in the South and commanded by American officers.
I was later commander of Chinese troops in America."

"What connection have you with the American Army?"

"My military books are used in the examinations at West Point
and Annapolis."

"But what official connection have you?"

"I have no official connection. That idea is erroneous."

It was probably the publication of this interview that caused the
U.S. Consul in Shanghai to call the attention of the U.S. Minister in
Peking to Lea's presence. The Minister, William J. Calhoun, who ironi-
cally was occupying the post that Lea had coveted a few years before,
suggested to Washington that he publish in local papers the articles of
the U.S. Code that forbade U.S. nationals to serve in foreign armies.[70]
The disposition of the Minister's cable is not known, but a vice-consul in
Shanghai is said to have warned Lea of the existence of the statutes.[71]

Lea's appearance on the scene in Shanghai created a problem not
only for U.S. officials but also for some of the revolutionary leaders. That
controversy had already begun before Sun and his party arrived in Shanghai. On December 16 it was reported from Singapore that Sun and Lea
disapproved of certain "offices" that had been assumed by some revolutionary leaders.[72] In speaking to Consul Anderson in Hong Kong, Sun
and Lea were more explicit. According to Anderson's dispatch, "Dr. Sun
. . . repudiates Wu Ting Fang and other Shanghai leaders as not authorized to represent and act for the revolutionary organization, the feeling
of the party being that Wu Ting Fang and various other leaders cast their
lot with the revolution only after its success became reasonably certain."[73] Thus, it was no coincidence that one of the questions in the
Shanghai interview alluded to this matter. When Lea was asked whether
he had met the revolutionary leaders since he arrived, he answered "all of
them." On further questioning he conceded that he had not yet seen Wu
T'ing-fang. He had intended to visit him but had not yet found the
time.[74]

From Lea's point of view, Wu T'ing-fang was not only an opportunistic latecomer to the revolution, but he had also assumed a role in two matters that Lea believed would fall in his own sphere of action. Wu had been charged with the negotiations with Yuan that were expected to result in the ouster of the Manchu regime and the establishment of a republic. He had also issued, on November 17, a "Manifesto to the Foreign World." According to Sun's and Consul Anderson's joint cable and confirming letter to the State Department, the negotiations with the Manchus and relations to foreign powers were the two domains of major interest to Lea. It is not known whether Sun, one of whose main concerns was a peaceful resolution of the conflict to forestall foreign intervention, shared Lea's antagonism against Wu, who had played a role in both men's earlier careers. While Chinese Imperial Minister in Washington, he was said to have opposed Lea's activities on behalf of the reformers. As the first Chinese lawyer in Hong Kong, he had known Sun through his brother-in-law, Ho Kai, who, as Sun's teacher, had greatly influenced the latter's thoughts on China's modernization.[75] Even though he had elected to become an official of the imperial government, Wu T'ing-fang's attitude toward the regime was ambivalent. Just as the Sino-Japanese War had helped to shape Sun's views on China's future, it had deeply impressed Wu. In July 1895 Wu came to the conclusion that China would never adopt reforms unless forced to do so by the foreign powers. In the interest of China's modernization, he was ready to accept their intervention even if it meant a loss of independence.[76] Thoughts of this nature may have remained with him throughout his official career.

It has been reported that Wu T'ing-fang showed the same animosity toward Lea as Lea had developed toward him. William Henry Donald, called "Donald of China," an Australian journalist and old China hand who had worked under the Manchus, Sun Yat-sen, and later under Chiang Kai-shek's regime, was present during the first meeting in Shanghai between Sun, Lea, and Wu. When Wu and others were shown into Sun's drawing room, they found him waiting together with "a strange-looking, small humpbacked man. . . . The visitors stared, for the deformed man had been introduced as General Homer Lea." Having learned from the newspapers that Sun was arriving with U.S. generals in tow, the visitors were surprised to find the leader of the revolution in such company and fell into an awkward silence. "Chinese do not like deformed people in any circumstance, but for [Sun] to have allied himself with a dwarf was, in their minds, beyond belief or excuse."[77]

It may be debatable whether Chinese have an abhorrence of deformed people, and it is questionable whether Donald's account, as related to a popular writer many years later, is literally true. Wu T'ing-fang most probably knew about Lea since his years in Washington and, therefore, could not have been surprised by his appearance when he saw him.

But regardless of its veracity, the report confirmed the antagonism or opposition against the outsider.

The arrival of Sun Yat-sen resolved the stalemate between the provincial delegates assembled in Nanking, concerning the election of a chief of state. On December 29 the delegates of 16 of the 17 rebellious provinces elected Sun the Provisional President of the Chinese Republic.

It has been reported that Sun preferred to establish a military government,[78] in accordance with the joint cable with Anderson to the State Department. To the probable regret of Lea, this idea was discarded in favor of a civilian government that Sun wanted to model after the U.S. presidential system. Others proposed a parliamentary regime under a prime minister, but in this case Sun won out.[79]

On January 1, 1912, in a solemn ceremony in Nanking, Sun took the oath of office. Lea accompanied him in a special train from Shanghai.[80] Although there is no report from Lea nor from any other source about his emotions, Lea must have felt at the pinnacle of his hopes and dreams.

At this point, U.S. military experts asked why the apparently well-trained imperial army was continually being defeated by a smaller but far more active force, evidently handled by excellent tacticians, notwithstanding $20 million spent on the imperial armies since the Sino-Japanese War. In explaining the success of this uprising, the War Department in Washington was said to have concluded that the victory of the revolutionary forces was due, in the main, to Homer Lea's military organization in the United States. It was believed that U.S. noncommissioned officers acting as their drill masters had found the Chinese in the United States very apt pupils. Both the drill masters and Chinese-American soldiers had been the backbone of the revolutionary forces and had made the victory possible.[81] Such reasoning, which, as we know, was based upon false presumptions, may betray a typical myopia of the military establishment when confronted with a popular revolution.

There is not even any evidence that Lea himself, after the ascendancy of Sun, had any military role and acted as Sun's chief of staff. He is said to have visited some military units in the company of Sun.[82] But this has not been confirmed, although at least one local commander issued orders to his troops to intensify training and strengthen discipline in view of the forthcoming inspection by Sun and a great American general.[83] At any rate, in preparation for his military role, Lea ordered still another military coat in Shanghai, which, however, he never had a chance to wear.[84] Ethel mentioned some years later that Sun had offered him "a place in the cabinet, but this was declined, as Lea preferred to remain as a friendly adviser only, his idea being that the bringing in of a foreigner might create dissension among the revolutionists."[85] Again there is no report, Chinese or Western, to support that statement. She also asserted that, after his arrival with Sun, Lea drafted "decrees, etc." for the new regime.[86] It does indeed appear that he took some actions in this respect. On December 29, 1911, even before the new government was formed, he cabled to Secretary Knox asking for its recognition by the United States: "Sun unanimously elected President by eighteen provinces. Court has yielded. We are now preparing the terms. I cabled you from Hongkong [together with Consul Anderson]. We want America to give recognition first. This is most important. Japan has volunteered to do this."[87] But no answer came as the United States was in no hurry to recognize Sun's government. In fact, recognition was delayed until half a year after Lea's death.

The lack of response from Washington did not discourage Lea. On January 9 he drafted for the signature of the Minister for Foreign Affairs a "Circular Note to the Powers" in which he again tried to have his country take action and have a special status in the developing affairs in China: "Desirous of ending civil war and bringing about an immediate restoration of peace, the President of the Republic of China has today addressed a note to the President of the Republic of the United States of America, requesting His Excellency to act as mediator between the people of China and the Manchu Dynasty."[88] There is no indication that the Circular Note was forwarded to the foreign powers, nor is there a record of a request of mediation sent to the U.S. President.

Also in January 1912 he drafted another "Circular Note to the Powers," requesting recognition of the Republic of China under promise to assume all obligations of the Manchu Government; to reform the currency and the legal and judicial system; to establish a national railroad net with the cooperation of Chinese and foreign capital; to open up all of China to foreign trade on an equal basis with Chinese commerce; and to eliminate all burdensome taxes on such trade except for customs duties.[89] Again, there is no record that the note was sent. In its stead, the Foreign Minister appointed by Sun addressed on January 17 his own note to the U.S. State Department asking for recognition at an early date based upon the fact that a firm republican government had been established.[90]

When he proposed that the U.S. President mediate the conflict between the Provisional Government in Nanking and the Imperial Government in Peking, Lea may have thought of President Theodore Roosevelt's mediation between Japan and Russia half a dozen years earlier. The situation was, of course, not identical. The conflict in 1905 existed between two sovereign powers, whereas now the United States would have become involved in a civil war. Lea's proposal can be understood as a desire to give his native country an advantage over competing foreign powers, as well as an attempt to strengthen his own standing with the administration in Washington and the new government in Nanking. Beyond that, however, any such action on the part of the U.S. President might have weakened the position of Yuan Shih-k'ai who, in effect, was acting as mediator and, by doing so, advanced his own prospects. Neither the military and members of the gentry, who had joined the revolution, nor the leaders of the T'ung Meng Hui, including Sun Yat-sen, wanted a prolonged, bloody civil war that would weaken the country and open the possibility of foreign intervention. Moreover, the revolutionaries were not sure that they would win a war with the northern armies under Yuan, which, in strength, were more or less equal to their forces in the south.[91] They were also conscious of their division into various factions, and Sun's group was by no means the strong and centralized organization that could have prevailed under a determined leadership.[92] For these reasons, there was a consensus that Yuan should be offered the presidency if he agreed to join the republicans.

For Sun, in particular, it mattered little who was to be the head of a Chinese republic as long as the Manchus lost their power. When still in Europe, he heard of Yuan's overtures to the revolutionaries and cabled his associates that he was in agreement with Yuan Shih-k'ai heading the revolutionary regime if he were willing to forsake the Manchus.[93] At about the same time, he expressed in his "Reminiscences" indifference as to who would assume the post of head of state: "Whether I am to be the titular head of all China, or to work in conjunction with another, and that other is Yuan-Shih-Kai, is of no importance to me. I have done my work . . . and China . . . will, in a short time, take her place amongst the civilized and liberty-loving nations of the world."[94] On January 15, Sun formally declared that he would resign if Yuan openly supported the republic and the Manchus abdicated. Twelve days later, several of Yuan's generals in the north joined the republican side, and after more negotiations Yuan was able to obtain the abdication of the last Manchu emperor on February 12. True to his word, Sun offered Yuan the presidency on the following day. Yuan was elected, inaugurated on March 10, and Sun relinquished the office on April 1.

Yuan's motives in abandoning the Manchus, it is generally agreed, were exactly opposite to Sun's in abandoning his claim to the office of president. While Sun did not care who held that office as long as China was a republic, Yuan wanted to head the government, whether it be monarchical or republican. He would not risk a long and costly civil war on behalf of the Manchus if he could gain his objective by betraying them and joining the republicans. He also was aware of the attitude of the foreign powers that favored him over any contenders. The Governments of Japan and Germany and, indeed, the United States were even willing to grant Yuan financial assistance if he were to make the attempt to subdue the rebellious southern provinces. But the British Government, acting through Sir Edward Grey, refused any help either to the Imperial Government in Peking or to Yuan as head of the northern armies without the consent of the revolutionary regime, which, of course, was not tendered. Under the circumstances the other powers also remained neutral, which left Yuan no choice but to accept a republic for which he had no liking. In this way, Sun's and Lea's efforts in London seemed to have borne belated fruit, although in November 1911 their mission appeared to be a complete failure.[95]

No direct information has become available as to Homer Lea's reaction to this turn of events, but it can be surmised that he disagreed with Sun's decision to abdicate. Not only would he be bereaved of the opportunity to test his military skills against Yuan but also to become Sun Yat-sen's chief of staff and to hold an important military or political position in the new China. After having worked so long and hard, he would be confronted again with a vacuum. All hopes and prospects would be gone.

An indication of Lea's disagreement with Sun's decision appears in a letter to him from the representative of the Associated Press, two days after Sun's declaration that he would resign in favor of Yuan if the latter brought about the abdication of the Manchu regime: "Tang shao yi [T'ang Shao-i, Yuan Shih-k'ais' representative in the negotiations with the revolutionaries] has an idea that you are advising the Dr. [Sun Yat-sen] against having any dealings with Yuan. How about it? . . . If the Manchu goes and a reasonable agreement is reached the Dr. will—he must eventually win out. Are you advising against Yuan or is this being done by Ike [Kyokichi, a Japanese friend of Sun]. . .?"[96] A further sign of Lea's opposition to a deal with Yuan and his advice to risk a military solution came more than half a year later in a letter to Homer and Ethel from a secretary of Sun, when Sun's friends and associates began to be disenchanted with Yuan. "I never forget [what the] General said when he is [sic] in Nanking—'Fight means peace.' "[97]

As it was, Lea did not learn of the abdication of the last Manchu and the imminent ascendancy of Yuan Shih-k'ai. On the day before the abdication was made known, Homer Lea suffered a stroke.

—10—

Final Days

In January 1912 Lea had been ill with influenza, but he had fully recovered when he suddenly collapsed on the morning of February 11. Within half an hour, the physician who examined him found him in a deep coma, with a very weak pulse and very low blood pressure. On the third day the coma even deepened and facial paralysis set in, as well as complete paralysis of the extremities. For five days he was completely blind. On the sixth day, the right eye and, on the following day, the left showed some reaction to light. Throughout this period the patient remained unconscious, except for brief intervals of semiconsciousness. After seven days the vision started to improve slowly. Lea's condition was still slowly improving on April 6 when the physician diagnosed the case as hemiplegia with cerebral embolism. He noted "no symptoms of any great defect in intelect [*sic*]" but found that the patient had "many maniacal ideas, . . . all of them . . . to a person aquainted [*sic*] with the extremely imaginative mind of General Homer Lea, easilly [*sic*] explainable." The physician, Dr. M. Urbánek, to judge from his name a Czech, wrote his report on stationery of the medical office of the Tientsin-Pukow Railway.[1] Given Sun's interest in the Chinese railroad system and his official connection with it some months later, it is likely that he engaged Dr. Urbánek to treat Lea.

The emotional strain and the distress caused by the turn of the political events in China, and any strenuous exertions that Lea might have made to stave it off, could have contributed to the collapse. A remark made by Ethel during his illness points to the effect that the change in Sun's and his own fortunes had on his equanimity: "Now that Sun is definitely decided to abdicate in order to bring about peace, we [Ethel and Sun] think it better that Homer be away,"[2] that is, leave China.

Nine days after the attack, Ethel wrote to her sisters: "He is slightly better now but for two days and nights we expected every breath to be his last. . . . We had absolutely given up all hope. . . . He is asleep most of the time now and very, very weak."[3] A few weeks later Lea was still paralyzed on one side, but he was not aware of it and ignorant of the seriousness of his illness. "His brain is too tired for anything to penetrate it. [The illness] is probably the only way he could get a rest for that grey matter of his."[4] And still a few weeks later, on March 31, Ethel's outlook changed from optimism to pessimism in two letters written that same day. "We begin electric treatments tomorrow and expect a good deal from them." In the second letter she confessed, "Homer is not gaining as I hoped and I begin to fear he will never be quite well again."[5]

Sun arranged for his secretary, J. Chockman, who had accompanied him from the United States and, therefore, knew the Leas well, to stay at Ethel's side and be of service to her. But he also came to visit whenever possible. "Dr. Sun of course has so many things to do. He can't be always coming over but he is naturally as pleased as I am that the General is going to get well," wrote Ethel.[6]

"Donald of China," who saw Lea when he was well enough to meet visitors, found him "frailer, seemingly smaller than ever before. But his eyes burned brightly and there was a new treble in his strange voice. For a time he talked spiritedly, and then looking out of his window where he could see rows of ancestral grave mounds, he said morosely: 'China is graves. They are all about us. Look at them. Graves, graves, graves.' The 'General' flung his arms in a wide arc. Then his mood changed. With a bony, crooked finger he reached out and tapped Donald on the head. 'Mark me,' he wheezed, 'we are going to have trouble with those Russian fellows. They are asking for a protectorate over Mongolia now. But that's not all. You just wait and see. They are the sort who have a destiny. There is always someone at some time or another on the march to conquer the world. They are that kind of people.' Donald rose to go, but Lea gripped him tightly by the arm. 'Buy me a big horse in Shanghai,' he begged. 'I must have a big horse—as big as you can get. And a big sword. I'll need them. The Russians are up to no good!' "[7]

Donald's account appears to confirm Dr. Urbánek's report of "maniacal ideas" that took hold of Lea during his illness. The concern with graves may be explainable in a man confronted with death. But then, years earlier Lea had been planning to write a novel, "The Romance of the Tombs," in which ancestral mounds played a role.[8] The remarks about the Russians may be less genuine. Donald's account was published during the Cold War period, when popular writers stressed Lea's preoccupation with Russia at the expense of his views on other matters.

By March 31 it was definitely decided that the Leas should return to the United States at an early date to avoid the heat of the summer. Ethel asked Agnes not to tell anybody that they were coming because she did not want "a bunch of reporters hanging around."[9] The couple departed from Shanghai on April 13 on the S.S. *Shinyo Maru* and arrived in San Francisco on May 6.[10] Sun arranged for Chockman to accompany them to Yokohama,[11] while a close friend and confidant of his, whose name was given as Jue Wu, stayed with them until they reached California.[12]

Lea's illness had become known in the United States. During the ship's stopover in Honolulu, the press learned that he was on board, nearly blind and partly paralyzed and confined to his stateroom.[13] Thus, his arrival could not be kept secret, notwithstanding Ethel's wishes. Reporters were at hand when he was taken from the boat in a wheelchair and, on his arrival in Los Angeles, from the train. "With no pomp or ceremony to mark a homecoming that was pitiful in the extreme," he was lifted into an automobile, with "a nurse, a physician, a relative and a friend or two . . . in attendance. . . . Met at the depot by a few friends who knew of his coming, General Lea could only smile at them, as if in benediction. His left side is entirely unresponsive to his will, and he was so weak that he could hardly raise his arms. To the . . . reporter who greeted him, General Lea looked his regrets at being unable to converse, and indicated his inability at this time to speak."[14]

Ethel did speak shortly to a journalist and confirmed that Lea had become paralyzed about three months earlier, "the shock coming without warning. I can not speak, of course, of my husband's relations with the new Chinese party, but it is true that he was a friend and adviser of Dr. Sun, whom we accompanied to China last year. Yes, China is getting along very well now under the new administration, and her future progress and prosperity are fully assured."[15]

It was quiet around Homer Lea during the last six months of his life. The Leas had moved into a cottage at Santa Monica not far from the beach. Homer's friends came to see him, and so did on occasion General Chaffee and a General Burton. Chockman wrote repeatedly inquiring about his health. Sun had also another individual ask about Lea's progress and wrote several times himself.[16] Ethel assured them that he was constantly improving. Toward the end of July he was, indeed, able to dictate a letter to Sun, in which he sounded like his old self: "I am now quite well enough to write you. . . . I have improved so far that I am quite confident, as are my doctors, that I will be able to return to China about the middle of September and will again devote myself to whatever tasks you have for me there." He wrote of having driven to Chinatown recently at the request of the Chinese of Los Angeles. He had heard there of a letter from Huang Hsing who mentioned the amalgamation of the northern and southern armies, whereby German officers serving with the northern armies were to be discharged and replaced by U.S. instructors. "Should you wish these [U.S.] officers immediately, inform me what the rate of pay is to be and I can see the Secretary of War and get permission for whatever number you might need. . . . Should you wish me to go to Washington, London and Paris before returning, instruct me accordingly."[17] Lea was obviously unaware of Yuan's ascendancy and Sun's loss of political and military power. It is also apparent that he was not conscious of the severity of his condition and that Ethel, not wishing to upset him, let him proceed with new schemes. It was later reported that he believed in his recovery until a few days before his death.[18]

On September 15 he wrote again to Sun, but no copy of that letter or of an enclosed memorandum has survived. In his answer, Sun expressed the hope that Lea's health would continue to improve so that they could meet in Paris in about two months. "The conditions in your memorandum are carefully noted. Several items need to be talked over between us when we meet."[19]

In his earlier letter, Lea had told Sun that he had not given any interviews since leaving Nanking and warned him not to believe any statements allegedly coming from him. But a week later he did see two journalists on two successive days. "A frail, crippled man," wrote the first, "sat in an invalid's chair on the beach at Santa Monica yesterday and studiously watched the reconstruction of the new Bristol Pier. To those around him the work was ordinary and without material significance; but to the cripple it portrayed the reconstruction of a nation—the rebuilding of China on a firm, substantial and modern governmental basis. The crippled watcher was General Homer Lea. . . . 'Do you see that pier out there in the ocean? That pier is China; and do you note the wonderful solidity of the new construction and the number of workmen, as busy as bees, making it firm? To me that represents the history of China, and the new constructive work shows its up-building.'. . . No one is more optimistic than General Lea over the future of China. . . . Several times since his return he has spoken before the developing organizations which are actively working for the Greater China."[20]

The second reporter had met Lea in better days a few years before. Now he found the little man to be thin, pale, and even smaller, as he huddled in the large invalid's chair. "But when I looked away from him and merely listened to his talk, there was no evident change in the man.

His brain is as agile and keen as it has ever been. His voice has that same impetuous, fiery quality of former years. The humor, the quaint optimism, and at times, the robust vulgarity of his phrases, are not changed. . . . His mind is as clear as a bell and as clean as an April sky-line. No intricacy of analysis is too subtle for him. His processes of reasoning, as we talked long and swiftly of the many national and military questions, were lucid and forceful. Whenever he made a point, he was able to call immediately three or four analogies. He was as glib with scientific data and statistics as a man who had come freshly from such records. There was no faltering, no hesitancy—not the slightest indication to show that his physical deterioration had in any way affected his mind."[21]

On Sunday, October 27, Homer Lea lost consciousness, probably due to another stroke, and he died on November 1, without regaining it. Two days later, his sister Hersa and a few friends, Robert J. Belford, Harry Carr, Ansel O'Banion, Isaac O. Levy, Charles Van Loan, and Marco Newmark, joined Ethel at the little seaside cottage, where the body lay on a bed, dressed in the uniform of a general of the Chinese army with a black cloak lined in red and a swagger stick on its side. "There was no service. Two men came in with a casket, placed in it the wasted little body that had been the home of so mighty a spirit and conveyed it to a crematory"[22] in a hearse followed by automobiles. A moment of silence in the chapel of the crematory was the entire ceremony, in accordance with Lea's wishes.[23]

From Sun Yat-sen came a letter to Mrs. Lea: "I am extremely grieved to learn from the newspapers that General Lea has passed away. I would have sent you a telegram to convey to you my deep sympathy and condolence, but for the fact that until now I never believed in the newspaper accounts to be true. In losing General Li [sic] I have lost a great and true friend. Miss Soong wishes to tender you her heart-felt sympathy in your bereavement."[24] The press carried a statement of Sun Yat-sen on Homer Lea's death:

> Unfortunately Mr. Lea was physically deformed but he possessed a wonderful brain. Although not a military man, he was a great military philosopher, well poise [sic] in high military problems. He helped me in a general way on military strategem [sic] with reference to the revolutionary propaganda. He commanded a profound farsight and insight in affairs military and was the author of a couple of books on high military tactics and strategem [sic]. Several of the prominent military men paid tribute to his professional production. General Roberts is one of his greatest admirers. He was a thoroughly sincere man and devoted his whole energy to the Chinese Revolution. Honest in his dealings, sympathetic in his opinions, frank and

resolute, he made a large number of friends among the Chinese. He helped me in Nanking until his death.[25]

It was said that Homer Lea wanted to be buried in China. Half a century after his death, his stepson, Joshua B. Powers, took the urn with his ashes, and another with the ashes of his mother, Ethel, who had died in 1934, to Taiwan. The urns were interred with high government officials being present at a ceremony.

——11——

Homer Lea's Political Philosophy

By the time Homer Lea reached adulthood, the position of the United States in world affairs had undergone a drastic change. The idea of this country's Manifest Destiny had found its fulfillment. The contiguous continental land mass had been settled and incorporated in the Union. Pioneers had gone west until they reached the barrier of the Pacific. Moreover, in the 1880s and 1890s, it seemed to many that the U.S. economy had grown to maturity and needed markets abroad if its expansion were to continue. Foreign trade required a merchant marine, and this, in turn, necessitated protection by a naval establishment. To engage in foreign trade, overseas trading posts had to be established, while the navy, to protect the trading routes, needed bases on foreign soil. Trading posts and naval bases were to be the cornerstones of a U.S. empire in the Pacific area. This movement culminated in the annexation of the Hawaiian Islands and the Philippines. Such forceful expansion meant war, and war required military preparedness. Alfred Thayer Mahan became the forerunner of a powerful group of ideologists and politicians, including men like Henry Cabot Lodge and Theodore Roosevelt, who were the advocates and protagonists of the new U.S. imperialism.

An earlier group of Americans who had called for overseas colonies had been motivated by theories of racial superiority. For them, the Anglo-Saxon race was destined to spread its rule over others due to its higher intellectual and physical endowments. Others relied on the will of providence, which called on them to propagate the tenets of Christian faith among less fortunate peoples. And still others discovered in the wider Teutonic race, which presumably included the British and the Americans together with the Germanic peoples, a superior genius for political organization that others lacked. Men like Lodge and Roosevelt adopted the racial bias of their precursors in advocating their imperialist ideas. But at the turn of the century, their youthful optimism flagged at times when they questioned whether increasing industrialization and affluence might not weaken the Anglo-Saxon stock in a world in which the masses of lesser peoples were multiplying so much faster.

Arrayed against the expansionist trend were people who might agree to the principle of Anglo-Saxon supremacy, but doubted whether militancy and war represented the preferred way for the promotion of the benefits of civilization to peoples not enjoying the blessings of democracy and American traditional values. They feared, moreover, that in the wake of militant imperialism the nation would be burdened by a large, colonial bureaucracy and a standing army and subjected to constant danger of war to maintain the foreign possessions. Colonies might also result in an influx of foreign populations who were unaware of U.S. customs, values, and institutions.

Among the leaders in the anti-imperialist camp, William James attacked the irrationalism of the apostles of expansion and war. Perhaps more than anybody else, Dr. David Starr Jordan, Homer Lea's occasional patron and political antagonist, was active in the anti-expansionist and pacifist movement. In numerous writings he deplored the effect of war on national welfare and development. In a reversal of social Darwinist thought, he blamed war for the survival of the unfittest by the elimination of the strong and courageous.

Whether for loss of interest in more territorial acquisitions or for moral compunctions, by the turn of the century the expansionist clamor died down considerably. Among those who fought this trend and struggled to keep the ideas of militancy and expansion alive, the voice of Homer Lea was the loudest. In *The Valor of Ignorance* he presented his own version of the need for territorial growth.

According to Homer Lea, the state as a political unit had its beginning in prehistoric times when primitive men fought each other and when, finally, one individual, stronger than his contenders, asserted himself by brute force. "It was when the brawniest paleolithic man had killed or subdued all those who fought and roamed in his immediate thickets that he established the beginning of man's domination over man, and with it the beginning of social order. . . . When the last blow of his crude axe had fallen and he saw about him the dead and submissive, he beheld the first nation; in himself the first monarch; in his stone axe the first law, and by means of it the primitive process by which, through all succeeding ages, nations were to be created and destroyed."[1] Lea maintained that no kingdom, no empire, no political unit, and no nation has come into existence except by physical force, by war, and none has vanished from the face of the earth except in the wreckage of defeat inflicted by stronger enemies. To survive, a nation must, therefore, remain strong, physically strong, just "as physical vigor constitutes the health in the individual." Individuals are strong because of their bodily condition, not because of their intellectual power or other immaterial attributes. And so the strength of a nation does not lie in its intellectual elite, no matter how great their accomplishments, but in raw, physical power that, in a political unit, is military strength. It is this that provides the basis for the existence of a nation.

As an individual's struggle for survival marks his whole life, so is war the normal state of a nation with "intervals of peace." The zenith of national power, the height of a nation's greatness, is reached in victories resulting from its military strength. But just as an individual's physical strength declines due to disease and old age, the health of a nation is subject to deterioration and decay when its militancy declines. Loss of militancy means the end of national existence, but death, which is inevitable in the individual, will not befall the nation that safeguards its militancy. Preservation of militancy means constant territorial expansion. There is no standstill for a nation. "National existence is governed by this invariable law: that the boundaries of political units are never . . . stationary—they must either expand or shrink. It is by this law of national expansion and shrinkage that we mark the rise and decline of a nation."

In the modern world, the preservation of militancy requires a conscripted standing army. Therefore, "if no provision is made by a nation for enforced military service among its inhabitants, the military capacity of a race or state decreases proportionately as is increased the complexity of its social organism and the diversity of its economic activities." Especially in our age of science, the military machine requires years to be put together, and more years to function until it is irresistible. There is no place anymore for volunteer forces, however patriotic and brave, for while "the spirit of militancy is born in a man . . . a soldier is made."

Permanent armies became necessary with the introduction of gunpowder and the growing complexity of armaments. The more complex the weapons, the more elaborate their manufacture and the longer the training of soldiers in their use. In fact, any new invention and every technical progress serves the science of war and its purposes. That nation is strongest that accomplishes the utmost utilization of scientific improvements. Thus "modern civilization began with the invention of gunpowder," or, as Heraclitus said, war is the father of all things.

The high cost of arming a nation and the diversion of a large part of its productive manpower to that purpose do not impoverish a nation. Wealth is not measured in higher or lower budgets but in a nation's natural resources, the level of intelligence of its people, and the productive means employed. Nor is the size of the productive population its measure. Technology and science are increased by the development of an arms industry, and so is the productive capacity of that part of the population engaged in it. For that reason it is erroneous to assume that a large military apparatus reduces the wealth of a nation by reducing the number of individuals in the productive process.

Industrialism, the development of industries and with them the material wealth of a country, is to be endorsed if used as a means to national power. But industrialization is merely the sustenance that the nation requires to achieve strength, no more, no less. It should not be considered the ultimate goal of a nation or, by itself, regarded as national power. Should it be made the national purpose, the nation must be compared to somebody who lives to eat rather than eats to live. "When a country makes industrialism an end it becomes a glutton among nations, vulgar, swinish, arrogant. . . . It is this purposeless gluttony, the outgrowth of national industry, that is commercialism. . . . While industry is the labor of a people to supply the needs of mankind, commercialism utilizes this industry for the gratification of individual avarice. . . . Commercialism sacrifices without the slightest compunction every principle and honor to gain the basest and paltriest possession of which man can boast." The degeneration of industrialism into commercialism means the final corruption of the state. Commercialism, a debased form of the struggle for survival on the level of individuals, is the death of a nation's militancy.

Already in nineteenth-century America, analogies had been drawn between biological principles and the view of the state as a living organism, with its growth to maturity and its eventual decay and death. The doctrine that the state, ever in motion, must either expand or shrink had also preceded Lea's dictum.[2] These theses were, as was Lea's theory of the origin of social order and war as the norm in the life of a nation, derived from Darwin's theories of life as a continuous struggle for existence and the survival of the fittest in that battle. They had found a strong echo in the United States in the second half of the century because they appeared to give validity to the U.S. social scene. Economically, that scene presented unbridled competition and laissez-faire capitalism. Intellectually, it had roots in the Calvinist ethos of individual self-interest as the way to reap material and spiritual rewards. Although nothing is known about Lea's private studies, he was obviously influenced by the environment of Darwinist and Spencerian thinking in formulating his political theories, as were earlier writers.

Lea's disparagement of materialistic business sentiment was shared to some degree by men like Theodore Roosevelt, Henry Cabot Lodge, and Alfred Thayer Mahan and more particularly by Brooks and Henry Adams. The Adams brothers, like Lea, were "on the periphery of American life."[3] In the former case, this was due to the brothers' inability to continue the family tradition of political service to the nation; in the latter case, Lea's deformity and illness had turned him from pursuing a "normal" life. His loathing of commercialism, or individual greed, was combined with a measure of anti-Semitism, which shows occasionally in his writings. It was not as consistent as that of the Adams brothers[4] and did not extend to his social life.

A comparison with the ideas of a more sinister historical figure, Adolf Hitler, is just as interesting or even more so. Lea's distinction between useful industrial activity and acquisitive commercialism was echoed in Hitler's similar categorization. The latter distinguished between purely acquisitive business activities beneficial only to individual enrichment, and creative labor in which he included industrial work as an occupation serving the purposes of the collectivity as represented by the state.[5]

There are more parallels in Lea's and Hitler's thinking. Lea believed that "whenever the wealth and luxury of a nation stand in inverse ratio to its military strength, the hour of desolation, if not at hand, approaches." According to Hitler, "the inner strength of a State coincides only in the very rarest cases with the so-called economic zenith, which usually announces . . . the already approaching decay of the State," and "whenever the economy was made the sole purpose of [the German] people's life, thus suffocating the ideal virtues, the State collapsed."[6] For Lea, national militancy or militarism was the underlying force in societal existence. The forms of intellectual, ideological, economic, and political life, the "temporary effulgences," or the phenomena of the superstructure in Marxist terminology, were subordinated to that force. "The militant spirit is a primordial element in the formative process and ultimate consummation of the nation's existence." Hitler used a similar picture when he called the "heroic virtues" the first circle of national existence.[7] Of course, Hitler could have borrowed more easily from German sources than from Homer Lea, and, as has been asserted, it may indeed be a peculiarity of amateur historians of ideas to detect an influence of Lea on Hitler.[8] Yet there existed a link between the two in the person of Karl Haushofer, the geopolitician, whom Hitler greatly admired. Haushofer knew Lea's books and quoted him frequently in his own. He also gave advice to Hitler and Rudolf Hess, Haushofer's personal friend and Hitler's secretary, while *Mein Kampf* was being written. Thus, it is entirely possible that Lea's thoughts had an influence on that treatise.[9]

Homer Lea had the distinction of having been the only one among American expansionist advocates to base the call for territorial growth on purely militaristic grounds. As such he might have been at home in Germany or Japan, countries with strongly developed military organizations, rather than in the United States with its infertile soil for a militaristic-oriented society. In Lea's time, his own country did not possess a substantial military establishment of a permanent nature. Even the civilian state apparatus functioned at a minimal level. The general tenor of society tended toward business, rather than toward political and much less toward military matters. Lea's picture of the militant nation, his radical militaristic thought, did not fit into the U.S. scene. Even if he had lived longer and continued to propound his militaristic notions, his theories still would not have become part of his country's mainstream thinking; nor is it likely that he would have become "a major figure in world military history," as someone has said. [10]

Dr. Jordan found *The Valor of Ignorance* cleverly written and containing many truths but some errors as well, "for I think," he told Lea, "that nations may as well quit and be called a public nuisance as to maintain their present armaments." [11] He advocated international arbitration as a means for avoiding war. Lea attacked and belittled that view as primitive and timid, calling its proponents misguided visionaries "who are so persistently striving through subservient politicians, through feminism, clericalism, sophism and other such toilers to drag this already much deluded Republic into that Brobdingnagian swamp from whose deadly gases there is no escape." For Homer Lea, the sources of war are always present and an integral part of the life of a nation. "They mark, in the life of political entities, the successive periods of their greatness or vicissitudes." War originates when two nations have been advancing on converging lines of interest and aggrandizement. Whenever the converging lines meet, "the struggle for supremacy, or even survival, is at hand." The inherent needs and wants of a people, the development of its political economy, the increase of militancy or, conversely, of commercialism, the degree of centralization or decentralization, and other factors determine the angle of convergence "and the speed by which nations thunder or creep toward the goal of their ideals and the summit of their greatness." No two nations move on parallel lines. The hour of their conflict is fixed by the angles of convergence and the speed with which they are advancing. It may take years, decades, or even centuries until the flash point is reached, but inevitably it will come. If any nation fails to advance along its line or even regresses, the surrounding nations move so much faster on their own lines of convergence in direct proportion to the increasing vulnerability of the declining country. The convergence is a natural law, another manifestation of the law of struggle and survival, which controls also all other life, plant or animal. Therefore, war is not the result of disputes per se but represents the struggle of humanity upward, the multiplication of individual efforts into one, and the aspirations of humanity's eternal strife toward greater and nobler ends, not of themselves as individuals but of their race. This law is unchangeable; it cannot be subverted or ignored. As a result, the causes of war cannot be removed or dealt with by arbitration. At best, arbitration addresses the symptoms of war, the overt disputes or disagreements that are nothing but the first signs of an approaching war, its preliminaries. Any attempt at the removal or settlement of such disputes leads merely to procrastination. Disputes among states with popular participation in their political life are even less amenable to arbitration because the popular will ignores reason and popular passions stall the hands of statesmen. The result is still more acute and speedier convergence, that is, war.

Dr. Jordan was obviously disturbed by Lea's views, and so he wrote to him again some weeks later suggesting that he read Sir Norman Angell's *Europe's Optical Illusion*, a book that in an enlarged edition appeared later under the title, *The Great Illusion*. Angell (1874–1967), winner of the Nobel Peace Prize, in 1933, was a prolific writer on war and peace and one of the world's foremost internationalists and pacifists. Of course, he took a view opposed to that of Lea. Angell argued that the economic interests of nations no longer require the expansion of their political boundaries because these do not coincide with economic frontiers any more. This renders military power and war futile because a nation cannot acquire economic advantages by force, and war, even when victorious, does not achieve national aims. Dr. Jordan was particularly concerned by Lea's assertion that in many cases the causes of war could be removed by the forceful absorption of small states into greater political units, a view contrary to that of Angell, and he suggested that "perhaps Angell could convert you, or else you convert him by answering his point of view."[12] There is no indication that Lea followed that suggestion. However, Angell, in later editions of his book, repeatedly and at some length discussed Lea's militaristic views. According to Angell, Lea's writings sounded like "a free translation of much nationalist literature of either France or Germany." He put Lea in the company of von Moltke, von Bernhardi, Mahan, and Theodore Roosevelt, as well as William James who, while decrying the irrationality of war, acknowledged the existence of militaristic instincts and ideals.[13] But Roosevelt, notwithstanding his own militaristic leanings, objected to Lea's unscrupulous deification of brute strength.[14] Commenting on Lea's prognosis of a Japanese victory over the United States unless measures were taken to avoid it, William James considered it foolhardy to disregard his views.[15]

Lea's views on war and their ideological background emerge also in the one article he wrote on military matters, "The Aeroplane in War," which was published in 1910.[16] He held the airplane to be completely useless in future military conflicts for two reasons: one, the "prevailing ignorance concerning the laws and forces that govern the conduct of war''; and the other, "a failure to comprehend that all engines and instruments of combat occupy but a limited and subordinated sphere" in war.

The laws and forces of war emanate, according to Lea, from the few dominant world powers whose decisions the minor states are bound to accept. The former are industrialized and urbanized societies, the latter mostly rural and underdeveloped. Because of the concentration of the population and their economic centers, the airplane is more effective against urbanized nations than against small, self-contained, and self-sufficient national units of a relatively primitive level of development, where airpower can do little damage to the military establishment and potential. The very simplicity of the economic structure of such a country, the dispersion of its population, and the relative independence of its various sections and sectors make it almost invulnerable against air attacks. Realizing their susceptibility to air warfare, the large powers adopted, in a convention at St. Petersburg in November 1908, an international agreement against bombardment from the air. Lea believed that the major countries would continue such prohibition in their own interests because, unless they did so, they would give smaller states a great advantage against larger national units.

There are several fallacies and inconsistencies in Lea's arguments. If war becomes inevitable when the converging lines of states meet, no international convention would remain an obstacle in an eventual conflict between major and minor powers or between two dominant world powers. Moreover, in his disregard or neglect of the economic and industrial factors of national existence in favor of the military and human elements, he did not question whether less developed or even rural societies possess the industrial and technological capacity to establish and organize an effective air force. He did, however, correctly foresee the effective limits of airpower when directed against rural or less developed political units, a lesson that the U.S. military learned in Vietnam half a century later.

Lea's second argument that mechanized warfare can play only a limited role shows his own limitations even more clearly. "Wars," he said in his article, "are between men and not the instruments they make use of in their combats." He had pressed the same argument in *The Valor of Ignorance*: "Warfare . . . has never been nor will it ever be mechanical. There is no such possibility as the combat of instruments. It is the soldier that brings about victory or defeat." Given the preponderant weight of the human element, weapons, regardless of their technologically advanced state, will not be the decisive factor. They do not guarantee victory if the militancy of the soldiers who use them is inferior to that of their enemies. Physical power, the brutality of all national development as expressed in war, depends on the patriotism of a nation's population, its fealty to race and country. Only those who have lost that militancy will turn to inanimate engines of war as an ineffectual subterfuge and evasion of the reality of militancy. Thus, the less militant a nation, the more it relies on machinery and equipment and neglects that one factor that remains constant in warfare throughout its endless changes—the soldier.

In his eagerness to extol the militant virtues of the soldier, Lea ignored the importance that he elsewhere attributed to the progress of science. He forgot his thesis that the utilization of scientific inventions for the purposes of war constitutes the strength of nations. The more complex the mechanical means of warfare, the smaller the difference between the technical apparatus needed in war or useful in peace, and the more necessary the training of armies in the use of armaments and their psychological adjustment to the new weapons systems; also, the more inevitable a permanent military establishment would be. But when confronted with a scientific invention that, in time, would alter the ways of warfare, the airplane, the untutored theorist of war drew back. Not having had any practical experience in military matters, nor the training that he himself found so indispensable for the modern military, he resorted to the romanticism that had led him, as a youngster, to study the campaigns and leadership qualities of Napoleon and the loyalty of his warriors. The amateur student of war fastened his views on romanticized conceptions of soldierly chivalry and heroism. His subordination of the other spheres of human endeavor to the purely military led him to ignore the lessons of the modern industrial age. It may be said to his credit, however, that he was not alone in placing excessive emphasis on the indomitable will to win at the expense of highly developed weaponry. General Foch of World War I fame, a professional with credentials better than Lea's, expounded similar ideas.

In Homer Lea's view, the vitality of a nation and the stability of its institutions require racial homogeneity. A country with racially heterogeneous elements that have diverging interests is doomed to deterioration and decay, unless the political power remains in the hands of a dominant racial elite. When the power slips from the hands of that elite and becomes diffused throughout the population, the ensuing political dissension leads eventually to territorial disintegration.

No country has ever experienced the degree of racial heterogeneity that prevails in the United States, and none suffers, writes Lea, from the same political, religious, and geographical diversity. The divergent elements of the population are unacquainted with the ideals that made the republic great. "The heterogeneous masses that now riot and revel within the confines of the Republic" are a danger to its existence because of their ignorance of "the primitive principles of the Republic, . . . the militant patriotism of those who in simple, persistent valor laid with their swords the foundations of this national edifice." The naturalization of these foreign elements is not a substitute for racial homogeneity because it does not erase the hereditary instincts, nurtured for centuries, that the immigrants bring to their new abode. To the contrary, those who forswear loyalty to the country of their birth do so merely for egoistic reasons and, therefore, cannot comprehend nor share in the collective values of their adopted land. They cannot acquire the patriotism that is the basis of the United States' greatness.

The non-Anglo-Saxon element that at the beginning of the Civil War had amounted to no more than one-twelfth of the total population had tripled by 1900 and continued to increase. Once it constitutes a majority, numerically as well as politically, "the ideal of national supremacy is lost in the endless controversies of internal legislation and petty ambitions." The union will begin to decay, and its decay will provoke its foreign adversaries to wage war against it.

The crumbling of national strength is hastened by the foreign elements' proclivity to crime. Already in Homer Lea's time, the immigrant foreigners congregated in the cities and, according to him, made them the centers of their criminal activities, in contrast to the rural districts with an overwhelmingly Anglo-Saxon population. Crime, he postulated, originates from the incomprehension of and the incompatibility with this country's institutions and traditional values, as well as from the lower moral status of the immigrant population. The superior portion of the population cannot "assimilate the inferior without the concomitant loss of superiority," and so "in this Republic there is, in addition to the deterioration by intermarriage, the infection of social contact, the erosive effect of inferior morals, a bastard patriotism" that cannot assure the preservation of the basic rights upon which the nation has been founded.

These foreign elements do not consider the needs of the national community but only their own interests. They do not work for the common good but pursue their individual wealth. The ensuing state-corrupting commercialism that does violence to the ancient virtues of the nation is, therefore, also of foreign origin. The opulence that comes from commercialism, instead of contributing to national power, is a danger to it, "for the arrogance that comes of it is only Hebraic, hence trade, ducats, and mortgages" are thought to be more valuable than armies and navies. Woe to the country when "an element alien in race, alien in aspiration and alien to the spirit of the government" gains the majority and proceeds to supplant the race that founded the republic and its traditional values and ambitions.

Whether they be of homogeneous or heterogeneous background, the masses are a danger to the state if they gain the control of the government. All energies are consumed in internal squabbles and contentions. Politicians fear to go against the local interests of their constituents, and, therefore, legislation responds to localized and sectional demands rather than to paramount national needs. Masses do not gain greater intelligence by their participation in governmental affairs. The mentality of the mob is irrational, "it is primitive, hence brutal. It is feminine, hence without reason. It is instinctive to the degree of an animal, and is cognizant only of its own impulses and desires." An individual can direct the collective effort toward the building and growth of the nation, but the rule of the "credulous and savage" masses will lead to its ruin.

An electoral populace not only imperils its own state but, by making the voice of the government inconsistent and incoherent, it also endangers the relations to other nations and makes rational, peaceful international intercourse impossible. It may lead the nation to arrogance, to irrational actions based on primitive prejudice, and to foolish disregard of the rights of others, while overestimating its own strength and neglecting military preparedness, thus inviting the disasters of war.

Lea's Cassandra-like warnings were not accompanied by proposals on how to meet the perils facing the United States and the Anglo-Saxon race, with the exception of calling for greater militancy and general conscription. By themselves, these would not lift the danger from inundation by foreign elements, nor would they solve the problems caused by popular rule, which is caused, in other words, by the misrule associated with democracy, or mobocracy, as Lea called it. When describing the consequences of a defeat of the United States at the hands of the Japanese invaders, he hinted at the form of government that he considered appropriate for his country: "The repulsed . . . forces will scatter, as heretofore, dissension throughout the Union, brood rebellions, class and sectional insurrections, until this heterogeneous Republic, in its principles, shall disintegrate, and again into the palm of re-established monarchy pay the toll of its vanity and scorn." The monarchy that he envisioned would be an austere military regime or dictatorship based upon the nation-building elite of the Anglo-Saxons.

As his militarism was "perhaps the closest American approximation to the German militarist writer General von Bernhardi,"[17] so was his political philosophy cast in the German mold of political romanticism, that is, his view of the state as a living organism, his harking back to the old virtues and the ideals of the forefathers, the emphasis on the heroic virtues, and the subordination of the individual to the collective unit, combined with the rejection of mass society and business mentality. Like that of all political romanticists, his outlook was a retrogressive and, in the political sense, reactionary ideology, which was out of step with the world he lived in and, above all, out of place in the pragmatic environment of an overwhelmingly Protestant, utilitarian, business-minded, and sci-ence-oriented United States. It is no wonder, then, that his writings found a relatively small echo at home and much better acceptance in Japan and Germany, where concepts of militant virtue and heroism were more compatible with a national mind not yet completely divorced from feudal, precapitalistic thinking.

—12—

Epilogue

Homer Lea was one of a number of Westerners who, since the beginning of the seventeenth century, went to China to act as advisers in the belief that they could make a contribution to the welfare and improvement of that country. In a few ways, Lea's approach to the Middle Kingdom was not unlike that of his predecessors; in most others, it was quite dissimilar. To begin with, almost all of these foreigners took up positions within the country, while Lea spent only a limited time there, though not necessarily by choice. Others went to China to remake that country in the image of the West, while he maintained that China should go its own way. He saw his contribution as merely a technical one, to bring to China the military training and organization developed in the West without, however, intruding upon the native development that, by itself, might lead to modernization. Contrary to others, he did not believe in the moral and spiritual superiority of the West, although he did assume that the country could gain materially by adopting Western scientific and technological advances. He avoided the tactlessness and arrogance that others displayed, and he deferred to the decisions made by his Chinese associates even when they did not favor his personal interests. In one important way, however, the most personal and revealing one, his attitude concorded with that of other Westerners whom fate had "cast adrift in those mysterious currents of the Orient Seas": essentially he was, as were the others, motivated less by a desire to help China than by the need to help himself.[1] Like many of the others, Homer Lea was willing to take risks in order to find in China a field for action that was denied to him at home. Changing the fate of China meant for him, as it had meant for others before him, changing his own world. In this limited sense Homer Lea did succeed: his youthful decision to champion the cause of China gave his life a direction and a meaning that, under ordinary circumstances, it would not have assumed.

Lea's contemporaries were impressed with the intensity of his dedication even when they disagreed with his actions and ideas. Dr. Jordan, who as an avowed pacifist disparaged Lea's militarism and his military career, nevertheless recognized his ardent determination, never rebuffed him personally, and, looking back at his life, found kind words for him: "One could hardly help a kindly feeling for the ambitious little romancer trying to make the most of his short life, limited physique and boundless imagination."[2]

Dr. Jordan's kindly feelings for Lea derived at least in part from the knowledge that all of his undertakings as a supporter and practitioner of reform and revolution in China had ended in failure. While he questioned whether Lea, with his many health problems, had been equal to the tasks he had set for himself, Jordan, like others, saw him as an interesting and exceedingly colorful individual—Lea was indeed called "one of the most picturesque personalities of his generation."[3]

The question remains, however, how he was able to evoke a friendly and often a positive response in such a large variety of people, at home as well as abroad. "When . . . three of modern China's greatest figures abide in a man of Lea's sort—it is a credit to Lea, not a deficit to K'ang, Liang, or Sun."[4]

To speak of "Lea's sort" is not exactly a compliment. It may connote a man of questionable character, and there were reasons why some people might have wanted to avoid him. Some of his public and private statements were of dubious and, at times, almost fraudulent nature; he was no military officer although he claimed the rank of general, and he generally lacked the credentials required in his public enterprises. But respectable citizens, community leaders, high military officers, recognized politicians, financiers, and statesmen did listen to him, did discuss with him his schemes, plans, and theories, and did support him. It is no wonder, then, that the three great Chinese figures should also have abided in him. They arrived in the West with little contact to non-Chinese to ask for moral and material support of their causes. Not being able to count on official assistance, they were ready to accept help from whatever quarter it was proffered. A man of Homer Lea's sort appeared to them a valuable ally. He was intelligent, active, smooth-tongued, apparently well connected with his compatriots, and known among Chinese in the United States as seemingly an expert in military philosophy, if not in military strategy and tactics. Moreover, all three men considered China and the Chinese people backward, materially and politically, when compared to the United States. As a result they may have experienced feelings of inadequacy when confronted with Americans of rank and position. Liang remained awkward and tongue-tied during his visit with J. P. Morgan. K'ang, self-confident and pompous, appeared to be less inhibited, but he, too, was easily impressed by rank or money and thus was taken in by a man like Falkenberg. Sun Yat-sen, considered and treated as an outsider by some in his own environment, was psychologically prepared to accept another outsider like Homer Lea. Sun, moreover, was a trusting man, somewhat naive and impractical when searching for foreign support, and he chose allies and companions indiscriminately. Thus, Sun and Lea developed a mutual trust and friendship[5] that were absent in Lea's relationship with K'ang. Beyond that, they both suffered from the frustrations of frequent failures and, in the end, Lea's life was, as Sun's has been described,[6] a somber story of shattered dreams.

At home, Lea's ephemeral fame rested perhaps more on his theories and writings than his putative military career and his dubious exploits in China, although those did excite the popular mind then and three decades later. His call for a stronger military and naval power in the Pacific coincided with the prevailing thinking in military and political circles. His prediction of an attack by Japan against the United States without declaration of war, his tracing correctly Japanese invasion routes in the Philippines, his anticipating the decline of the British Empire, and his prophetic words about Russian aggressiveness, although he was not alone in such predictions, made him a hero during the dark days of World War II and the period of the Cold War. The uniqueness of his home-grown militarism is still remembered in books on war and militarism.

But again a few questions are called for to arrive at a better understanding of the personality, the life, and the attitude of Homer Lea: What moved him to make and persist in the relentless efforts to succeed, efforts that oftentimes were not restrained by doubts or scruples? What made him exalt raw physical strength and political power? How did this man, possessed of a weak and stunted body, come to turn his restless mind to military problems, to war and victory? What prompted him to decry what he considered sickness in the body politic and decay and decadence of nations? Why did he condemn mass democracy, ask for disenfranchisement of the common people, and call for the rule by a racial elite?

Answers to some of these questions were provided by a contemporary of his, Randolph Bourne who, like Lea, was a hunchback, tried to make a name for himself in the annals of his times, and died a young man. But unlike Lea who never drew attention to his deformity or permitted others to refer to it, Bourne tried to come to terms with his bodily state. In his essay, "The Handicapped," written while still an undergraduate, Bourne discussed the influence of his affliction on his life and his attitude: "When one . . . is in full possession of his faculties and can move about freely, bearing simply a crooked back and an unsightly face, he is perforce drawn into all currents of life. . . . He has all the battles of a stronger man to fight, and he is at a double disadvantage in fighting them. He has constantly with him the sense of being obliged to make extra efforts . . . and he is being haunted with a constant feeling of weakness and low vitality. . . . He is never confident of himself . . . and yet his environment and circumstances call out all sorts of ambitions and energies in him which, from the nature of his case, are bound to be immediately thwarted. This attitude is likely to keep him at a general low level of accomplishment unless he have an unusually strong will, and a strong will is perhaps the last thing to develop under such circumstances. . . . I suffered tortures in trying to learn to skate, to climb trees, to play ball, to conform in general to the ways of the world. I never resigned myself to the inevitable, but overextended myself constantly in a grim determination to succeed."[7]

Bourne's physical impairments "filled him with a profound sympathy for all who are dispised and ignored in the world" and made him "understand the feelings of all the horde of the unpresentable and the unemployable, the incompetent and the ugly, the queer and the crotchety people who make up so large a proportion of human folk."[8] According to his friend, Van Wyck Brooks, the "physical disability that had cut Bourne off from the traditional currents and preoccupations of American life had given him a poignant insight into the predicament of all those who, like him, could not adjust to the industrial machine."[9] Bourne died a political radical and an outspoken pacifist.

Unlike Bourne, Lea never conceded that his infirmities influenced his attitude toward the world or played a role in his vital decisions, but nevertheless he conformed, though unknowingly, to Bourne's image of the handicapped possessed of strong will power. Less than a year before his death, when he seemed to be within reach of the goal for which he had struggled during his short life, the editorial of a Far Eastern newspaper expressed Bourne's thought, as it related to Lea, in a different way. Homer Lea, said the paper, "is one of the men who bids fair to serve in history as a proof that the intellect is greater than the body, that in fact no physical deficiencies can retard the progress of a bold and ambitious mind."[10] Dr. Jordan put it in these words: "The very qualities that dwarfed him in the eyes of his neighbors added to his stature" when his dreams appeared to have become reality.[11]

The compensatory drive led Lea, like Bourne, also to an underprivileged group of humanity. But differing from Bourne's social concerns, his were entirely political. In the 1890s the Chinese minority in California lived a precarious life on the margin of society. Lea felt attracted to these queer and unrepresentable outsiders, and through them he became aware of the political misfortunes of their homeland. At the same time, too, political and commercial attention had turned to the Orient. In particular, Americans had become more conscious of China, the largest and, potentially, the richest country in the East. "Between 1895 and 1905, China had moved from the periphery to the heart of American concern."[12] It was a mark, though a bizarre one, of Lea's sensitivity to the trends of the times that he adopted China's struggle against a tyrannical regime and the encroachments by the Western powers as his lifework.

The physical debility that drew him to a politically weak group of people made him also extoll physical and political strength. Hence his admiration of virility in individuals and of political and military power in nations: "As physical vigor represents the strength of man in his struggle for existence, in the same sense military vigor constitutes the strength of nations. . . . As manhood marks the height of physical vigor among mankind, so the military successes of a nation mark the zenith of its greatness."[13] Thus, the infirm and crippled Homer Lea became one of the foremost militarists of his time.

The glorification of strength and power, owed, as it were, to a grim effort to compensate for his own weak bodily state, did not necessarily have to lead to Lea's extremist and outlandish theories. In Bourne's case, too, his physical condition may have contributed to his turning away from the mainstream of American thought in favor of political radicalism and socialism. But while remaining on the ideological fringe, Bourne kept the rational outlook of the intellectual, whereas Lea's utterances in their stridency and shrillness have an irrational tinge. This has been explained as the result of a pathological condition that affects many civilian militarists, particularly Homer Lea, "much the weirdest figure among the American, and probably all, civilian militarists." According to this theory, such individuals often suffer from psychosomatic disorders; they see in society a reflection of their own sick or sickly condition and, not knowing of a remedy for their unhealthy state, invent a sure and radical cure for the world around them. As a result of this transference of their own pathological condition, these civilian militarists come to consider the "armed forces . . . the healthiest of all males when they themselves are struck by ill health. . . . They want to join armed bodies in vicarious ways, or have others join them, thus to win back health. The lonely unconventional thinker craves for, exalts, prescribes for others, the male lonely-hearts society, the most orthodox, tight-knitted company, after contemporary society has been found hateful, mercenary, commercial, demagogical, democratic, decadent, lacking in a sense of honor and order or respect for 'birth.' "[14] Surely, Lea falls into this category of espousers of the military and of war.

Ultimately, Homer Lea was a tragic figure, but his tragedy was not simply that of his malformed body and his physical debility, nor his inordinate drive to excel and his failing to achieve many of his goals. Others of healthy constitution and endowed with greater intellect and as strong an ambition as his also experience failure. Thus, a man of Bourne's gifts and maturity could rightfully hope that his achievements and failures would "be flowing from the common lot of men, not from his own particular disability."[15] But in the case of Homer Lea, also a gifted individual, personal weaknesses, whether physical, emotional, or educational, circumscribed his accomplishments and determined his disappointments, because he was unable or unwilling to accept and adjust to the limits that his infirmities imposed on him. As a result, his frailties influenced his actions, which were often bizarre, and his thoughts, which were largely eccentric. The refusal to recognize his particular personal reality, which he had already shown as a youth, compelled him, in later years, to overreach and deceive himself about the scope of his physical, intellectual, and political powers and resources. That same trait drove him also, on various occasions, to mislead others. To one observer, his flagrant misstatements were not the prevarications of an impostor but the product of the inflated ego of a brilliant mind.[16] But his strong ego was owed to his maladjustment rather than to his intellect, which, if not brilliant, was certainly active and sharp. Lea's ardent desire to succeed made him a desperate gambler, and so he did not hesitate to dissemble, dissimulate, or lie whenever he thought that deceit might further his aims, which it usually did not. He was also an amateur in such attempts, just as he was a dilettante as a military man and a strategist, as a political theorist and a practicing politician. He was no impostor, though, and his life was not a fraud because he sincerely believed in himself and the causes he championed. To repeat Dr. Jordan's conclusion: "One [can] hardly help a kindly feeling for the ambitious little romancer trying to make the most of his short life, limited physique, and boundless imagination."[17]

——Appendix I——
Sun Yat-sen's Letters to Homer Lea

1

38, Spofford Alley
San Francisco, Cal.
February 24, 1910.

My dear General:—

Your letter of the 21st reached me this morning. I will come to see
you and Mr. B. as soon as I settle my affair in this city. When I come I shall
let you know some days before hand.

Many thanks for your noble feeling towards our cause.

Very truly yours
Sun Yat Sen

2

On Sea, March 24, 1910

My dear General:—

In my former letter I informed you that someone posessing some
very important documents of a certain military Power. Just before my

---

The unedited letters in Appendices I and II were given to the Hoover Institution on War, Revolution and Peace by Joshua B. Powers and Laurence Boothe.

sailing I received a list of the same, herewith I am enclosed with a translation. The list only given 12 kinds but there are others besides, all amount to more than thirty big books. All are the latest work of the General Staff of the Power. I think it is the most valuable thing that any rivalry Power could get. Would you try to find out whether the War Department of this country would avail this opportunity of obtaining these secret documents?

With best regards,

I am
Very truly yours,
Y. S. Sun

List:

1   Orders for mobilization of the active army and navy of all Japan.
2   Orders of coast defence.
3   Active orders of high commands during war.
4   Regulation and orders of telegraphic corps in battle field.
5   Regulations and orders of the sanitary corps in battle field.
6   Regulations and orders for Field Artilleries.
7   Regulations and orders for General telegraphic corps.
8   Important schedules.
9   Details of regulations of active officers.
10   Orders of the Chief Inspector of military training.
11   Orders and regulations of the line of communication.
12   Orders for heavy artilleries and siege guns.

Besides the above there are more than ten of other kinds of very important military matters.

3

April 10, 1910

My Dear General:

I arrived here already more than two weeks and have received information from C--- concerning the affair of C--- The cause of its failure is owing to the too hot-headed men of the first regiment. The time fixed for the uprising was only known to a few of the leaders on both sides; the others only informed that business will start as soon as it can be arranged and did not give any definite date. When the date arrived we were short of funds to bring in the armed men to the city and the authorities at the same time got reumor of something and took precaution by having all

the munitions of the new army to be sent back to the city and a mechanism of their rifles also taken away so as to render them useless. At that
time our men held a council and decided to change the time into the
sixth day after the New Year, for the authorities intended to restore the
mechanism and munitions on the fifth day, when N.Y. vacation expired
and ordinary official business began. And by the sixth day our men can
arrive in the city on foot, then a co-operation on both sides, and our
business would be a sure success. But on New Year day some dispute
happened to take place between some men of the 2nd R and the police.
The 1st R, however, thought that the real business is going to begin or
have been misinformed that the authorities had discovered the whole
affair, and rose as one man and marched into the city to attempt to seize
the arsenal and recover the mechanism and ammunition, but were prevented and shot down by the T- R garrison. Killed and wounded were
more than two hundred. The fight was a most unequal one. The entire
force deprived of the mechanism and munitions could not reply a shot
and have to retreat back to their camp and search for whatever residue
arms and munitions. They found a few dozen rifles and 70000 cartridges
in the target ground and used that to give a feeble resistance during the
third day. The 2nd and 3rd R saw their comrades slaughtered by the T--
but could not render any assistance for they themselves are also deprived
of the fighting mechanism. But notwithstanding this some of the individuals cast their lots with their comrades and joined the unequal fight.
Seven out of the eleven battalions took part in the fight. There were only
four that did not take part and they were surrounded before they could
do anything. Now the people of the whole K-t- is aroused in indignation
against the officials and demand the restoration of every soldier and pun-
ishment of the T for the massacre. It is reported owing to fear of a general
uprising of all the new army the government has yielded to the popular
demand of K-t. Immediately after the C affair there were mutinies in
S- T- and K-s provinces. Now the government is ordering four divisions
to be completed in K-t this year so that we shall have more chances to put
our men in.

   I have just received word from S.C. that wonderful progress has
been made along the frontier of Y and K by our agents. The soldiers and
people of that region are very enthusiastic in support of the cause and
they thought they are ready now to do anything and urge us to start the
general movement at once. I have sent word to them to wait until our
affairs here are settled.

   At present there is trouble in Hunan but I don't know anything
about it. But this indicates that the soldiers in the Y are also ready to do
anything. If there is no properly directed movement for them to join,
they will join any mischievous movement that happens to take place in
the meantime, such as that have occurred in C-

How is our scheme getting on? When can Mr. B. let us know any-thing definite?

With best regards etc.

(This letter available only as a typewritten copy.)

4

Honolulu, May 9th, 1910

My dear General:—

I just received news from China today says that the remnant of the 1st regiment about 7000 men have safely returned to their home in Kan-chow, near Kwang Chow Wan, the French Concession. They at once be-gan propogading work and have already got more than 10.000 followers. They have collected about a thousand rifles with 200 cartridges each from their own district. The rest of the 1st regiment also returned to their re-spective districts, next numerous to Kanchow men are those of Haifung and Lufung, the two coast districts of the Waichowfu. They also working in their own villages and also got more than 10.000 followers. At any time the Kanchow and Waichow men are ready for business.

The two undisbanded regiments of the new army in Canton are go-ing to be sent for garrison duty to the Kanchowfu. They ammunition is still not restore to them, but when they go off for their garrison duty this must be restored to them. Then we may make good use of those men and their weapons.

Mr. Hu, the party manager in Hong Kong, has went to Singapore with Messers Huang and Chao, late regimental commander of Canton recently.

I am sorry to tell you that one of my secretaries Mr. Wang Chiang Wei, with some others had been captured in Peking, and Mr. Wang has been sentenced of imprisonment for life. The only hope for him now is the capture of Peking by our army.

I will go to Hilo tomorrow noon and return here in a week of time. When you start for the East?

With best regards to you and Miss Power.

Very truly yours
Y. S. Sun

5

Honolulu, May 24, 1910

My dear General Lea:—

I am going to leave this Islands for Japan on the 30th this month by S. S. Mongolia. I shall stay there for a while to wait for news from you and at the same time to do what I can to prepare the way for the future.

I just received information from China that some of our comrades have already taken measure to secure concessions for cultivation from French authority in Kwang Chow Wai before they know anything of our proposition out here. The French government there are inviting anyone to go and develope the land, each application for concession will give three acres of land. But application must be sent three months before any answer is given.

I am also informed that there is a certain firm in Hong Kong who would undertake to supply any kind of arms and will guarantee to deliver any part in the coast of Kwangtung Province; thus it will save us a good deal of trouble of transporting the arms ourselves. If we arrange to buy from that firm, goods can be delivered to the spot where we need before we pay the price. This is the most sure and convenient way, if we could succeed in raising the loan in America, I should like you to see this Hong Kong firm first before we enter into contract with any others. We may use the Hong Kong firm either as a whole supplier or as merely a transporter. For they have ships and godowns in every port in the Far East as well as license to carry and store arms legally to and in anywhere.

My temporary address in Japan is as follows: Y. S. Sun, c/o Mr. K. H. Ike, No. 10, Nakanocho, Akasaka, Tokio, Japan. I will write again as soon as I arrive there.

With the best regards to you and Miss Power.

Very truly yours,
Y. S. Sun

6

Penang, Aug. 11, 1910.

My dear General:—

Your letter of June 18 safely reached me here yesterday. The commissioned officers are now recalled back to the army to train new recruits for two divisions of the Kwangtung army, which must be completed within a year of time. Most of them return except a few very mark men, who are now with me here. We could recover our position in the Canton army very soon and with a much greater strength than before. The numbers of men in the Haifung and Lufung districts are increasing day by day, so I could not tell you the exact number. But it is pretty certain that all able adultmen could be enlisted into the cause. And farther east all the districts in Chowchow fu, and Kia Yung Chow are ready to join. This part of Canton produce the best fighting men. It numbers about several millions. The Chowchow people had once been employed by the England and French armies during their invasion to Peking in 1860, and proved to be the best fighting material. The Taku forts were captured by storming by these Chowchow men.

The vallages within the triangle shape of country between Hong Kong, Fumoon, and Waichow, having been strongly armed with modern rifles, are promise to assist with all their arms, number at least 30.000. But ammunition must be provided for them.

The threatening uprising in the Yangtse valley have been stopped by me during my sojourn in Japan, as I have informed you when I wrote from there. At first they promised to keep quiet up to winter but now I can make them to wait longer until our plan for raising funds is succeeded. So you can go on with our original plan.

Some trouble is going on in the province of Yunnan now. I have sent a man from here by way of Burma to stop them last week. I think he could succeed in making them keep quiet for a time. Please send me a copy or two of your late book, "the Valor of Ignorancy", as the copy which I had have been took away by a friend.

I intended to stay here for two or three months within that time you may address your letters to me as follow:—

Mr. Chung San
c/o Tek Cheang
197 Beach Street
Penang
Straits Settlements

With my kindest regards to you and Miss Power.

Very truly yours
Y. S. Sun

7

Penang, Straits Settlements,
Sept. 5, 1910.

My dear General:—

I just received a letter from Mr. B. dated June 25, New York, which gives very encouraging news; but since that time neither of you send me any word, as I had arranged in a letter to you from Japan; so I supposed Mr. B's project might have been failed or delayed. I wrote to Mr. B. in reply asking him to send me $50.000 in advance from his own account, if he think that the project of raising fund is sured. Then when the matter settled he may have his money back in two folds as interest for his risk. For I need the money for preparatory work very much, if I can have this sum now I can do a work ten times much as the same money can do in a few month after.

As I have told you in my last letter that encouraging news came from every part in China. Cooperation could be easily obtained in many districts along the Kwang tung coast. We can start a movement with a much easier and quicker way than that as we have arranged in the Long Beach Hotel, and with much less expenses. I feel sure that Canton city can be captured from the outset. That will save us all the trouble for a preparation of means and ways to attack it, after the movement is commenced, from out side, for it can be captured by surprise within at any time. In possession of that city we possess at least a hundred thousand of modern rifles and sufficient quantity of ammunitions, and many hundred pieces of modern artilleries, and rifle and cartilage factories, and besides plenty of ready money and vast resources of material supplies. Most of the leaders are very reluctant to do anything other than capture that city from the very start. I think also that that city is the main object from the beginning and besides it is much easier to capture it at the beginning than afterward. The money use for this purpose will much less than the other scheme which we worked out in America.

Now if Mr. B's New York project failed I want you try some other way to get me half a million dollar (gold), for the Canton scheme only, put the others aside for a while, until we achieve our first object. Can you succeed in raising that amount of money in the shortest possible time? If not try to get as much as you can, but in any case send fifty thousand at once for preparatory work.

Since I stopped the movement of this summer in the Yangtse Valley and South China, in conforming to your advice, all our hopes are concentrated in the American project. I shall be much obliged for you to let me know at once if your's and Mr. B's schemes both failed, so that I may take independent measure in the immediate future.

With kindest regards to you and Miss Power.

> Very truly yours
> Chungsan

Address:-   Cable address
  Chungsan   Tekcheang
    c/o Tek Cheang   Penang
      197 Beach Street
        Penang
          Straits Settlements

P.S. If any money order also to the same name. In case of telegraphic communication use A.B.C. code latest edition (5th) by adding 269 to the figure of every word find the result and send that as cipher. When receiving any message deduct 269 from each word and the result will be the decipher message.

P.S. Before starting the movement from Canton it is a vital important for us to secure a perfect understanding of the English Government. To do this you and I must go to London and work together. If the project of getting money in America is succeeded and the 50.000 duly sent to me I will at once set the others to work and I myself go to London immediately to meet you there. And also have everything to be arranged beforehand in the city.

If all your schemes failed get me as many letters of introduction to Manila as you can and send them to me here at once. Much obliges.

8

Penang, Sept. 29, 1910

My dear General:—

Your letter of August 7, to Hong Kong, is in receipt. Hereafter do not send any letter to the Hong Kong address, but direct to here.

In regard to as Mr. B's appointment as financial agent, if the project could not succeed the same have to be recalled, as I was asked to return the signature in that case.

I want you to go on the other plan we spoke about and try to secure some money for us as quick as possible. Under the present circumstances I think a quarter million of gold dollars will be quite enough for the whole thing, even less than that may enable us to do some wonderful work.

Since I returned to the Far East I always try to stop premature movement in every part of China, on condition that I will supply the money in winter. If this condition can not be fulfilled it will be a great blow to my influence. I hope you would urge Mr. B. to send me the sum I asked in a former letter from his account. By this my influence could be saved from discredit. If he can do a little more the whole thing can be carried out to a successful issue.

I am now waiting for your introduction to go to Manila. Did you send it already? I have written you to ask for it quite a long time ago. I didn't think I can spare to come over to the United States again at present for everything in here are so unsettled. And I am fear I shall be unable to stop the uprising in the coming winter, although I still try in that direction, on account of want of money. If this winter movement can be postponed I will come over from Manila in the end of this year.

Very sincerely yours,
Chung San

Address:—
c/o Tok Cheang, 197 Beach Street, Penang, Straits Settlement.

9

Penang, November 7, 1910.

My dear General:—

Your letter of September 18, and the book and magazines have duly received some days ago; and after that Mr B's letter arrived which informed me that sydicate would meet early in October. But that month has already passed and yet up to this time there is still no definite news from him, so I do not expect much from his side. I want you to go on your own way to get the means for our movement as soon as possible. Of course I will not wait if any opportunity turn up, but it is very difficult to push matter forward without the necessary means. Since I been here I have improved the condition of the preparatory work many ways. And now we can make a sure success with far less money than we first proposed. I think even a tenth of our original sum would be enough. Can you get that any way quick? I am going try to raise some money here, if I can get barely enough to bigin, even far from a making of our success, I will start the business at once.

In regard to the translation of your book I will tell my Japanese friend to begin at once. I think we may make something in that way. As to the Chinese edition there will be no hope of making any profit out of it, for Chinese publishers only offer from 3 to 5 Mexican dollars to a thousand words of the best translation, because copyright are not effective in China. Your book after translated perhaps will make about 100.000 words (characters) which only amount to 500 Mexican or 250 American dollars, but at least take one for three months to finish it. But your book contains valuable knowledge which will be indispensable for the Chinese at the present age. I will try to get some one to bring out a Chinese edition after the Japanese is come off.

And in regard to your observations of aeroplane in war I have read it several times with much appreciation. All your reasoning are perfectly sound, I agreed with you entirely in your first part, but as to part second "as a means of reconnaissance" you missed out one thing that is aeroplane and dirigible balloon can take very good photographs which will help a commander to form a perfect opinion of the enemy's situation. For instance in the battles of Lean Yang and Mukden the Japanese force are less one third then the Russians but the former showed a bold front and enveloped the latter on both wings which made the Russian commander thought that the Japanese are more numerous than him. The Japanese line extending over 100 miles, which the Russian captive balloon cannot see. If the Russian had used dirigible or aeroplane to take photograph they could at once detect out the Japanese number during these long battles.

And about the Chinese Government in concerning the force you had trained in America, I think most likely, if such force is still under your command, they would like to get it over and transport it to China and to destroy it, as they had done once in the first Wusung Shanghai railway case, to buy it up in the pretention to control the line, but immediately the transaction is finished turned up the rails and shipped them together with the locomotors and cars to Formosa and left there to rot. And for the present Government to maintain such force as your four regiments under they service is the most untenable thing under the present situation of China. And I think the whole thing is propped up by Chang Yim Fang, the present Chinese Minister in Washington, for his own good. Be careful for all Chinese you come in contact with in America, and under no circumstance to let any one know of the relation between you and I.

I hope to hear good news from you soon.

With kindest regards to you and Miss Power.

Very truly yours
Y. S. Sun

10

Aug. 10, 1911

My dear General:—

Your letters from Washington and Weisbaden are in receipt. I was exceedingly glad to hear that you had made such a great success with the Government and the Senator, and more so to hear that your eyes are getting better rapidly. This last bit of news is most important for it relieves my anxiety very much.

As soon as I received your Washington letter I had at once sent word to my men in China to work accordingly. But before my letter reaches them I have received several cablegrams and letters from them states that more than ten divisions of the new army outside of Peking are sure, and all the Chinese divisions in the Capitol are very promising. Recently one of our men General Wu Lu Ching, is gave command of the sixth division in Peking. And many officers from the Province of Chile hitherto served in the various divisions in other provinces are now returned home to take service in the Peking Army in order to work for the purpose of cooperation with the other divisions when the movement took place. Thus you see they are working hard for the same object before they knew our plan. I expect great result could be obtained in that direction very soon.

There are none who would divide power with me at present, all leaders of different provinces are only too welcome for me to take up general command, in fact they only fear is that I would not accept that position. Lately I received many letters urging me to return to the East soon and start the movement quick. The only thing left to be done now is the way of getting the necessary fund for the starting.

In regard to the effect of the renewal of the Anglo-Japanese alliance to our affair, I don't think it makes any different at all. It shows that Japan is not yet ready to take independent action to shape the affairs of the Far East to suit her own purposes. At present her own people is over-burdened with increased taxation and the Japanese Government needs perhaps ten years more of time to consolidate and develope Korea and Manchuria, and needs also the money and peace at this juncture. So there is time for us to regenerate China before the new conqueror is ready. And I hope you would be quick to see your English friends and get the means for us to work on.

I am going to leave San Francisco soon and travel eastward again expect to reach New York on end of October.

With best regards to you both
Y. S. Sun

11

Idaho, Sept. 25, 1911

My dear General:—

Your letter of August 29th reached me here yesterday. I was very glad to hear that your eyes are getting better.

It is still my intention to establish headquarters in Paris or London if I can find the means. General Hwang had not been ordered to Europe yet as he has much to do in China.

Recently there is great trouble happened in Szechuan caused by the railway dispute between the people and government. Our headquarters in the south has been greatly disturbed because there is rumor that the Army in Szechuan has joined the fracas. If that is true our men proposed to start the Yu Nan Army in follow suit first, then the Canton Army after.

But I don't that is true as we never intend that the Szechuan Army should take the initiation in the national movement and it was quite unprepared in that respect. According to official report that the new Army in Szechuan disobeyed the Viceroy's order to fight, but did not join the people, it adopts a neutral position, I think that is what really happened.

In regard to how and when and where to obtain the necessary funds, I really cannot form an decision. I only hoping to get it as soon as possible.

After I ending my journey at New York I will try to come over to Europe to see what could be done with France and England.

Please write me again to New York address c/o Sing Fat Co. 1127 Broad way.

With my best regards to you both.

Very truly yours
Y. S. Sun

12

21 Yates Road, Shanghai
27th June, 1912

Dear Mrs. Lea,

I am indeed very glad to learn that you and the General had a pleasant trip home, and what makes me more glad still is to hear that the General's health is getting stronger daily and the doctors opine that he will be able to walk about in another time. By the time this letter reaches you, you will be spending your time in the beach, and I have no doubt that a change of air and the sunshine will do much to hasten his recovery.

By to-morrow's "Shinyo Maru", my son and two daughters will be leaving for the States to prosecute further studies. Sun Fo will go to the University of California, to take up what course of studies it is not yet decided. I trust during his sojourn in the States, he will have occasions to meet your people.

Things in China are gratually getting into proper shape, the bickerings of the political parties in Peking resulting in the enforced retirement of the Premier are nothing very serious. I trust and hope everything will work on smoothly once again before long.

I have tried to eschew politics as much as possible, I intend to devote all my energies to develope the natural resources of this country, and particularly to the construction of railways. I hope to succeed.

With very kind wishes to you and the General,

Yours truly,
Sun Yat Sen

13

491 Avenue Paul Brunat,
Shanghai, October 13th, 1912.

My dear Lea:

I am very happy to receive your letter of September 15th and also a letter from Mrs Lea written two weeks earlier, for both of which I thank you very much. I hope your health will continue to improve and we may meet in Paris in about two months from now.

When Mr Mitchell's telegram came I was up in Pekin. It was transmitted by my friend to Pekin from Shanghai. I was under the impression that it was a telegram sent by Mr Mitchell from Shanghai. Accordingly I wired back to him trying to make an appointment for a long interview. On my return I found that Mr. Mitchell had not been to Shanghai at all. Mrs Lea's letter made it all plain.

The conditions in your memorandum are carefully noted. Several items need to be talked over between us when we meet.

My visit to the north has been a great success as you must have learned from the press. There is far better understanding between the south and the north as a result of this visit. General Huang has been up there also where he was enthusiastically received too. He is just now back to Shanghai.

Some of the Shansi bankers have approached me to see whether it would be possible to start an industrial bank. It is hoped that they would raise five million dollars for the purpose. I am now exchanging letters with General Yen of Shansi on the matter.

With warmest regards and best wishes to Mrs Lea and yourself,

Sincerely yours,
Y. S. Sun

General Homer Lea,
Ocean Park, Cal.

—Appendix II—

Sun Yat-sen's Letters to Charles B. Boothe

1

San Francisco, March 21, 1910.

My dear Mr. Boothe:—

Thank you very much for your kind letter of the 19th inst. and the clipping etc. enclosed in it.

I only arrived San Francisco this morning, for I have been stopped on way in Bakersfield, Hanford, and Fresno. I am going to sail by S.S. Korea tomorrow noon for Honolulu. My address there will be:-Y. S. Sun c/o The Liberty News, P. O. Box 1020, Honolulu, Territory Hawaii, and telegraphic address Losun, Honolulu. I hope to hear good news from you soon.

With best regard to you and Mrs Boothe and Miss Boothe.

I am
Very sincerely yours
Sun Yat Sen

2

Honolulu, T. H., April 5, 1910

My dear Mr. Boothe:—

Your kind letter of March 24, with clippings from the New York World and La Follettes, and a letter of Dr. Y. are in receipt. I have the

New York World's article it is very interesting and enclosed herewith I return it to you.

In regard to Dr. Y. I did informed him of our conference but did not tell him anything particularly. I told him that you intended to go to the East soon, so he may hear all from you. Now in this case I leave the matter entirely to your decision.

My son is well and still studies in school here I think some day he may come over the States to see you.

With kindest regards

Very truly yours
Sun Yat Sen

3

Honolulu, T. H., May 24 1910

My dear Mr. Boothe:—

I am going to leave here for Japan on the 30th this month by S.S. "Mongolia." I shall stay in Japan for a while to wait you answer, and at the same time do what I can to prepare the way of working in the near future. My temporary address is as follow: Y. S. Sun, care of Mr. K. H. Ike, No. 10, Nakanocho, Akasaka, Tokio, Japan. I will write you again and give you my permanent address, if I establish any, as soon as I arrive there.

With the best regards to you and all your family.

Very truly yours
Sun Yat Sen

4

Tokyo, June 22nd, 1910

My dear Beach:—

Your letter of May 12, reached me at Honolulu just on the day of my departure from the Islands. I arrived in Japan already a fortnight, since that time the Peking Government left no stone unturned to get out of this country. The Japanese Government feels rather trouble for my staying here, the minister of foreign affairs positively objected my prsence in Tokyo, but the minister of war have contrary opinion. On the day of my arrival a cabinet meeting took place and the war department prevailed and I was allowed to stay, but that was before the Peking Government try to do anything. As now the Peking Government impresses the foreign office here so hard, I think I have to leave here on my own accord in order to relieve the uneasiness of the Government here.

Before my arrival some of our leaders have already come to meet me. I told them you view of stopping all premature movements, they all agreed and promised to send word to their own provinces to stop them immediately. I think all such kind of movement can be stopped up to the winter of this year. So we still have many peaceful months to work.

I am preparing to leave here, but friends in connection with the war department wish me to stay a little longer. So my program is very unsettled now, but will write you at once when things are decided.

In case your work is accomplished before I can communicate to you wher my about you can cable to Hong Kong as follow:-

Chungkokpo, Hong Kong
Ahmi Settled

The agent in Hong Kong will forward such a cable to me at once wherever I may happen to be.

The document signed by representatives of various provinces is ready in here I will send it to you soon.

> With my best regards
> Very truly yours
> Chungsan

5

Singapore, July 15, 1910

My dear Mr. Boothe:—

I left Japan at the end of June, and arrived here two day before. During my stay in Japan and on my way called at Shanghai and Hong Kong have met many leaders, they are very willing to comply your wishing by waiting quietly for a time, if there is hope for a successful move soon.

At present I have no matter of important to tell you, except that one of our comrades, formerly a captain of a cruiser in the Chinese navy, is now promoted into the chief command of the whole Chinese fleet. If time come, I am sure, he would co-operate with us. How is matter getting on in your part, and what is the result of your New York tour? I am waiting eagerly for definite news from you.

My temporary address in Singapore is as follow:-
                     Y. S. Sun
                         c/o Kong Ye Chiong
                             77 Cecil Street
                                 Singapore
                                     Straits Settlements
         Cable address
             Enghock Singapore
         With my best regards

                                                 Very truly yours
                                                 Y. S. Sun
P.S. I may pay a visit to Manila in the coming few months, can you give
me introduction to see some of your friends there? And I should like you
would ask your friend, the former general in the Phillipine, to give me
some introduction to the officials there, if you think adviseable.

     Kang Yu Wei is staying at Singapore at present, he been here al-
ready two months before my arrival.

6

                                         Penang, Straits Settlements,
                                         Sept. 4, 1910.

Dear Sir:—

     Your letter of June 25, from New York, only reached me here yester-
day. I was glad to hear that the result of your visiting to the East is a most
satisfactory one. Your former letters to Hawaii were received during my
sojourn in Japan. I had replied them all, and besides I had wrote once or
twice to either you or the General before I left Japan, in regarding to the
rumour which you referred.

     In my former letters I either told you or the General that I was just
in time, when in Japan, to stop all premature movements in the Yangtse
valley and South China. The leaders from different parts of China all
agreed with me to wait until our project in America succeeded.

     The signatures which I promised to obtain has sent you by regis-
tered post from Yokohama, I have no doubt it has reached you long before now.

     Everything must have been settled by this time. What is the final
result now? Is it succeed or fail, in any case I should like to know the

result as soon as possible, so that I may take independent measure in the future.

If you think that our project of raising the funds will be surely succeeded and final settlement is only a question of time, I should like you would advance me a sum of $50.000 American dollars from your own account for the preparatory work. For this will facilitate me to do a great deal of that part of the work, and perhaps ten times of that money may not done the same amount of work in a few months later. If you would advance this sum, when the project is succeeded, you may have twice of it back as interest for the risk you run.

There will be no disturbance take place in the Yangtse valley and South China up to the coming winter; so you may be sure that there is nothing to disturb you in the meantime.

I shall be in Penang in the coming two or three months, and within that time I cannot come to meet you, even our project succeed, unless the above sum of $50.000, could be sent here beforehand.

Our position among the army in Canton has been recovered since the last failure, and will be much stronger than before within a very short time. The attitude of all other armies in the Empire are the same and with more eagerness to look for a signal of a general movement.

Recently the army in Sin Chiang (East Turkistan) has broke out into mutiny. This is a part of the previous arrangement of the summer movement with the Yangtse valley, which I have so effective stopped in conforming to your advice when I was in Japan. This out lying part of China is too far away from our means of communication, for we cannot use the government telegraph line and our messengers have not enough time to reach there.

With kindest regards

Very truly yours
Chungsan

P.S. The telegraphic code (269) which you gave me at Los Angeles, I found it not very suitable for our use. I think we better use the ABC. code latest edition with modification of our own design. I suggest to add 269 to each figure by sender, and receiver can subtract the same in decipher.

Address:-   Cable address:-

Chungsan   Tekcheang, Penang
   c/o Tek Cheang
      197 Beach Street
         Penang
            Straits Settlements
Money order also for Chungsan

7

Penang, November 8, 1910

My dear Mr. Beach:—

Your letter of September 26 is in receipt, but the cablegram you mentioned did not reached me. By what address did you send it?

October is now over, how is the result of the Syndicate meeting? As up to this time there is no definite news from you, I fear, in spite of your hard work for our cause, the New York project might have been failed through. Have you some other way to obtain money for us? We are not in need of so large a sum as we first proposed in your house, for many of the preparatory works have been done since my returning here. I think from one tenth to one fifth of the original amount would be enough to carry out the whole business to a successful end, say half million dollars in gold will be just about the amount we need at the present moment. A small sum must have been easier and quicker to raise than a big one, wouldnt you think so? If you can get this sum within three months from date, it will be just in time for our purpose. After that we will not wait, but take independent measure to do what we can by any means. In case we could succeed in gaining a permanent footing before you conclude any loan, then the condition of the same must be entirely modified. But if nothing could be done or the attempt failed in our part, then the condition will be continued as we have arranged in Los Angeles.

Situation in China is the same so I have no news to tell you.

In regard to Momento I agreed with you entirely.

I hope to hear good news from you soon.

With kindest regards

Very truly yours
Chung San

Cable address
    Tekcheang
        Penang

8

December 16,1910

My dear Mr. Beach:—

Your letters of Oct. 21, and Nov. 1, 1910, had reached me a few days before my departure from Penang. As you did not send any cablegram after your letters, I think the question is decided that we could not succeed in that line.

We are now taking independent measure of our own to start the great movement in the coming few months. But we are in great need of help at present. Can you do anything for us by your own means? Another few hundred thousand could make us carry out everything perfectly through. But at any case whether we have the money or not, I am sure of our success in the next move.

I left Penang on the 6 December on way to Europe, and will enter the Red Sea by tomorrow. After I finished my business in Europe I will proceed to America and thence to China. I will communicate with you as soon as I reach American shore. If you would do something for us with your own means I will come direct to see you at Los Angeles.

With kindest regards

Very truly yours
Chungsan

9

Vancouver, B.C., March 6, 1911.

My dear Mr. Beach:—

I intended to write you long before this but always so busy and so unsettled about future plan that I could not do so. Now I am go to leave here about a week of time and will stop over on way in Kamloops, Galgary, Winnipeg, Toronto and Montreal, thence to New York. I expect to reach New York in a month of time. My address there will be Y. S. Sun, Care of Sing Fat Co, 1127, Broadway, New York. During the meantime communication can be forwarded through Tai Hon Yat Bo, Vancouver. B.C.

As you cannot get for our the necessary funds in time we must start the movement with our own means. I am now working in raising money from my own countrymen and have succeeded in getting more than half we need already, and hope to get the other part along my way east. As soon as money is enough we will set to work at once.

How is you plan of getting money? Is it still any hope of doing something in a smaller scale than our original plan? If so I hope you would do something for us at once. If you could not do anything before my arrival at New York I have to ask you to send back that paper which signed my comrades, by registering post to the address which I gave above, for I have promised to my comrades to return their signatures in case of failure of raising the intending funds.

With kindest regards

                                        Yours very truly
                                        Y. S. Sun

Notes

Abbreviations

Boothe Papers = The Papers of Charles B. Boothe, Hoover Institution on War, Revolution and Peace, Stanford University.

LC = Library of Congress, Washington, D.C.

NA = National Archives, Washington, D.C.

Pardee Papers = The Papers of George C. Pardee, Bancroft Library, University of California, Berkeley.

Powers Papers = The Papers of Joshua B. Powers, Hoover Institution on War, Revolution and Peace, Stanford University.

PRO = Public Record Office, Kew Richmond, Surrey, England.

Chapter 1

1. *San Francisco Call*, April 22, 1900, mag. sec., pp. 1, 7.
2. Ibid.
3. *San Francisco Call*, April 21, 1901, mag. sec., pp. 1, 3. See also *National Cyclopedia of American Biography*, vol. 2, p. 50.
4. See, for example, *New York Sun*, June 28, 1905, p. 2.
5. Clare Boothe, "Introduction" to Homer Lea, *The Valor of Ignorance* (New York: 1942), p. 8.
6. Carl Crow, *China Takes Her Place* (New York, 1944), p. 60.
7. See Zella Armstrong, *Notable Southern Families* (Chattanooga, Tenn., 1926), vol. 3, p. 71, and copy of undated statement by Watson C. Lea, Powers Papers.
8. See Harry Carr, *Riding the Tiger. An American Newspaper Man in the Orient* (Boston, 1934), p. 169.
9. Copy of undated statement by Watson C. Lea. Powers Papers.
10. Copy of undated statement by Marco Newmark. Powers Papers.
11. Ibid.
12. Copy of undated statement by Hund. Powers Papers.
13. Frederick L. Chapin, "Homer Lea and the Chinese Revolution," Harvard Undergraduate Thesis, April 1950, p. 6.

14. Copy of undated statement by Marco Newmark. Powers Papers.

15. Marshall Stimson, "A Los Angeles Jeremiah. Homer Lea: Military Genius and Prophet," *Quarterly of the Historical Society of Southern California* (March 1942): 6.

16. Ibid.

17. Ibid.

18. Copy of letter by Homer Lea to President Jordan, Stanford University, June 2, 1897. Powers Papers.

19. Ibid.

20. Copy of letter by Guy W. Wadsworth to President Jordan, June 4, 1897. Powers Papers.

21. Copy of letter by Homer Lea to President Jordan, Stanford University, June 2, 1897. Powers Papers.

22. Will Irwin, *The Making of a Reporter* (New York, 1942), p. 19.

23. Robert Sullivan, "Nobody Listens to a Prophet," *New York Daily News*, December 28, 1941, p. 40.

24. Ermal Lea Green, "She Knew Him Well," *Saturday Evening Post*, May 23, 1942.

25. *St. Louis Post-Dispatch*, May 19, 1905, pt. 2, p. 13.

26. U.S. Passport No. 55866 of June 22, 1911. Powers Papers.

27. Chapin, "Homer Lea," p. 34.

28. David Starr Jordan, *The Days of a Man* (Yonkers, N.Y., 1922), vol. 2, p. 32.

29. Irwin, *Making of a Reporter*, p. 19.

30. Personal communication by Joshua B. Powers to the author. See also membership card of Homer Lea in the Automobile Club of Southern California, exp. date August 1, 1911. Powers Papers.

31. Copy of letter from Dr. H. W. Hunsacker, San Francisco, to Stanford University, May 15, 1898. Powers Papers.

32. *Daily Palo Alto*, January 25 and September 15, 1898.

33. See copy of statement of registrar of Stanford University. Powers Papers.

34. *San Francisco Call*, April 22, 1900, mag. sec., pp. 1, 7.

35. Letter by No [Ng] Poon Chew to Dr. Jordan, *New York Evening Post*, December 19, 1912, p. 6; and Ng Poon Chew, "The Real Homer Lea," *Oriental Review* 3 (January 1913): 171–72.

36. See L. Eve Armentrout-Ma, "Chinese Politics in the Western Hemisphere, 1893–1911. Rivalry Between Reformers and Revolutionaries in the Americas," Ph. D. dissertation, University of California, Davis, 1977, pp. 124 (n. 65), 160.

37. Carl Glick, *Double Ten. Captain O'Banion's Story of the Chinese Revolution* (New York, 1945), pp. 48–57, mentions Homer Lea's membership in the Pao Huang Hui, while Chapin, "Homer Lea," p. 14, speaks of him as a

member of the Chih Kung T'ang. Both assertions, while probably correct, cannot be substantiated.

38. "Students Notebook." Powers Papers.

39. Homer Lea, "The Reawakening of China," unpublished manuscript. Powers Papers.

40. *Philadelphia Inquirer*, June 26, 1905, p. 2.

41. Homer Lea, *The Valor of Ignorance* (New York, 1909), p. 18.

42. Homer Lea, *The Vermilion Pencil* (New York, 1908), p. 144.

43. Copy of letter from Ethel Lea to Joshua Powers, August 15, 1911. Powers Papers.

44. Homer Lea, "The Defenses of China," unpublished manuscript. Powers Papers.

45. *San Francisco Call*, April 22, 1900, mag. sec., pp. 1, 7.

46. Ibid.

47. Ibid.

48. *San Francisco Call*, June 23, 1900, p. 1.

49. See n. 35 above.

50. *San Francisco Call*, June 23, 1900, p. 1.

Chapter 2:

1. *San Francisco Call*, June 23, 1900.

2. *Stanford Alumnus* 1 (June 1900): 164.

3. *New York Tribune*, July 30, 1900, p. 3.

4. *New York Tribune*, July 28, 1900, p. 3.

5. For example, Professor Harold Z. Schiffrin, in a letter to the author dated March 2, 1982, is not at all certain that Lea was in China in the summer of 1900.

6. Jordan, *Days of a Man*, vol. 2, pp. 32–34.

7. Sun Yat-sen, "My Reminiscences," *Strand Magazine* (London) 42 (March 1912): 301–7.

8. Governor Henry A. Blake to Foreign Office, August 3, 1900. PRO, FO 17/1718, pp. 365–66.

9. See C. Martin Wilbur, *Sun Yat-sen. Frustrated Patriot* (New York, 1976), p. 311, n. 50.

10. Armentrout-Ma, "Chinese Politics," pp. 242–43.

11. *Kuo Fu Nien P'u Tseng Ting Pen* [A Chronological Biography of the Father of the Country], Lo Chia-lun and Huang Chi-lu, eds. (Taipei, 1969), vol. 1, pp. 175–76.

12. See Chapin, "Homer Lea," p. 113.

13. *San Francisco Call*, April 21, 1901, mag. sec., pp. 1, 3.

14. J. O. P. Bland, *Recent Events and Present Politics in China* (Philadelphia, 1912), p. 255.

15. Glick, *Double Ten*, p. 159.

16. Jung-pang Lo, *K'ang Yu-wei. A Biography and a Symposium* (Tucson, 1967), pp. 271–72.

17. Personal communication to the author, October 15, 1980.

18. See Thomas William Ganschow, "A Study of Sun Yat-sen's Contacts with the United States Prior to 1922," Ph. D. dissertation, Indiana University, March 1971, p. 39.

19. See summary of statement by Ethel Lea in Herbert H. Gowen and Joseph Washington Hall, *An Outline History of China* (New York, 1926), pp. 352–53.

20. Letters from Homer Lea to Dr. David Starr Jordan, April 23 and May 6, 1909. Stanford University Archives.

21. See below pp. 220–22.

22. Robert Leo Worden, "A Chinese Reformer in Exile: The North American Phase of the Travels of K'ang Yu-wei, 1899–1909," Ph. D. dissertation, Georgetown University, 1972, p. 100.

23. See letter from the Chinese Empire Reform Association, San Francisco, to President William McKinley, July 18, 1900. NA, Dept. of State, Microcopy 179, Roll 1077.

24. Richard O'Connor, *Pacific Destiny* (Boston, 1969), pp. 306–8.

25. Clare Boothe, "Introduction" to 1942 edition of Lea, *Valor of Ignorance*, pp. 15–16; and Clare Boothe, "Ever Hear of Homer Lea?" *Saturday Evening Post* 214 (March 7, 1942): 72.

26. See Chapin, "Homer Lea," pp. 20–21.

27. Ng Poon Chew, "Letter to Dr. Jordan," *New York Evening Post*, December 19, 1912, p. 6.

28. *San Francisco Call*, April 9, 1901.

29. Letter from Ng Poy Kee [Ng Poon Chew] to Homer Lea, May 13, 1912. Powers Papers.

30. *San Francisco Call*, April 21, 1901.

31. Ibid.

32. See Tse Tsan Tai, *The Chinese Republic. Secret History of the Revolution* (Hong Kong, 1924), p. 20.

33. See Lowell Thomas, *Born to Raise Hell: The Life Story of Tex O'Reilly, Soldier of Fortune* (New York, 1936), p. 176.

34. Yung Wing, *Diary for the Year 1902*, Connecticut State Library, Hartford (Microfiche); and Yung Wing, *My Life in China and America* (New York, 1909).

35. Consul-General Sir J. Swettenham to the Marquess of Salisbury, March 29, 1900. PRO, CO 273/264.

36. *San Francisco Call*, April 21, 1901.

37. *San Francisco Call*, April 9, 1901.

38. *Sun* (Santa Cruz), April 9, 1901.

39. *China Press* (Shanghai), December 28, 1911, in NA, General Records, Record Group 59, M98, Roll 1008.

40. Lo, *K'ang Yu-wei*, p. 186.

41. Governor Henry A. Blake to Foreign Office, August 3, 1900. PRO, FO 17/1718, pp. 365–66.

42. Lo, *K'ang Yu-wei*, p. 185.

43. *Stanford Alumnus* 2 (February 1901): 75.

44. Will Irwin, "White Leader of Chinese," *New York Sun*, June 28, 1905, p. 2.

45. Irwin, *Making of a Reporter*, p. 19.

46. Boothe, "Introduction" to Lea, *Valor of Ignorance*, pp. 16–17.

47. Letter from H. G. Otis to Homer Lea, May 24, 1909. Powers Papers.

48. Lowell, *Born to Raise Hell*, p. 176.

49. Ibid.

50. See letter of K. Aishi to Homer Lea, January 11, 1901. Powers Papers.

51. L. Eve Armentrout, "The Canton Rising of 1902–1903: Reformers, Revolutionaries, and the Second Taiping," *Modern Asian Studies* 10 (January 1976): 97.

52. Letter to the author, July 23, 1982.

53. Edmund B. D'Auvergne, *Pierre Loti* (New York, 1926), p. 178.

54. Pierre Loti, *Les Derniers Jours de Pékin* (Paris, 1902).

55. D'Auvergne, *Pierre Loti*, p. 178.

56. François de Tessan, "Loti en Amérique," *Demain* (Paris) (1924): 184–85. See also *Independent* 73 (September 26, 1912): 712.

57. De Tessan, "Loti en Amérique," and François de Tessan, *Promenades au Far-West* (Paris, 1912), pp. 162–73.

58. See outline of *The Vermilion Spider*. Powers Papers.

59. Lea, *Vermilion Pencil*, p. 111.

60. Lowell, *Born to Raise Hell*, pp. 175–76.

61. Harold Z. Schiffrin, *Sun Yat-sen and the Origins of the Chinese Revolution* (Berkeley, 1968), p. 230.

62. Lowell, *Born to Raise Hell*, pp. 175–76.

63. Ibid., p. 176.

64. Letter from Ethel Lea to her sister Agnes, August 8, 1911. Powers Papers.

65. Frederick L. Chapin, "Homer Lea, Unpublished Manuscript," p. 278. Powers Papers.

66. Letter from Ethel Lea to her sister Agnes, February 22, 1912. Powers Papers.

67. Marco R. Newmark, *Jottings in Southern California History* (Los Angeles, 1955), p. 138.

68. Jordan, *Days of a Man*, vol. 2, pp. 33–34.

69. See letter of K. Aishi to Homer Lea, January 11, 1901. Powers Papers.

70. *San Francisco Call*, April 9, 1901.

71. *San Francisco Call*, April 21, 1901, mag. sec., pp. 1, 2.

72. *San Francisco Chronicle*, April 22, 1901, p. 4.

73. Letter from No [Ng] Poon Chew to Dr. Jordan, *New York Evening Post*, December 19, 1912, p. 6; and Ng Poon Chew, "The Real Homer Lea," *Oriental Review* 3 (January 1913): 171–72.

Chapter 3

1. *San Francisco Call*, April 21, 1901. See also *San Francisco Call*, April 9, 1901 and the *Sun* (Santa Cruz), April 9, 1901.

2. Undated letter from Sir Brian Leighton to Homer Lea. Powers Papers.

3. See letter from K'ang Yu-wei to Homer Lea, October 10, 1904. Powers Papers.

4. Armentrout, "The Canton Uprising," p. 97; Armentrout-Ma, "Chinese Politics," p. 204; Tse, *Chinese Republic*, pp. 21–22.

5. Letter from S. Y. Hsu to Homer Lea, May 9, 1903. Powers Papers.

6. Letter from Homer Lea to President Theodore Roosevelt, August 6, 1903. Powers Papers.

7. See Joseph R. Levenson, *Liang Ch'i-ch'ao and the Mind of Modern China* (London, 1959). pp. 70–76.

8. *San Francisco Chronicle*, October 18, 1903, p. 20; and *Sacramento Union*, October 19, 1903, p. 8.

9. Letter from Homer Lea to Governor George C. Pardee, September 24, 1903. Pardee Papers.

10. *Los Angeles Times*, October 21, 1903.

11. *Los Angeles Times*, October 23, 1903.

12. *Los Angeles Times*, October 25, 1903.

13. *Los Angeles Times*, October 30, 1903.

14. *Los Angeles Herald*, October 30, 1903, p. 11.

15. *Los Angeles Times*, October 30, 1903, p. 2.

16. See p. 59 below.

17. Leong Kai Chew (Liang Ch'i-ch'ao), "The Educational Reformation of China," *Independent* 55 (October 15, 1903): 2441–42.

18. Levenson, *Liang Ch'i-ch'ao*, p. 62.

19. Lo, *K'ang Yu-Wei*, p. 188.

20. *Los Angeles Times*, March 30, 1905, p. 2. See also p. 58 below.

21. *Los Angeles Examiner*, March 16, 1905.

22. *St. Louis Post-Dispatch*, May 19, 1905, p. 2.

23. Glick, *Double Ten*.

24. Letter from Carl Glick to Captain Fred Rheinstein, May 5, 1945. Powers Papers.

25. Glick, *Double Ten*, p. 23.

26. *Who's Who in America, 1908–1909* (Chicago, 1908), 5th ed. pp. 304–5.

27. Letter from Sun Yat-sen to Homer Lea, September 29, 1910. Powers Papers.

28. Lee Shipper, "Leaside," *Los Angeles Times*, April 10, 1945, pt. 2, p. 4.

29. From articles of incorporation of Western Military Academy, as quoted by Worden, "Chinese Reformer," pp. 125–26.

30. Glick, *Double Ten*, pp. 101, 222.

31. Letter from Homer Lea to Governor George C. Pardee, October 7, 1905. Pardee Papers.

32. See Lo, *K'ang Yu-wei*, p. 181; Hellmut Wilhelm, "The Poems from the Hall of Obscured Brightness," in Lo, *K'ang Yu-wei*, p. 339, n. 110; and Chapin, "Homer Lea," pp. 115–16.

33. *San Francisco Chronicle*, May 18, 1905, p. 9.

34. *St. Louis Post-Dispatch*, May 19, 1905, pt. 2, p. 13.

35. Letter from Ansel O'Banion to A. H. Powers, March 23, 1943. Powers Papers.

36. See Parade Report (Form No. 16) of Company A, First Infantry, First Brigade, Imperial Army, of November 15, 1904. Powers Papers. See also Parade Report from Ralph J. Faneuf, Captain Commanding, Company C, First Infantry, First Brigade, Imperial Army, August 21, 1905. Powers Papers.

37. See General Order No. 8, Headquarters First Brigade, C.I.A., of November 1, 1904. Powers Papers.

38. Letter from Lieutenant W. W. Rhein to Lieutenant General Homer Lea, January 16, 1905. Powers Papers.

39. Letter from Major George W. Gibbs to General Homer Lea, January 6, 1905. Powers Papers.

40. Letter from secretary of English, Chinese Empire Reform Association, Baltimore, Md., to General Homer Lea, December 20, 1904. Powers Papers.

41. See report from Company A, Second Infantry Regiment, St. Louis. Powers Papers.

42. See General Order No. 8, Headquarters First Brigade, C.I.A., of November 4, 1904. Powers Papers.

43. See *Review of Reviews* 37 (June 1908): 767.

44. Letter from John M. York to John Alton, December 18, 1904. Pardee Papers.

45. Letter from Adjutant General of California to Roger S. Page, December 18, 1904. Pardee Papers.

46. *Los Angeles Times*, December 31, 1904, p. 6.

47. *Los Angeles Times*, January 4, 1905, p. 2.

48. *Los Angeles Times*, January 3, 1905, p. 2.

49. *Los Angeles Times*, January 4, 1905, p. 2.

50. Glick, *Double Ten*, p. 132.

51. See Schiffrin, *Sun Yat-sen and the Origins*, pp. 20, 22, 211, and 212, about the politically ambiguous attitudes of some Chinese imperial officials.

52. *Los Angeles Times*, January 4, 1905, p. 2.

53. *Los Angeles Times*, June 7, 1905, p. 2.

54. *Los Angeles Times*, March 19, 1905, p. 6; and *Los Angeles Examiner*, March 19, 1905, p. 23.

55. *Los Angeles Times*, January 20, 1905, pp. 1, 8.

56. Glick, *Double Ten*, pp. 108–11.

57. Statement by K'ang Yu-wei made in 1899, quoted in Worden, "Chinese Reformer," p. 94.

58. Letter from K'ang Yu-wei to Homer Lea, October 10, 1910. Powers Papers.

59. Letter from K'ang Yu-wei to Homer Lea, February 18, 1905. Copy in Chapin, "Homer Lea," p. 135.

60. *St. Louis Post-Dispatch*, May 19, 1905, pt. 2, p. 13.

61. *San Francisco Call*, April 9, 1901.

62. *Morning Oregonian* (Portland), February 14, 1905, p. 8.

63. Letter from K'ang Yu-wei to Homer Lea, February 18, 1905. Copy in Chapin, "Homer Lea," p. 135.

64. See Shelley Hsien Cheng, "The T'ung-meng hui: Its Organization, Leadership and Finances, 1905–1912," Ph. D. dissertation, University of Washington, Seattle, 1962, p. 124.

65. *Los Angeles Times*, March 13, 1905, p. 1 and March 14, 1905, p. 2.

66. *Los Angeles Examiner*, March 16, 1905.

67. *Los Angeles Herald*, March 14, 1905, p. 12.

68. *Los Angeles Examiner*, March 16, 1905.

69. *Los Angeles Times*, March 19, 1905, p. 6.

70. *Los Angeles Examiner*, March 19, 1905, p. 23.

71. *Los Angeles Examiner*, March 22, 1905, p. 7.

Chapter 4

1. *Los Angeles Times*, March 25, 1905, pt. 2, p. 2.

2. *Los Angeles Times*, March 29, 1905, p. 10.

3. See letter from Senator George C. Perkins to Adjutant General Corbin, August 30, 1899. NA, Records of the Adjutant General's Office, Record Group 94, File No. 223380.

4. Letter of R. A. Falkenberg to President William McKinley, March 7, 1899. Ibid.

5. Letter of R. A. Falkenberg to the Secretary of War, July 10, 1899. Ibid.

6. *Los Angeles Times*, April 11, 1905, pt. 2, p. 1.

7. Letters from R. A. Falkenberg to War Department, December 6, 1893 and to Assistant Adjutant General, January 14, 1894, quoted by Worden, "Chinese Reformer," p. 134.

8. Letters from R. A. Falkenberg to President William McKinley, March 7, April 27, and June 1, 1899. NA, Record Group 94, File No. 223380.

9. Letter from R. A. Falkenberg to Secretary of War, July 10, 1899. Ibid.

10. Ibid.

11. Letter from R. A. Falkenberg to Secretary of War, July 22, 1899. Ibid.

12. Letter from R. A. Falkenberg to President William McKinley, March 7, 1899. Ibid.

13. Letter from Acting Secretary of War to R. A. Falkenberg, April 10, 1899. Ibid.

14. Letters from R. A. Falkenberg to President William McKinley, April 24, June 1 and 23, 1899; to Secretary of War, June 19, July 10 and 22, 1899; to Assistant Secretary of War, August 10, 1899; to Senator Elihu Root, August 10 and 17, 1899; to the President's secretary, George B. Cortelyou, July 29, 1899. Ibid.

15. Cable from R. A. Falkenberg to Senator Elihu Root, August 17, 1899; cable from Senator G. C. Perkins to Adjutant General, August 19, 1899, and letter from Adjutant General to Senator Perkins, August 22, 1899; letters from Senator Perkins to Adjutant General and from Adjutant General to Senator Perkins, August 30, 1899; from R. A. Falkenberg to Senator Root, November 1, 1899. Ibid.

16. Letters from Mrs. R. A. Von Falkenberg to War Department, November 4, 1899, and from Assistant Adjutant General to Mrs. R. A. Von Falkenberg, December 4, 1899. Ibid.

17. Letter from R. A. Falkenberg to Secretary of State John Hay, October 6, 1900, and copy of letter from R. A. Falkenberg to Emperor of Germany, Mikado of Japan, and Queen of England, September 14, 1900. NA, Record Group 59, Misc. Letters, Microcopy 179, Roll 1084.

18. Letters from R. A. Falkenberg to Governor George C. Pardee, July 27, 1903; and from Governor Pardee to R. A. Falkenberg, July 21, 1903. Pardee Papers.

19. Letter from R. A. Falkenberg to Governor George C. Pardee, February 17, 1904. Pardee Papers.

20. Petition to Governor George C. Pardee, May 7, 1904. Pardee Papers.

21. Letter from Governor George C. Pardee to Jing Poo Hai, Chinese Consul General in San Francisco, February 25, 1905. Pardee Papers.

22. *Los Angeles Times*, March 30, 1905, pt. 2, p. 1.

23. *San Francisco Chronicle*, April 3, 1905, p. 4.

24. *Los Angeles Times*, March 30, 1905, pt. 2, p. 1.

25. Ibid.

26. Ibid.

27. *Los Angeles Times*, March 31, 1905, p. 7.

28. Ibid. and April 2, 1905, p. 4.

29. *Los Angeles Times*, April 3, 1905, p. 4.

30. *Los Angeles Times*, April 7, 1905; and *Los Angeles Examiner*, April 8, 1905.

31. *Los Angeles Times*, April 8, 1905, pt. 2, p. 6.

32. *Los Angeles Examiner*, April 8, 1905.

33. Ibid.

34. *Los Angeles Times*, April 11, 1905, pt. 2, p. 1.

35. See n. 17 above.

36. *Los Angeles Times*, March 30, 1905, pt. 2, p. 1.

37. *Los Angeles Times*, April 8, 1905, pt. 2, p. 6. See also *San Francisco Chronicle*, April 3, 1905, p. 4.

38. *San Francisco Chronicle*, April 3, 1905, p. 4.

39. *Los Angeles Times*, March 30, 1905, pt. 2, p. 1, and March 31, 1905, p. 7. See also *San Francisco Chronicle*, April 3, 1905, p. 4.

40. *San Francisco Chronicle*, May 4, 1905, p. 9, and p. 67 below.

41. See Feng Tzu-yu, *Chung-hua min-kuo k'ai-kuo-ch'ien ko-ming shih* [History of the Chinese Revolution before the Establishment of the Chinese Republic] (Shanghai, 1946), vol. 2, p. 107.

42. Glick, *Double Ten*, pp. 137–55.

43. Carl Glick and Hong Sheng-Hwa, *Swords of Silence. Chinese Secret Societies—Past and Present* (New York, 1947), pp. 167, 183–84.

44. See letters from Carl Glick to Richard E. Fuller, July 25, 1945; Richard E. Fuller to Carl Glick, July 28, 1945; Carl Glick to Richard E. Fuller, August 4, 1945; Hugh A. Matier to Carl Glick, August 11, 1945; Hugh A. Matier to Ansel O'Banion, August 11, 1945; Richard E. Fuller to Carl Glick, August 13, 1945. Carl Glick Papers. The University Libraries, University of Iowa, Iowa City. See also Glick and Hong, *Chinese Secret Societies*, pp. 184–85.

45. *New York Times*, May 15, 1904, p. 2.

46. Copy of letter from Edmund F. English, no address, April 22, 1904. NA, Microcopy 92, Roll 126.

47. Letter from Edmund F. English to S. R. Van Sant, St. Paul, Minn., May 23, 1904. Van Sant Papers, Minnesota State Archives. Quoted by Worden, "Chinese Reformer," p. 140, n. 53.

48. See letters from Secretary of State John Hay to Chinese Minister Sir Chentung Liang Chen, May 23, 1904. NA, Microcopy 99, Roll 14; John Hay to Secretary of the Treasury Leslie M. Shaw, June 2, 1904. NA, Microcopy 40, Roll 162; J. M. Bixbie to Secretary of War H. W. Taft, May 26, 1904, and Assistant Adjutant General E. R. Hills to J. M. Bixbie, June 4, 1904. Records of the Adjutant General's Office, Record Group 94, File 530187; W. T. G. Neal to U.S. Minister in China, Edwin Conger, June 8, 1904, and Edwin Conger to Secretary of State John Hay, June 24, 1904. NA, Microcopy 92, Roll 126; R. L. Flanigan to

Secretary of War, July 7, 1904; E. R. Hills to Major R. L. Flanigan, July 13, 1904. NA, Records of the Adjutant General's Office, Record Group 94, File 538315; E. Y. Webb to Secretary of War, September 2, 1904; Military Secretary, War Department, to E. Y. Webb, September 6, 1904. NA, Record Group 94, File 919711; Telegram from Colonel Jackson, U.S., to Military Secretary, October 10, 1904; Assistant Adjutant General to Colonel Jackson, October 14, 1904. NA, Records of the Adjutant General's Office, Record Group 94, File 932916.

49. Secretary of State John Hay to Chinese Minister Sir Chentung Liang Chen, May 23, 1904. NA Microcopy 99, Roll 14; and to Secretary of the Treasury Leslie M. Shaw, June 2, 1904. NA, Microcopy 40, Roll 162.

50. Letters from Fernand Parmentier to Secretary of State John Hay, July 1, 1904, and to Associated Press June 2, 1904. NA, Record Group 59, Misc. Letters, Microcopy 179, Roll 1216.

51. *Philadelphia Inquirer*, December 28, 1904, pp. 1–2.

52. *Fresno Morning Republican*, April 22, 1905, p. 12.

53. *San Francisco Call*, April 22, 1905, and *San Francisco Chronicle*, April 22, 1905, p. 3.

54. Letters from Governor Pardee to W. D. Crichton, May 4, 1905; W. D. Crichton to Governor Pardee, May 5, 1905; Dr. Chester Rowell to Governor Pardee, May 5, 1905; Governor Pardee to G. W. Jones, May 10, 1905; Governor Pardee to Dr. Chester Rowell and W. D. Crichton, May 10, 1905. Pardee Papers.

55. Telegram from Homer Lea to Governor Pardee, April 25, 1905. Pardee Papers.

56. Telegram from Homer Lea to Dr. David Starr Jordan, n.d. Stanford University Archives.

57. *St. Louis Globe-Democrat*, May 19, 1905, p. 1.

58. *Fresno Morning Republican*, May 16, 1905, p. 5, and June 17, 1905, p. 10. See also *San Francisco Chronicle*, May 18, 1905, p. 9.

59. Letter from Homer Lea to G. W. Jones, May 18, 1905. Pardee Papers.

60. Letters from G. W. Jones to Chinese Empire Reform Association, Fresno, May 22, 1905 and to Governor Pardee, May 22, 1905; Governor Pardee to G. W. Jones, May 30, 1905; private secretary of Governor Pardee to G. W. Jones, June 1, 1905. Pardee Papers.

61. *St. Louis Globe-Democrat*, May 19, 1905, p. 1.

62. *St. Louis Republic*, May 20, 1905, p. 2.

63. Letter from R. A. Falkenberg to Governor Pardee, May 18, 1905. Pardee Papers.

64. Letters from W. H. Eckley to Governor Pardee, May 24, 1905; Governor Pardee to R. A. Falkenberg, May 25, 1905, and to W. H. Eckley, May 30, 1905; R. A. Falkenberg to Governor Pardee, June 15, 1905; Governor Pardee to R. A. Falkenberg, June 16, 1905; R. A. Falkenberg to Governor Pardee, August 30, 1905. Pardee Papers.

65. Letter from R. A. Falkenberg to Department of State, October 30, 1905. NA, Record Group 59, Misc. Letters, Microcopy 179, Roll 1266.

66. Statement by R. A. Falkenberg to the Nevada State Senate, n.d.; letters from R. A. Falkenberg to President Theodore Roosevelt, January 16, 1908, and to Assistant Secretary of State, February 9, 1908. NA, Microcopy 862, Roll 735.

67. *San Francisco Chronicle*, April 3, 1905, p. 4, and May 4, 1905, p. 9.

68. *San Francisco Chronicle*, May 4, 1905, p. 9.

69. Letter from W. A. Hammel, L.A. Chief of Police, to Military Secretary, June 20, 1905. See also letters and notes from W. H. Eckley to Governor Frank W. Higgins, May 25, 1905; secretary of Governor Higgins to William H. Loeb, Jr., secretary of the President, May 27, 1905; William H. Loeb, Jr., to War Department, May 29, 1905; War Department to Judge Advocate General, May 31, 1905; Judge Advocate General's Office to Military Secretary, War Department, June 3, 1905; Lieutenant General Chaffee, Chief of Staff, to Military Secretary, June 7, 1905; Military Secretary to L.A. Chief of Police, June 8, 1905; Lieutenant General Chaffee to Military Secretary, June 20, 1905; Military Secretary to Judge Advocate General, June 28, 1905; Judge Advocate General to Military Secretary, June 30, 1905; Acting Secretary of War to Secretary of State, July 3, 1905; Military Secretary to Governor Higgins, July 3, 1905; Acting Secretary of State to Acting Secretary of War, July 14, 1905; Acting Secretary of War to Secretary of State, July 18, 1905. NA, Record Group 94, File 1019722. See also *New York Times*, June 21, 1905, p. 4.

70. *Evening Post* (New York), June 20, 1905, p. 1.

71. *New York Tribune*, June 23, 1905, p. 7.

72. *New York American*, June 25, 1905, p. 37.

73. Letter from R. J. Faneuf to Governor Pardee, September 28, 1905. Pardee Papers.

74. Letter from Homer Lea to Governor Pardee, October 7, 1905. Pardee Papers.

75. Ibid.

76. Ibid.

77. See pp. 74–75 below.

78. Letters of California Assistant Adjutant General to Governor Pardee, October 9, 1905, and Governor Pardee to Homer Lea, October 13, 1905. Pardee Papers.

Chapter 5

1. *Los Angeles Examiner*, April 8, 1905.

2. Stimson, "Los Angeles Jeremiah," pp. 6–7.

3. Worden, Chinese Reformer, p. 265.

4. *St. Louis Republic*, May 19, 1905, p. 3.

5. *St. Louis Globe-Democrat*, May 20, 1905, p. 3; *St. Louis Republic*, May 20, 1905, p. 3; see also *Ninety-First Annual Report of the American Baptist*

Missionary Union, 1904–1905 (Boston, 1905), as cited by Worden, "Chinese Reformer," p. 153.

6. See Jordan, *Days of a Man*, vol. 2, pp. 33–34.

7. *St. Louis Post-Dispatch*, May 19, 1905, pt. 2, p. 13.

8. Ibid.

9. *Chicago Daily Tribune*, May 24, 1905, p. 7; *Chicago Daily Herald*, May 24, 1905, p. 3; *Chicago Daily News*, May 23, 1905, p. 8.

10. *Inter-Ocean* (Chicago), May 25, 1905, p. 12; *Chicago Daily Tribune*, May 25, 1905, p. 16.

11. *Los Angeles Times*, June 11, 1905, p. 4.

12. *Chicago Daily Journal*, May 23, 1905, p. 1.

13. Letters from Homer Lea to Dr. David Starr Jordan, May 10 and June 3, 1905. Stanford University Archives.

14. See Worden, "Chinese Reformer," p. 158, and *Pittsburg Gazette*, June 18, 1905, p. 2 and June 19, 1905, p. 3.

15. Diary of Secretary John M. Hay, June 15, 1905, in John Milton Hay Papers, Container 1, Library of Congress.

16. *New York Daily Tribune*, June 25, 1905, p. 3.

17. Glick, *Double Ten*, p. 133.

18. See letter from K'ang Yu-wei to President Theodore Roosevelt, September 14, 1905 and January 30, 1906, reprinted in Worden, "Chinese Reformer," apps. C and D, pp. 281–305.

19. See Worden, "Chinese Reformer," p. 163.

20. *Baltimore American*, June 10, 1905, p. 15; June 11, 1905, p. 8; June 12, 1905, p. 12; *Baltimore Sun*, June 11, 1905, p. 16; June 12, 1905, p. 12.

21. *Pittsburg Dispatch*, June 18, 1905, p. 2, and June 19, 1905, p. 3.

22. *Public Ledger* (Philadelphia), June 24, 1905, p. 3; see also *Philadelphia Inquirer*, June 25, 1905, p. 2, and *North American* (Philadelphia), June 25, 1905, p. 3.

23. *Public Ledger* (Philadelphia), June 24, 1905, p. 3; see also *Philadelphia Free Press*, June 25, 1905, p. 3.

24. *Philadelphia Inquirer*, June 26, 1905, pp. 1–2; see also *Public Ledger* (Philadelphia), June 26, 1905, p. 2.

25. *Philadelphia Inquirer*, June 25, 1905, p. 2.

26. *Philadelphia Inquirer*, June 26, 1905, pp. 1–2.

27. *Chicago Daily Tribune*, June 26, 1905, p. 3.

28. *New York Times*, June 13, 1905, p. 9.

29. *New York Herald*, June 28, 1905, p. 5.

30. *New York Sun*, June 28, 1905, p. 2.

31. *New York Tribune*, July 5, 1905, p. 4.

32. *Los Angeles Times*, June 26, 1905, p. 2.

33. *Boston Journal*, July 6, 1905, p. 6, and July 10, 1905, p. 3; *Boston Globe*, July 6, 1905, evening ed., p. 11; July 7, 1905, p. 14; July 10, 1905, p. 3; *Boston Herald*, July 10, 1905, p. 7.

34. *Hartford Courant*, July 14, 1905, p. 8.

35. *Hartford Courant*, July 17, 1905, pt. 2, p. 11, and July 20, 1905, pt. 2, p. 1; *Hartford Times*, July 20, 1905, p. 3.

36. *Hartford Courant*, July 17, 1905, pt. 2, p. 11.

37. *Hartford Courant*, July 18, 1905, pt. 2, p. 1.

38. *Hartford Courant*, July 20, 1905, p. 18.

39. *New York Tribune*, July 23, 1905, p. 4.

40. *Hartford Courant*, July 26, 1905, p. 8.

41. See enclosure to letter from R. A. Falkenberg to State Department, October 30, 1905. NA, Record Group 59, Misc. Letters, Microcopy 179, Roll 1266.

42. *New York Tribune*, January 20, 1906, p. 2.

43. Newmark, *Jottings in Southern California*, p. 139.

44. Armentrout-Ma, "Chinese Politics," pp. 386, 414. According to her personal communication to the author, Dr. Ma relied on statements by Dr. Jung-pang Lo who was said to have spoken "with some of these former cadets." Lo was the grandson of K'ang Yung-wei.

45. Glick, *Double Ten*, pp. 231–44, 253–57.

46. Ibid., p. 278.

47. Criminal Case File No. 828, Minute Books, vols. 18–20, Records of the Federal District Court of California. Federal Records Center, Laguna Niguel, Calif.

48. Letter of Homer Lea to Ethel Powers, September 20, 1908. Powers Papers.

49. See n. 41 above.

50. Letter from H. G. Otis to Homer Lea, May 24, 1909. Powers Papers.

51. Letter from Ansel O'Banion to A. H. Powers, May 9, 1943. Powers Papers.

52. Glick, *Double Ten*, p. 286.

53. See Chün-tu Hsüeh, *Huang Hsing and the Chinese Revolution* (Stanford, 1961), p. 79.

54. Letter from Sun Yat-sen to Homer Lea, November 7, 1910. Powers Papers.

55. Letter from G. W. Gibbs to Homer Lea, September 4, 1912. Powers Papers. Fred C. Husman, previously captain of Company A of the Chinese Imperial Reform Army in St. Louis, mentioned in a letter of July 24, 1942 to Captain A. E. O'Banion that "things as you know blew up about 1910 with the change of feeling towards a wider move with Dr. Sun." Glick Papers, University of Iowa Library, Iowa City, Iowa.

56. See Gowen and Hall, *History of China*, p. 352.

57. Kwang Ching Liu, *Americans and Chinese. A Historical Essay and a Bibliography* (Cambridge, Mass., 1963), p. 29.

58. *New York Times*, November 25, 1911, p. 5.

59. *New York Times*, December 29, 1911, p. 5. See also p. 170 below.

60. See Chapin, "Homer Lea," p. 86.

61. *Hartford Courant*, July 20, 1905, p. 18.

62. Chapin, "Homer Lea," pp. 87, 91.

63. Letter from Homer Lea to Charles B. Boothe, April 7, 1908. Boothe Papers.

64. Letter from Charles B. Boothe to K'ang Yu-wei, June 14, 1909. Boothe Papers.

65. Letter from Ansel O'Banion to A. H. Powers, March 22, 1943. Powers Papers.

66. See Chapin, "Homer Lea," pp. 89–90.

67. Letter from Charles B. Boothe to Yung Wing, March 6, 1909. Boothe Papers.

68. Letter from W. W. Allen to Charles B. Boothe, January 21, 1909. Boothe Papers.

69. Sun Yat-sen, "My Reminiscences," p. 305.

70. Armentrout-Ma, "Chinese Politics," pp. 163, 286, 311, 313, 316. See also p. 33 above.

71. Letter from Homer Lea to Ethel Powers, September 20, 1908. Powers Papers.

Chapter 6

1. Letter from Homer Lea to Governor Pardee, October 7, 1905. Pardee Papers.

2. See letter from Homer Lea to David Starr Jordan, May 10, 1908. Stanford University Archives. See also his letter to W. G. Jones, May 18, 1905. Pardee Papers.

3. *San Francisco Chronicle*, October 31, 1905, p. 15.

4. *Los Angeles Times*, June 7, 1905, pt. 2, p. 1.

5. Irwin, *Making of a Reporter*, p. 21.

6. Lea, *Vermilion Pencil*, pp. 28–32.

7. Ibid., p. 144.

8. Ibid., pp. 327–28.

9. Irwin, *Making of a Reporter*, p. 21.

10. Homer Lea, "The Red Dawn of China," unpublished manuscript, pp. 9–10. Powers Papers.

11. *New York Times*, lit. sec., March 14, 1908, p. 13, and June 13, 1908, p. 340.

12. *Outlook* 88 (April 11, 1908): 767.

13. *Nation* 86 (April 1908): 354.

14. Roger Daniels, *The Politics of Prejudice. The Anti-Japanese Movement in California and the Struggle for Japanese Exclusion* (Berkeley, 1962), p. 141, n. 30.

15. Handwritten note by Joshua B. Powers, in Chapin, "Unpublished Manuscript." Powers Papers.

16. Green, "She Knew Him Well."

17. Newmark, *Jottings in Southern California*, pp. 140–41.

18. Verbal communication to author by Joshua B. Powers.

19. Handwritten note by Joshua B. Powers, in Chapin, "Unpublished Manuscript." Powers Papers.

20. Letter from Homer Lea to Ethel Powers, September 20, 1908. Powers Papers.

21. Chapin, "Unpublished Manuscript," p. 261. Powers Papers. Documentary evidence of date and place of marriage is not available, but all subsequent passports in possession of Joshua B. Powers and other official documents give her name as "Mrs. Ethel Lea."

22. Willard Huntington Wright, "Homer Lea Sorely Stricken," *Los Angeles Times*, August 4, 1912, pt. 5, p. 21.

23. Personal communication to the author.

24. Lea, *Vermilion Pencil*, pp. 28–32.

25. Chapin, "Unpublished Manuscript." Powers Papers. The letter itself cannot be found.

26. Letter of Ethel Lea to her sisters Agnes and Mamie, March 16, 1912. Powers Papers.

27. Newmark, *Jottings in Southern California*, p. 144.

28. Undated deposition by Marco Newmark. Powers Papers.

29. Undated deposition by Watson Lea. Powers Papers. See also Mary L. Roberts, "Oregon Relative Tells of War Prophet," *Portland Journal*, March 22, 1942.

30. Lea, *Valor of Ignorance*, p. 344.

31. Green, "She Knew Him Well."

32. Letter from Homer Lea to Charles B. Boothe, April 7, 1908. Boothe Papers.

33. Letter from Homer Lea to Ethel Powers, September 20, 1908. Powers Papers.

34. Letter from Charles B. Boothe to W. W. Allen, February 3, 1909. Boothe Papers.

35. See publishing contract between Harper & Brothers and Homer Lea, June 17, 1909. Powers Papers.

36. Letter from Charles B. Boothe to W. W. Allen, February 12, 1909. Boothe Papers.

37. Letter from Sun Yat-sen to Charles B. Boothe, July 15, 1910. Boothe Papers.

38. Letters from W. W. Allen to Charles B. Boothe, March 31, 1910, Boothe Papers; Sir Tollemache Sinclair to Homer Lea, May 3, 1911; Clarence W. McIlvaine of Harper & Brothers, London, to Homer Lea, October 26, 1912. Powers Papers.

39. Letter from Sun Yat-sen to Homer Lea, November 7, 1910. Powers Papers.

40. Marius B. Jansen, *The Japanese and Sun Yat-sen* (Cambridge, Mass., 1967), p. 253, n. 77.

41. Letter from Koki H. Ike to Homer Lea, November 10, 1911. Powers Papers, Chapin, "Unpublished Manuscript," p. 257.

42. See news release by Japanese publisher as reprinted in *World Peace Foundation Pamphlet Series*, vol. 2, 1912, p. 4.

43. John Costello, *The Pacific War, 1941–1945* (New York, 1982), p. 32, refers to Lea's assessment as the basis of U.S. military strategy in the Pacific. For similar predictions by others and a more critical view of Lea see Daniels, *Politics of Prejudice*, pp. 71–74. See also George E. Mowry, *The Era of Theodore Roosevelt, 1900–1912* (New York, 1958), pp. 188–89.

44. See Louis Morton, "The War Plan Orange," *World Politics* 11 (January 1959): 221–23; Richard D. Challener, *Admirals, Generals, and the American Foreign Policy, 1898–1914* (Princeton, 1973), pp. 30–34; and Costello, *Pacific War*, p. 32.

45. William Reynold Braisted, *The United States Navy in the Pacific, 1909–1922* (Austin, Tex., 1971), pp. 30–35.

46. Letter from Lord Roberts to Homer Lea, March 5, 1910. Powers Papers.

47. Robert Young, "The Impudence of Charlatanism," *Japan Chronicle* (Kobe), February 11, 1912, reprinted with a letter to the editor from Dr. David Starr Jordan, January 10, 1912, in *World Peace Foundation Pamphlet Series*, vol. 2, 1912.

48. See Wilbur, *Sun Yat-sen*, p. 68, and Schiffrin, *Sun Yat-sen and the Origins*, p. 139. For the author's view see p. 134 below.

49. Letter from Sun Yat-sen to Homer Lea, March 24, 1910. Powers Papers.

50. Glick, *Double Ten*, pp. 192–208.

51. *San Francisco Chronicle*, November 19, 1910, p. 1. See also *San Francisco Call*, November 18, 1910, pp. 1–3, and November 19, 1910, p. 1; and *San Francisco Examiner*, November 19, 1910, p. 1.

52. Valeriu Marcu, "American Prophet of Total War," *American Mercury* 54 (April 1942): 474.

53. Charles A. Willoughby and John Chamberlain, *MacArthur, 1941–1951* (New York, 1954), p. 19. See also *Reports of General MacArthur. The Campaigns of MacArthur in the Pacific*, prepared by his General Staff (Washington, D.C. 1966), vol. 1, pp. 3, 174–76.

54. Willoughby and Chamberlain, *MacArthur*, p. 1.

55. Clare Boothe, "Ever Hear of Homer Lea?" *Saturday Evening Post* 214 (March 14, 1942): 27, 38–40.

56. Homer Lea, "Preface" to *The Day of the Saxon* (New York, 1912, 1942).

57. Letter from Clarence W. McIlvaine to Homer Lea, March 18, 1912. Powers Papers.

58. Letter from Lord Roberts to Homer Lea, November 13, 1911. Powers Papers.

59. Letter from Clarence W. McIlvaine to Homer Lea, October 26, 1912. Powers Papers.

60. Homer Lea, *Des Britischen Reiches Schicksalsstunde. Mahnwort eines Angelsachsen*. Aus dem Englischen mit einer Einführung von Graf E. Reventlow (Berlin, 1913).

61. See letter from J. Chockman to Homer and Ethel Lea, July 5, 1912. Powers Papers.

62. Letter from John S. Phillips to Homer Lea, October 7, 1912. Powers Papers.

63. Letter from Homer Lea to Lord Roberts, April 15, 1910. National Army Museum, London.

64. Lea, *Day of the Saxon*, p. 5.

65. See pp. 186–87 below.

66. Robert Strausz-Hupé, *Geopolitics and the Struggle for Space and Power* (New York, 1942), p. 248.

67. Edward Mead Earle, "Introduction" to *Makers of Modern Strategy. Military Thought from Machiavelli to Hitler* (Princeton, 1943), p. xi.

68. Lea, *Valor of Ignorance*, p. 27. See also p. 184 below.

69. Strausz-Hupé, *Geopolitics*, p. 249.

70. Reventlow, "Introduction" to Lea, *Britischen Reiches*, p. xliii.

Chapter 7

1. See letters from Charles B. Boothe to Governor Pardee, May 12, 1905, Pardee Papers; and to K'ang Yu-wei, June 14, 1909, Powers Papers.

2. Julian Hartt, "American Plot for China Revolt Revealed," *Los Angeles Times*, October 13, 1966.

3. See letters from Homer Lea to Charles B. Boothe, April 7, 1908; and from Charles B. Boothe to Homer Lea, September 11, 1908. Boothe Papers.

4. Letter from Homer Lea to Charles B. Boothe, September 21, 1908. Boothe Papers.

5. Ibid.

6. Homer Lea, "The Boycott—China's Mighty Weapon," *Van Norden's Magazine* 3 (July 1908): 49–57.

7. Letter from Homer Lea to Charles B. Boothe, September 21, 1908. Boothe Papers.

8. See *Kuo-Fu Nien P'u Tseng Ting Pen*, vol. 1, p. 299; and Lo Hsiang-lin, "Kuo-fu yü Han-ma Li Chiang-chün" [The Father of the Country and General Homer Lea], in *Kuo-fu yü Ou-Mei chih yu-hao* [The Father of the Country and His European and American Friends], (Taipei, 1951).

9. Homer Lea, "How Socialism Failed in China," *Van Norden's Magazine* 3 (September 1908): 107–113 and 3 (October 1908): 81–85.

10. See Margaret Field, "The China Boycott of 1905," *Center for East Asian Studies*, Harvard University, 11 (December 1957): 63–98. See also Harold

Z. Schiffrin, *Sun Yat-sen. Reluctant Revolutionary* (Boston, 1980), pp. 112, 276.

11. See, for instance, John Meskill, ed., *The Patterns of Chinese History* (Lexington, Mass., 1965), pp. 55–69; Frederic Wakeman, Jr., *The Fall of Imperial China* (New York, 1975), pp. 55–70; and Schiffrin, *Reluctant Revolutionary*, p. 17.

12. Lea, "How Socialism Failed," p. 108.

13. Homer Lea, "Can China Fight?" *The World To-Day* 12 (February 1907): 137–46.

14. See Ralph L. Powell, *The Rise of Chinese Military Power, 1895–1912* (Princeton, 1955), p. 338. See also Payson J. Trent, *The Far East. A Political and Diplomatic History* (New York, 1935), p. 421, and Mary Clabaugh Wright, ed., "Introduction," *China in Revolution: The First Phase, 1900–1913* (New Haven, 1968), pp. 27, 35–36.

15. Lea, "How Socialism Failed," pp. 108–9.

16. Letter from Homer Lea to Charles B. Boothe, October 5, 1908. Boothe Papers.

17. Letter from W. W. Allen to Charles B. Boothe, November 15, 1908. Boothe Papers.

18. Letter from Homer Lea to Ethel Powers, September 20, 1908. Powers Papers.

19. Letters from Charles B. Boothe to K'ang Yu-wei, June 14, 1909; and to Yung Wing, June 11, 1909. Boothe Papers.

20. Letter from Adna R. Chaffee to Homer Lea, May 18, 1909. Powers Papers.

21. Letter from H. G. Otis to Homer Lea, May 24, 1909. Powers Papers.

22. Letters from Homer Lea to David Starr Jordan, April 23 and May 6, 1909. Stanford University Archives.

23. See letters from Homer Lea to Charles B. Boothe, September 21 and October 5, 1908. Boothe Papers.

24. See Tse, *Chinese Republic*, p. 25.

25. Letter from Charles B. Boothe to Yung Wing, December 28, 1908. Boothe Papers.

26. Letter from W. W. Allen to Charles B. Boothe, November 25, 1908. Boothe Papers.

27. Letter from Yung Wing to Charles B. Boothe, October 21, 1908. Boothe Papers.

28. Letter from Yung Wing to Homer Lea, December 4, 1908. Boothe Papers.

29. Letter from Charles B. Boothe to W. W. Allen, February 12, 1909. Boothe Papers.

30. Letter from Yung Wing to Charles B. Boothe, December 14, 1908. Boothe Papers.

31. Yung Wing, "Letter of invitation," n.d. Boothe Papers.

32. Letter from Yung Wing to Charles B. Boothe, December 14, 1908. Boothe Papers.

33. Letter from W. W. Allen to Charles B. Boothe, January 29, 1909. Boothe Papers.

34. Letter from Yung Wing to Charles B. Boothe, January 25, 1909. Boothe Papers.

35. Letter from Charles B. Boothe to W. W. Allen, January 3, 1909. Boothe Papers.

36. Letter from Charles B. Boothe to W. W. Allen, January 3, 1909. Boothe Papers.

37. See Worden, "Chinese Reformer," pp. 229–30, for speculations about the death of the Kuang-hsü Emperor.

38. See ibid., pp. 227–28, 231–34.

39. Letter from Yung Wing to Charles B. Boothe, January 4, 1909. Boothe Papers.

40. Letters from Yung Wing to Charles B. Boothe and Homer Lea, January 16, 1909; and to Charles B. Boothe, January 25, 1909. Boothe Papers.

41. Letter from W. W. Allen to Charles B. Boothe, January 21, 1909. Boothe Papers.

42. Letter from Yung Wing to Charles B. Boothe and Homer Lea, January 16, 1909. Boothe Papers.

43. See Ganschow, "Sun Yat-sen's Contacts," pp. 54–59.

44. Letter from Yung Wing to Charles B. Boothe and Homer Lea, January 16, 1909. Boothe Papers.

45. Letter from Yung Wing to Charles B. Boothe, January 25, 1909. Boothe Papers.

46. Letter from Charles B. Boothe to W. W. Allen, January 25, 1909. Boothe Papers.

47. Yung Wing, "Wants of China," n.d. Boothe Papers.

48. Letter from W. W. Allen to Charles B. Boothe, January 2, 1909. Boothe Papers.

49. Yung Wing, "Wants of China," n.d. Boothe Papers.

50. W. W. Allen, "A Plan. (Revision No. 1)," January 27, 1909. Boothe Papers.

51. Letters from W. W. Allen to Charles B. Boothe, January 12 and 29, 1909. Boothe Papers.

52. Letter from Charles B. Boothe to W. W. Allen, December 28, 1908. Boothe Papers.

53. Letters from W. W. Allen to Charles B. Boothe, January 29 and February 1, 1909. Boothe Papers.

54. Letter from Charles B. Boothe to W. W. Allen, February 3, 1909. Boothe Papers.

55. Letter from W. W. Allen to Charles B. Boothe, January 21, 1909. Boothe Papers.

56. Letter from Charles B. Boothe to W. W. Allen, February 3, 1909. Boothe Papers.

57. Yung Wing, "A plan to negotiate a loan," undated four-page document. Boothe Papers.

58. Allen, "A Plan."

59. Letter from W. W. Allen to Charles B. Boothe, February 13, 1909. Boothe Papers.

60. Letter from Charles B. Boothe to W. W. Allen, February 3, 1909. Boothe Papers.

61. Letter from W. W. Allen to Charles B. Boothe, February 6, 1909. Boothe Papers.

62. Letters from W. W. Allen to Charles B. Boothe, February 6 and 13, 1909. Boothe Papers.

63. Letter from W. W. Allen to Charles B. Boothe, February 6, 1909. Boothe Papers.

64. Ibid.

65. Letters from Yung Wing to Charles B. Boothe, February 19 and 22, 1909. Boothe Papers.

66. Letter from W. W. Allen to Charles B. Boothe, January 29, 1909. Boothe Papers.

67. Letter from Charles B. Boothe to Yung Wing, March 6, 1909. Boothe Papers.

68. Letters from Yung Wing to Charles B. Boothe, June 5, 1909, and from Charles B. Boothe to Yung Wing, June 11, 1909. See also letters from Charles B. Boothe to W. W. Allen, February 12, 1909; from Charles B. Boothe to Yung Wing, February 12 and 15, 1909 and March 6, 1909; and from W. W. Allen to Charles B. Boothe, March 1, 1909. Boothe Papers.

Chapter 8

1. Letter from Yung Wing to Charles B. Boothe, September 14, 1909. Boothe Papers.

2. Letter from Charles B. Boothe to Yung Wing, October 2, 1909. Boothe Papers.

3. Letter from Yung Wing to Charles B. Boothe, October 20, 1909. Boothe Papers.

4. Letter from Charles B. Boothe to Yung Wing, December 23, 1909. Boothe Papers.

5. See Yen-p'ing Hao, "The Abortive Cooperation Between Reformers and Revolutionaries (1895–1900)," *Papers on China*, vol. 15, Harvard University East Asian Research Center, December 1961, p. 103. See also pp. 23–24 above.

6. Tse, *Chinese Republic*, p. 18.

7. Yung Wing, *Diary for the Year 1902*, entry on April 10, 1902.

8. See the Chinese source quoted by Wilbur, *Sun Yat-sen*, p. 68; see also Schiffrin, *Reluctant Revolutionary*, p. 139.

9. See Shelley Hsien Cheng, "The T'ung-meng-hui: Its Organization, Leadership and Finances, 1905–1912." Ph.D. dissertation, University of Washington, 1962, p. 124.

10. Letter from W. W. Allen to Charles B. Boothe, January 21, 1909. Boothe Papers.

11. Letter from W. W. Allen to Charles B. Boothe, March 14, 1910. Boothe Papers.

12. See Harold Z. Schiffrin, "The Enigma of Sun Yat-sen," in Mary Clabaugh Wright, ed., *China in Revolution: The First Phase, 1900–1913* (New Haven, 1968), pp. 467–71.

13. Letter from Yung Wing to Sun Yat-sen, February 15, 1910. Boothe Papers.

14. Letter from Sun Yat-sen to Homer Lea, February 24, 1910. Boothe Papers.

15. Letters from Yung Wing to Charles B. Boothe, March 4, 16, and 28, 1910. Boothe Papers.

16. Letter from Sun Yat-sen to Charles B. Boothe, April 5, 1910. Boothe Papers.

17. Letter from Yung Wing to Charles B. Boothe, May 26, 1910. Boothe Papers.

18. Letter from Yung Wing to Charles B. Boothe, November 10, 1910. Boothe Papers.

19. Tse, *Chinese Republic*, p. 28.

20. See Edmund H. Worthy, Jr., "Yung Wing in America," *Pacific Historical Review* 34 (1965): 286.

21. See letters from Sun Yat-sen to Ethel Lea, November 14, 1912; December 23, 1913; June 17, September 13, and December 31, 1914; November 10, 1915; January 11 and October 19, 1916; August 5, 1921; and February 11, 1922. Powers Papers. There may have been others. Ethel Lea's letters to Sun Yat-sen have not been preserved.

22. Eulogy by Sun Yat-sen on the death of Homer Lea. *China Press* (Shanghai), November 6, 1912. Powers Papers.

23. See Schiffrin, *Reluctant Revolutionary*, p. 31.

24. Ibid., p. 5.

25. See Schiffrin, "Enigma of Sun Yat-sen," pp. 466–70, and *Reluctant Revolutionary*, pp. 4–6, 270–71. See also Wilbur, *Sun Yat-sen*, p. 75.

26. Wilbur, *Sun Yat-sen*, p. 7.

27. Sun Yat-sen, *Kuo fu ch'üan chi* [The Complete Works] (Taipei, 1973), vol. 5, p. 121.

28. See letter from Sun Yat-sen to Charles B. Boothe, March 21, 1910. Boothe Papers.

29. Untitled three-page document, dated March 12, 1910. Boothe Papers.

30. See Cheng, "T'ung-meng-hui," p. 337, and Schiffrin, *Reluctant Revolutionary*, p. 140.

31. See Hsüeh, *Huang Hsing*, pp. 80–81.

32. See Jean Chesneaux, *Secret Societies in China in the Nineteenth and Twentieth Centuries* (Ann Arbor, 1971), pp. 42–43.

33. See Yoshihiro Hatano, "The New Armies," in Mary Clabaugh Wright, ed., *China in Revolution: The First Phase 1900-1913* (New Haven, 1968), p. 207.

34. Hsüeh, *Huang Hsing*, pp. 77, 80.

35. Document entitled "Memorandum of March 14, 1910." Boothe Papers.

36. Handwritten notes by Homer Lea. Boothe Papers.

37. Power-of-Attorney, signed in Los Angeles, California, March 14, 1910. Boothe Papers.

38. Letter from Charles B. Boothe to W. W. Allen, July 19, 1910. Boothe Papers.

39. Letter from Sun Yat-sen to Homer Lea, September 5, 1910. Boothe Papers.

40. Hsüeh, *Huang Hsing*, pp. 79–80.

41. Letters from Sun Yat-sen to Homer Lea, May 9 and 24, 1910. Powers Papers. See also Hsüeh, *Huang Hsing*, p. 79.

42. Hsüeh, *Huang Hsing*, pp. 52–53, 82.

43. Letter from Sun Yat-sen to Homer Lea, September 25, 1911. Powers Papers.

44. "Memorandum of March 14, 1910." Boothe Papers.

45. Letter from Sun Yat-sen to Homer Lea, May 9, 1910. Powers Papers.

46. Letter from Sun Yat-sen to Homer Lea, May 24, 1910. Powers Papers.

47. Letter from Sun Yat-sen to Charles B. Boothe, May 21, 1910. Boothe Papers.

48. Copy of letter from Sun Yat-sen to Homer Lea, April 10, 1910. Boothe Papers.

49. Letter from W. W. Allen to Charles B. Boothe, April 4, 1910. Boothe Papers.

50. Letter from Charles B. Boothe to Sun Yat-sen, May 12, 1910. Boothe Papers.

51. Ibid.

52. Letter from W. W. Allen to Charles B. Boothe, April 4, 1910. Boothe Papers.

53. Letter from Charles B. Boothe to Sun Yat-sen, May 12, 1910. Boothe Papers.

54. Letter from Homer Lea to W. W. Allen, June 13, 1910, and telegram to Charles B. Boothe, June 21, 1910. Boothe Papers.

55. Letters from Sun Yat-sen to Charles B. Boothe, June 22 and September 4, 1910. Boothe Papers.

56. Letter from W. W. Allen to Charles B. Boothe, July 23, 1910. Boothe Papers.

57. Letter from W. W. Allen to Charles B. Boothe, July 12, 1910. See also Charles B. Boothe to W. W. Allen, July 19, 1910. Boothe Papers.

58. Letter from Sun Yat-sen to Charles B. Boothe, September 4, 1910. Boothe Papers.

59. Letter from Sun Yat-sen to Homer Lea, September 5, 1910. Boothe Papers.

60. Letter from Sun Yat-sen to Homer Lea, September 29, 1910. Powers Papers.

61. Letter from Sun Yat-sen to Homer Lea, November 7, 1910. Powers Papers. See also Sun Yat-sen to Charles B. Boothe, November 8, 1910. Boothe Papers.

62. Letter from Charles B. Boothe to Sun Yat-sen, October 21, 1910. Boothe Papers.

63. Letter from Homer Lea to Charles B. Boothe, September 21, 1910. Boothe Papers.

64. Letters from Charles B. Boothe to C. B. Hill, January 12, 1911, and from C. B. Hill to Charles B. Boothe, March 3, 1911. Boothe Papers.

65. See Hsüeh, *Huang Hsing*, pp. 83–84.

66. Letter from Sun Yat-sen to Charles B. Boothe, November 8, 1910. Boothe Papers.

67. Letter from Charles B. Boothe to Sun Yat-sen, December 16, 1910. Boothe Papers.

68. Letter from Homer Lea to Charles B. Boothe, September 21, 1910. Boothe Papers.

69. Letter from Sun Yat-sen to Charles B. Boothe, March 6, 1911. Boothe Papers.

70. Letter from Charles B. Boothe to Sun Yat-sen, April 13, 1911. Boothe Papers.

71. See Foster Rhea Dulles, *China and America. The Story of Their Relations Since 1784* (Princeton, 1946), pp. 126–32.

72. Letter from Sun Yat-sen to Homer Lea, September 5, 1910. Boothe Papers.

73. Letters from Charles B. Boothe to Yung Wing, June 11, 1909, and from Homer Lea to Charles B. Boothe, June 26, 1910. Boothe Papers.

74. Letter from Charles B. Boothe to Sun Yat-sen, September 26, 1910. Boothe Papers.

75. Homer Lea, "The Aeroplane in War," *Harper's Weekly* 54 (August 20, 1910): 8–9; 54 (August 27, 1910): 11, 26.

76. See p. 99 above.

77. Letter from Sir Tollemache Sinclair to Homer Lea, May 3, 1911. Powers Papers.

78. See letter from Sun Yat-sen to Homer Lea, August 10, 1911. Powers Papers.

79. See undated draft of a letter from Homer Lea to Senator Elihu Root, probably of November 2, 1911. Powers Papers.

80. See report from the Division of Far Eastern Affairs, State Department, to Secretary of State Philander Knox, November 14, 1911. NA, Knox Papers.

81 Ibid.

82. Letter from Sun Yat-sen to Homer Lea, August 10, 1911. Powers Papers.

83. Letter from Senator Elihu Root to Homer Lea, September 19, 1911. Powers Papers.

84. Letter from Sun Yat-sen to Homer Lea, September 25, 1911. Powers Papers.

Chapter 9

1. Letter from Sun Yat-sen to Homer Lea, August 10, 1911. Powers Papers.

2. Letter from Homer Lea to an unnamed friend, August 18, 1911. Powers Papers.

3. Ibid.

4. Letter from Ethel Lea to Joshua B. Powers, September 3, 1911. Powers Papers.

5. Lea, *Day of the Saxon*, p. 132.

6. Letter from the Military Attaché, U.S. Embassy, Berlin, to Homer Lea, August 9, 1911. Powers Papers.

7. Letter from Homer Lea to an unnamed friend, August 11, 1911. Powers Papers.

8. Letter from the military attaché, U.S. Embassy, Berlin, to Homer Lea, August 9, 1911. Powers Papers.

9. See map in Powers Papers. Another map refers to the maneuvers of the Second Imperial Guard Division, held in the fall of 1910 near Berlin.

10. See Ethel Lea's handwritten notes to her sister Agnes on copy of Homer Lea's letter to an unnamed friend, August 11, 1911. Powers Papers.

11. Clare Boothe, "Introduction" to Lea, *The Valor of Ignorance*, 1942 edition, p. 26.

12. Letter from Homer Lea to an unnamed friend, August 11, 1911. Powers Papers.

13. Sun Yat-sen, *Memoirs of a Chinese Revolutionary* (London, 1927), pp. 219–20. See also Leonard S. Hsü, *Sun Yat-sen. His Political and Social Ideals* (Los Angeles, 1933), pp. 78–79.

14. Hsü, *Sun Yat-sen*, pp. 78–79, and Sun Yat-sen, *Memoirs*, p. 220.

15. See Ganschow, "Sun Yat-sen's Contacts," pp. 73–75.

16. See Ethel Lea in Gowen and Hall, *History of China*, p. 352, and Chapin, "Unpublished Manuscript," p. 274. The cable has not been preserved.

17. Letter from Ethel Lea to her sister Agnes, October 23, 1911. Powers Papers.

18. See letter from Homer Lea to Ethel, quoted in Chapin, "Unpublished Manuscript," p. 275. The letter cannot be found.

19. Undated letter from Homer Lea to Lord Roberts, written on stationery of Savoy Hotel, London, probably written on October 19, 1911. National Army Museum, London.

20. Letter from Lord Roberts to Homer Lea, March 5, 1910. National Army Museum, London.

21. Letter from Homer Lea to Lord Roberts, April 15, 1910. National Army Museum, London.

22. See undated letter from Homer Lea to Lord Roberts, n. 6 above.

23. See letter from Harold F. Wyatt to Homer Lea, October 4, 1911. Powers Papers. See also *Times* (London), November 16, 1911, p. 3.

24. See letter from Charles Beresford to Homer Lea, March 8, 1912. Powers Papers.

25. Letter from Ethel Lea to her sister Agnes, October 23, 1911. Powers Papers.

26. Ibid. and Chapin, "Unpublished Manuscript," p. 278. Powers Papers.

27. See publishing contract with Harper & Brothers, October 25, 1911. Powers Papers.

28. *Times* (London), October 28, 1911, p. 8.

29. Cable from Sun Yat-sen to Homer Lea, October 31, 1911. Powers Papers.

30. Cable from Sun Yat-sen to Homer Lea, November 1, 1911. Powers Papers.

31. Letter from Homer Lea to Lord Roberts, Wednesday, n.d., probably of November 2, 1911. National Army Museum, London.

32. Undated copy of letter from Homer Lea to Senator Elihu Root, probably of November 2, 1911. Powers Papers.

33. See letters from Sir Edward Grey's secretary to Lord Roberts, November 7, 1911, and from Lord Roberts to Homer Lea, November 8, 1911. Powers Papers.

34. Letter from Lord Roberts to Homer Lea, November 8, 1911. Powers Papers.

35. Chapin, "Unpublished Manuscript," p. 284.

36. Ibid., p. 262.

37. See Tse, *Chinese Republic*, p. 25.

38. See letter from Sir Edward Grey to Sir J. Jordan, November 14, 1911. PRO, FO 371/1095.

39. Ibid. See also copy in Powers Papers.

40. Schiffrin, "Enigma of Sun Yat-sen," p. 472.

41. See letter from Sir Edward Grey to Sir J. Jordan, November 14, 1911. PRO, FO 371/1095. The statement has not survived.

42. Ibid.

43. See p. 147 above.

44. Sun Yat-sen, *Memoirs*, p. 222.

45. See Wilbur, *Sun Yat-sen*, p. 313, n. 80. Hsü, *Sun Yat-sen*, p. 80 translates the phrase as "an American friend."

46. See Wilbur, *Sun Yat-sen*, p. 66.

47. Cable from Sun Yat-sen to Homer Lea, November 1, 1911. Powers Papers.

48. Letter from C. S. Addis to Homer Lea, November 18, 1911. Powers Papers.

49. Report from Division of Far Eastern Affairs to Secretary of State Philander Knox, November 14, 1911. NA, Knox Papers.

50. Letter from Ethel Lea to her sister Agnes, November 16, 1911. Powers Papers.

51. Letter from F. N. Mande to Homer Lea, November 19, 1911. Powers Papers.

52. Letters from Lord Stanhope to Homer Lea, November 17 and 19, 1911. Powers Papers.

53. Letter from Lord Stanhope to Ethel Lea, February 12, 1913. Powers Papers.

54. Letter from Ethel Lea to her sister Agnes, November 16, 1911. Powers Papers.

55. Ibid.

56. See Wilbur, *Sun Yat-sen*, p. 66.

57. Letter from Sun Yat-sen to Homer Lea, August 10, 1911. Powers Papers.

58. *New York Times*, November 25, 1911, p. 5.

59. Letter from Ethel Lea to her sister Agnes, November 26, 1911. Powers Papers.

60. Gowen and Hall, *History of China*, p. 352.

61. *Singapore Free Press*, November 20, 1911, editorial.

62. *Penang Gazette*, December 14, 1911. NA, General Records, Record Group 59, Roll 1084.

63. *Straits Times* (Singapore), December 16, 1911. p. 2.

64. *Singapore Free Press*, December 18, 1911.

65. See letter from Anderson to Secretary of State, December 21, 1911. NA, Record Group 59, Roll 1016.

66. See telegram from Anderson to Secretary of State, December 21, 1911. NA, General Records, Microcopy 329, Roll 8.

67. Letter from Senator Elihu Root to Homer Lea, December 19, 1911. Powers Papers.

68. *South China Morning Post* (Hong Kong), December 22, 1911, p. 7.

69. *China Press* (Shanghai), December 28, 1911. NA, General Records, Record Group 59, M 98, Roll 1008.

70. See telegram from Calhoun to Secretary of State, December 28, 1911. NA, State Department Records, Microcopy 329, Roll 8.

71. Chapin, "Homer Lea," p. 108. Chapin mentions reports in the San Francisco press of an injunction issued by the district court in Shanghai enjoining Lea from aiding the revolutionaries.

72. *Straits Times* (Singapore), December 16, 1911, p. 9.

73. See telegram from Anderson to Secretary of State, December 21, 1911. NA, General Records, Microcopy 329, Roll 8.

74. *China Press* (Shanghai), December 28, 1911. NA, General Records, Record Group 59, M 98, Roll 1008.

75. See Schiffrin, *Sun Yat-sen and the Origins*, pp. 20–22, 120 (n. 81), 329–30, and Schriffrin "Enigma of Sun Yat-sen," p. 446.

76. Edward J. M. Rhoads, *China's Republican Revolution. The Case of Kwangtung, 1895–1913* (Cambridge, Mass., 1975), pp. 38–39.

77. Earl Albert Selle, *Donald of China* (New York, 1948), pp. 107-9.

78. T'ang Leang-li, *The Inner History of the Chinese Revolution* (London, 1930), pp. 92–93.

79. See Hsüeh, *Huang Hsing*, p. 127.

80. Feng Tzu-yu, *Ko-ming i-shih* [Fragments of the History of the Revolution] (Taipei, 1965), vol. 1, p. 376.

81. "Rebels Were Drilled Here," *New York Times*, December 29, 1911, p. 5. See also p. 85 above.

82. Heinrich Herrfahrdt, *Sun Yatsen. Der Vater des Neuen China* (Hamburg, 1948), p. 57.

83. Lo Hsiang-lin, "Kuo-fu yü," p. 99.

84. Letter from J. Chockman to Ethel Lea, June 15, 1912. Powers Papers.

85. Gowen and Hall, *History of China*, p. 352.

86. Ibid.

87. Telegram from Homer Lea to Secretary of State Knox, December 29, 1911. LC, Knox Papers.

88. Draft of communication from the Office of the Minister of Foreign Affairs, January 9, 1912. Powers Papers.

89. See draft of Circular Note to the Powers, n.d., with Lea's handwritten changes. Powers Papers.

90. See note from Chinese Foreign Minister Wang Ch'ung-hui to Secretary of State Knox, January 17, 1912. NA, Knox Papers.

91. See Ernest P. Young, "The Rise of Yuan Shih-k'ai," in Wright, ed., *China in Revolution*, p. 430; and Harley F. MacNair, *China in Revolution. An Analysis of Politics and Militarism Under the Republic* (New York, 1968), pp. 31–32. According to Cheng, "T'ung-meng-hui," pp. 297–301, the southern armies allied with the revolutionaries had an advantage over the troops in the north.

92. See Schiffrin, "Enigma of Sun Yat-sen," pp. 466–67.

93. See Hsüeh, *Huang Hsing*, pp. 124–25. The date of the cable, November 12, 1911, indicates that it was sent from London and not from Paris, as Hsüeh believes. See also Wilbur, *Sun Yat-sen*, p. 297, n. 27.

94. Sun Yat-sen, "My Reminiscences," p. 307.

95. Young, "Yuan Shih-k'ai," pp. 428–33; and Chin-Tung Liang, *The Chinese Revolution of 1911* (Jamaica, N.Y., 1962), p. 27.

96. See letter from J. Russell Kennedy to Homer Lea, Shanghai, January 17, 1912. Powers Papers.

97. Letter from J. Chockman to Homer and Ethel Lea, August 24, 1912. Powers Papers.

Chapter 10

1. Medical report by M. Urbánek, M.D., Nanking, April 6, 1912. Powers Papers.

2. Letter from Ethel Lea to her sister Agnes, March 31, 1912. Powers Papers.

3. Letter from Ethel Lea to Agnes, February 20, 1912. Powers Papers.

4. Letter from Ethel Lea to Agnes, March 8, 1912. Powers Papers.

5. Two letters from Ethel Lea to Agnes, March 31, 1912. Powers Papers.

6. Letter from Ethel Lea to Agnes, March 8, 1912. Powers Papers.

7. Selle, *Donald of China*, p. 124.

8. See outline of Homer Lea, "The Romance of the Tombs." Powers Papers.

9. Letter from Ethel Lea to Agnes, March 31, 1912. Powers Papers.

10. *San Francisco Chronicle*, May 7, 1912, p. 5; and *Los Angeles Times*, May 8, 1912.

11. Letter from J. Chockman to Homer and Ethel Lea, May 28, 1912. Powers Papers.

12. *San Francisco Chronicle*, May 7, 1912, p. 5.

13. *Los Angeles Times*, May 2, 1912; and *New York Times*, May 2, 1912, p. 5.

14. *Los Angeles Times*, May 8, 1912, and May 18, 1912, p. 5.

15. *San Francisco Chronicle*, May 7, 1912, p. 5.

16. See letters from J. Chockman to Homer and Ethel Lea, May 28; to Ethel, June 15; to Homer and Ethel, July 5 and August 24, 1912. Letter from W. C. Chen to Ethel Lea, April 4, 1912. Letters from Sun Yat-sen to Ethel Lea, June 27 to Homer, and October 13, 1912. Powers Papers.

17. Letter from Homer Lea to Sun Yat-sen, July 27, 1912. Powers Papers. There were German instructors in the northern armies of the empire. See Christopher Hibbert, *The Dragon Wakes. China and the West, 1793-1911* (New York, 1970), p. 371.

18. Harry C. Carr, "Death Overpowers Odd World Figure," *Los Angeles Times*, November 2, 1912, p. 2.

19. Letter from Sun Yat-sen to Homer Lea, October 13, 1912. Powers Papers.

20. D. W. Green, "What Gen. Homer Lea Has to Say," *Los Angeles Examiner*, August 3, 1912, pp. 1-2.

21. Willard Huntington Wright, "Homer Lea Sorely Stricken," *Los Angeles Times*, August 4, 1912, pt. 5, p. 21.

22. Newmark, *Jottings in Southern California*, p. 144.

23. See scrapbook on funeral. Powers Papers.

24. Letter from Sun Yat-sen to Ethel Lea, November 14, 1912. Powers Papers.

25. Statement by Sun Yat-sen in *China Press* (Shanghai), November 6, 1912. Powers Papers.

Chapter 11

1. All quotations in this chapter are from *The Valor of Ignorance* unless other sources are given.

2. See Albert K. Weinberg, *Manifest Destiny. A Study of Nationalist Expansionism in American History* (Chicago, 1963), pp. 192-223.

3. See John P. Mallan, "Roosevelt, Brooks Adams, and Lea: The Warrior Critique of Business Civilization," *American Quarterly* 8 (Fall 1956): 221–23.

4. Ibid.

5. See Adolf Hitler, *Mein Kampf* (New York, 1939), pp. 197, 281–82.

6. Ibid., p. 199.

7. Ibid.

8. See Alfred Vagts, *A History of Militarism* (New York, 1959), p. 455.

9. See Strausz-Hupé, *Geopolitics*, pp. 29, 75, 249.

10. Mallan, "Roosevelt," p. 225.

11. Letter from David Starr Jordan to Homer Lea, December 7, 1909. Stanford University Archives.

12. Letter from David Starr Jordan to Homer Lea, January 31, 1910. Stanford University Archives.

13. See Norman Angell, *The Great Illusion* (New York, 1913), pp. 161, 212–13, 232, 284.

14. Theodore Roosevelt, "Preparedness Against War," *Works* (New York), vol. 20, p. 155.

15. William James, *The Moral Equivalent of War*, Association for International Conciliation, Pamphlet Series No. 27, February 1910.

16. Lea, "Aeroplane in War," pp. 11, 26.

17. Richard Hofstadter, *Social Darwinism in American Thought* (Boston, 1955), p. 190.

Chapter 12

1. For motivations and attitudes of foreign advisors and helpers in China, see Jonathan D. Spence, *To Change China: Western Advisers in China 1620–1960* (Boston, 1969), pp. 291–93.

2. David Starr Jordan, *Days of a Man*, vol. 2, p. 30.

3. Paul Kaufman, "Homer Lea," *Dictionary of American Biography* (New York, 1933), Vol. 6, p. 70.

4. Worden, "Chinese Reformer," p. 150.

5. For Sun's personality see Schiffrin, *Reluctant Revolutionary*, p. 5, and Schiffrin, "Enigma of Sun Yat-sen," pp. 443, 466, 469, 470. See also Wilbur, *Sun Yat-sen*, p. 75; and Marius B. Jansen, *The Japanese and Sun Yat-sen* (Cambridge, Mass., 1954), p. 59. For bases of Sun's and Lea's friendship see p. 138 of this book.

6. Wilbur, *Sun Yat-sen*, p. 290.

7. Randolph Bourne, *The Radical Will. Randolph Bourne, Selected Writings 1911–1918* (New York, 1977), pp. 73, 75.

8. Ibid., p. 79.

9. Van Wyck Brooks, *Randolph Bourne. History of a Literary Radical and Other Essays* (New York, 1920), p. xiv.

10. *Straits Times* (Singapore), December 18, 1911, p. 6.

11. David Starr Jordan, *Unseen Empire* (Boston, 1912), p. 6.

12. Marilyn Blatt Young, *The Rhetoric of Empire. American China Policy, 1895–1901* (Cambridge, Mass., 1968), pp. 228–29.

13. Lea, *Valor of Ignorance*, p. 11.

14. Vagts, *History of Militarism*, pp. 455–56.

15. Bourne, "The Handicapped," in *Radical Will*, p. 87.

16. Division of Far Eastern Affairs to Secretary of State Knox, November 14, 1911. LC, Knox Papers.

17. Jordan, *Days of a Man*, vol. 2, p. 30.

BIBLIOGRAPHY

Angell, Norman. *The Great Illusion*. New York, 1913.

Armentrout, L. Eve. "American Involvement in Chinese Revolutionary Activities, 1898–1913." M.A. thesis, California State University, Hayward, 1972.

————. "The Canton Rising of 1902–1903: Reformers, Revolutionaries, and the Second Taiping." *Modern Asian Studies* 10 (January 1976): 83–105.

Armentrout-Ma, L. Eve M. B. "Chinese Politics in the Western Hemisphere, 1893–1911: Rivalry Between Reformers and Revolutionaries in the Americas." Ph. D. dissertation, University of California, Davis, 1977.

Armstrong, Zella. *Notable Southern Families*. Vol. 3, Chattanooga, 1926.

Baltimore American.

Baltimore Sun.

Bland, J. O. P. *Recent Events and Present Policies in China*. Philadelphia, 1912.

Charles B. Boothe Papers. Hoover Institution on War, Revolution and Peace, Stanford, Calif.

Boothe, Clare. "Ever Hear of Homer Lea?" *Saturday Evening Post* 214 (March 14, 1943): 27, 38–40, 42.

————. "Introduction" to Homer Lea, *The Valor of Ignorance*. New York, 1942.

Boston Globe.

Boston Herald.

Boston Journal.

Bourne, Randolph. *The Radical Will: Randolph Bourne, Selected Writings, 1911–1918*. New York, 1977.

Braisted, William Reynold. *The United States Navy in the Pacific, 1909–1922*. Austin, Tex., 1971.

Brooks, Van Wyck. "Introduction" to *Randolph Bourne, History of a Literary Radical and Other Essays*. New York, 1920.

Carr, Harry C. "Death Overpowers Odd World Figure." *Los Angeles Times*, November 2, 1912, pp. 1–2.

―――. *Riding the Tiger. An American Newspaper Man in the Orient.* Boston, 1934.

Challener, Richard D. *Admirals, Generals and American Foreign Policy, 1898–1914.* Princeton, 1943.

Chapin, Frederic L. "Homer Lea and the Chinese Revolution." Undergraduate thesis, Harvard University, April 12, 1950.

―――. "Homer Lea. Unpublished Manuscript." Joshua B. Powers Papers. Hoover Institution on War, Revolution and Peace, Stanford, Calif.

Cheng, Shelley Hsien. "The T'ung-meng-hui: Its Organization, Leadership and Finances, 1905–1912." Ph. D. dissertation, University of Washington, Seattle, 1962.

Chesneaux, Jean. *Secret Societies in China in the Nineteenth and Twentieth Centuries.* Ann Arbor, 1971.

Chicago Daily Journal.

Chicago Daily News.

Chicago Daily Tribune.

China Press (Shanghai).

Chong, Key Ray. "The Abortive American-Chinese Project for Chinese Revolution, 1908–1911." *Pacific Historical Review* 41 (February 1972): 54–70.

Costello, John. *The Pacific War, 1941–1945.* New York, 1982.

Crow, Carl. *China Takes Her Place.* New York, 1944.

Daily Palo Alto.

Daniels, Roger. *The Politics of Prejudice. The Anti-Japanese Movement in California and the Struggle for Japanese Exclusion.* Berkeley, 1962.

D'Auvergne, Edmund B. *Pierre Loti.* New York, 1926.

Dingle, Edwin J. *China's Revolution.* New York, 1912.

Dulles, Foster Rhea. *China and America. The Story of Their Relations Since 1784.* Princeton, 1946.

Earle, Edward Mead. *Makers of Modern Strategy. Military Thought from Machiavelli to Hitler.* Princeton, 1943.

Federal District Court of California, Records. Federal Archives and Records Center, Laguna Niguel, Calif.

Feng Tzu-yu. *Chung-hua min-kuo k'ai-kuo-ch'ien ko-ming shih* [History of the Chinese Revolution before the Establishment of the Republic]. Vol. 2. Shanghai, 1946.

———. *Ko-ming i-shih* [Fragments of the History of the Revolution]. Vol. 1. Taipei, 1953.

Field, Margaret. "The Chinese Boycott of 1905." *Center for East Asian Studies.* Harvard University, Vol. 11, December 1957.

Fresno Morning Republican.

Ganschow, Thomas William. "A Study of Sun Yat-sen's Contacts with the United States Prior to 1922." Ph. D. dissertation, Indiana University, 1971.

Glick, Carl. *Double Ten. Captain O'Banion's Story of the Chinese Revolution.* New York, 1945.

Carl Glick Papers. University Libraries, University of Iowa, Iowa City.

Glick, Carl, and Hong Sheng-Hwa. *Swords of Silence. Chinese Secret Societies—Past and Present.* New York, 1947.

Gowen, Robert H., and Joseph Washington Hall. *An Outline History of China.* New York, 1926.

Green, D. W. "What Gen. Homer Lea Has to Say." *Los Angeles Examiner*, August 3, 1912, pp. 1–2.

Green, Ermal Lea. "She Knew Him Well." *Saturday Evening Post*, May 23, 1942.

Hao, Yen-p'ing. "The Abortive Cooperation Between Reformers and Revolutionaries (1895–1900)." *Papers on China.* Harvard University East Asian Research Center, vol. 15, December 1961.

Hartford Courant.

Hartford Times.

Hartt, Julian. "American Plot for China Revolt Revealed." *Los Angeles Times*, October 13, 1966.

Hatano, Yoshihiro. "The New Armies." In Mary Clabaugh Wright, ed., *China in Revolution: The First Phase, 1900-1913.* New Haven, 1968.

John Milton Hay Papers. Library of Congress, Washington, D.C.

Herrfahrdt, Heinrich. *Sun Yatsen. Der Vater des Neuen China.* Hamburg, 1948.

Hibbert, Christopher. *The Dragon Wakes. China and the West, 1793-1911.* New York, 1970.

Hitler, Adolf. *Mein Kampf* (U.S. ed.). New York, 1939.

Hofstadter, Richard. *Social Darwinism in American Thought*. Boston, 1955.

Hsiao, Kung-chüan. *A Modern China and a Modern World. K'ang Yu-wei, Reformer and Utopian, 1858–1927*. Seattle, 1975.

Hsieh, Winston, "Triads, Salt Smugglers and Local Uprisings: Observations on the Social and Economic Background of the Waichow Revolution of 1911." In Jean Chesneaux, ed., *Popular Movements and Secret Societies in China, 1840–1950*. Stanford, 1972.

Hsü, Immanuel C. Y. *The Rise of Modern China*. New York, 1975.

Hsü, Leonard S. *Sun Yat-sen. His Political and Social Ideals*. Los Angeles, 1933.

Hsüeh, Chün-tu. *Huang Hsing and the Chinese Revolution*. Stanford, 1961.

Huang Chen-wu. *Hua Ch'iao yü Chung-kuo ko-ming* [Overseas Chinese and the Chinese Revolution]. Taipei, 1963.

Huang Chi-lu, "Chung-kuo ko-ming chih yu, Homa Li Chiang-chün" [General Homer Lea, a Friend of the Chinese Revolution]. In *Chuan-chi wen-hsüeh* [Biographical Literature]. Taipei, 1969.

Hudson, Maxim. *Defenseless America*. New York, 1915.

Independent (New York).

Inter-Ocean (Chicago).

Irwin, Will. *The Making of a Reporter*. New York, 1942.

———. "White Leader of Chinese." *New York Sun*, June 28, 1905, p. 2.

James, William. *The Moral Equivalent of War*. Association for International Conciliation Pamphlet Series, no. 27, February 1910.

Jansen, Marius B. *Japan and China from War to Peace, 1894–1972*. Chicago, 1975.

———. *The Japanese and Sun Yat-sen*. Cambridge, Mass., 1967.

Jordan, David Starr. *The Days of a Man*. Yonkers, N.Y., 1922.

———. "Letter to the Japan Chronicle," January 10, 1912. Reprinted with an editorial from the *Japan Chronicle* (Kobe), February 11, 1912, *World Peace Foundation Pamphlet Series*, vol. 2, no. 5, 1912.

———. *Unseen Empire*. Boston, 1912.

David Starr Jordan Papers. Stanford University Archives, Stanford University Libraries, Stanford, Calif.

Kaufman, Paul. "Homer Lea," *Dictionary of American Biography*. New York, 1933. Vol. 6, p. 70.

Philander Chase Knox Papers. Library of Congress, Washington, D.C.

Kuo Fu Nien P'u Tseng Ting Pen [A Chronological Biography of the Father of the Country]. Lo Chia-lun and Huang Chi-la, eds., 2 vols. Taipei, 1969.

Lea, Homer. "The Aeroplane in War." *Harper's Weekly* 54 (August 20, 1910): 8–9 and 54 (August 27, 1910): 11, 26.

———. "The Boycott—China's Mighty Weapon." *Van Norden's Magazine* 3 (July 1908): 49–57.

———. *Des Britischen Reiches Schicksalsstunde. Mahnwort eines Angelsachsen*. Aus dem Englischen mit einer Einführung von Graf E. Reventlow. Berlin, 1913.

———. "Can China Fight?" *World To-Day* 12 (February 1907): 137–46.

———. *The Day of the Saxon*. New York, 1912, 1942.

———. "The Defenses of China." Unpublished manuscript. Joshua B. Powers Papers, Hoover Institution on War, Revolution and Peace, Stanford, Calif.

———. "How Socialism Failed in China." *Van Norden's Magazine* 3 (September 1908): 107–13 and 3 (October 1908): 81–85.

———. "The Legacy of Commodore Perry." *North American Review* 197 (January 1913): 741–46.

———. "The Red Dawn of China." Unpublished manuscript. Joshua B. Powers Papers, Hoover Institution on War, Revolution and Peace, Stanford, Calif.

———. *The Valor of Ignorance*. New York, 1909, 1942.

———. *The Vermilion Pencil*. New York, 1908.

Levenson, Joseph R. *Liang Ch'i-ch'ao and the Mind of Modern China*. London, 1959.

Liang Ch'i-ch'ao (Leong Kai Chew). "The Awakening of China." *Independent* 55 (May 28, 1903): 1267–68.

———. "The Educational Reformation of China." *Independent* 55 (October 15, 1903): 2441–42.

Liang, Chin-Tung. *The Chinese Revolution of 1911*. Jamaica, N.Y., 1962.

Liu, Kwang Ching. *Americans and Chinese. A Historical Essay and a Biography*. Cambridge, Mass., 1963.

Lo Hsiang-lin. "Kuo-fu yü Han-ma Li Chiang-chün" [The Father of the Country and General Homer Lea]. In *Kuo-fu yü Ou-Mei chih yu-hao* [The Father of the Country and His European and American Friends]. Taipei,
1951.

Lo, Jung-pang. *K'ang Yu-wei. A Biography and a Symposium*. Tucson, 1967.

Loan, Charles E. Van. "General Homer Lea." *Harper's Weekly* 57 (January 4,
1913): 7.

Los Angeles Examiner.

Los Angeles Herald.

Los Angeles Times.

Lü Fang-shang. "Ho Ma Li Tang An Chien Shu" [A Brief Account of the Homer
Lea Papers]. In Huang Chi-lu, ed., *Yen chiu Chung-shang Hsien-sheng ti
Shih Liao yü Shih Hsüeh* [Historical Materials and Historiography of the
Study of Sun Yat-sen]. Taipei, 1975.

MacArthur, Douglas. *Reports of General MacArthur. The Campaigns of MacArthur in the Pacific*. Vol. 1. Prepared by his General Staff. Washington,
D.C., 1966.

McKee, Delber L. *Chinese Exclusion Versus the Open Door Policy, 1900–1906*.
Detroit, 1977.

MacNair, Harley F. *China in Revolution. An Analysis of Politics and Militarism
Under the Republic*. New York, 1968.

Mallan, John P. "Roosevelt, Brooks Adams, and Lea: The Warrior Critique of
Business Civilization." *American Quarterly* 8 (Fall 1956): 216–30.

Marcu, Valeriu. "American Prophet of Total War." *American Mercury* 54 (April
1942): 473–78.

Merk, Frederick. *Manifest Destiny and Mission in American History*. New York,
1963.

Meskill, John, ed. *The Pattern of Chinese History*. Lexington, Mass., 1965.

Morning Oregonian (Portland).

Mowry, George E. *The Era of Theodore Roosevelt, 1900–1912*. New York, 1958.

Nation.

The National Cyclopedia of American Biography. Vol. 2, pp. 500–1.

Newmark, Marco R. *Jottings in Southern California History*. Los Angeles, 1955.

Newsweek.

New York American.

New York Daily News.

New York Evening Post.

New York Herald.

New York Sun.

New York Times.

New York Tribune.

Ng Poon Chew. "Letter to Dr. Jordan." *New York Evening Post*, December 19, 1912, p. 6.

_____. "The Real Homer Lea." *Oriental Review* 3 (January 1913): 171–72.

The Ninety-First Annual Report of the American Baptist Missionary Union, 1904–1905. Boston, 1905.

North American (Philadelphia).

O'Connor, Richard. *Pacific Destiny.* Boston, 1969.

Outlook.

George C. Pardee Papers. Bancroft Library, University of California, Berkeley.

Penang Gazette.

Philadelphia Free Press.

Philadelphia Inquirer.

Pittsburgh Dispatch.

Pittsburgh Gazette.

Powell, Ralph E. *The Rise of Chinese Military Power, 1895–1912.* Princeton, 1955.

Joshua B. Powers Papers. Hoover Institution on War, Revolution and Peace, Stanford, Calif.

Public Ledger (Philadelphia).

Public Record Office, Kew Richmond, Surrey, England.

Reventlow, Graf Ernst von. "Homer Lea. Was Er Wollte und Was Er War." Introduction to Homer Lea, *Des Britischen Reiches Schicksalsstunde.* 2nd. ed., Berlin, 1917.

Rhoads, Edward J. M. *China's Republican Revolution. The Case of Kwangtung, 1895–1913*. Cambridge, Mass., 1975.

Field Marshal Lord Roberts Papers. National Army Museum, London.

Roberts, Mary L. "Oregon Relative Tells of War Prophet." *Portland Journal*, March 22, 1942.

Roosevelt, Theodore. "Preparedness Against War." *Works*. Vol. 20. New York.

Sacramento Union.

St. Louis Globe-Democrat.

St. Louis Post-Dispatch.

St. Louis Republic.

San Francisco Call.

San Francisco Chronicle.

San Francisco Examiner.

Schiffrin, Harold Z. "The Enigma of Sun Yat-sen." In Mary Clabaugh Wright, ed., *China in Revolution: The First Phase, 1900–1913*. New Haven, 1968.

————. *Sun Yat-sen and the Origins of the Chinese Revolution*. Berkeley, 1968.

————. *Sun Yat-sen. Reluctant Revolutionary*. Boston, 1980.

Selle, Earl Albert. *Donald of China*. New York, 1948.

Shipper, Lee. "Leaside." *Los Angeles Times*, April 10, 1945, pt. 2, p. 4.

Singapore Free Press.

South China Morning Post (Hong Kong).

Spence, Jonathan D. *To Change China. Western Advisors in China, 1620–1960*. Boston, 1960.

Stanford Alumnus.

Stimson, Marshall. "A Great American Who Saw It Coming." *Christian Science Monitor*, March 7, 1942, p. 6.

————. "A Los Angeles Jeremiah. Homer Lea: Military Genius and Prophet." *Quarterly of the Historical Society of Southern California* (March 1942): 5–13.

Straits Times (Singapore).

Strausz-Hupé, Robert. *Geopolitics. The Struggle for Space and Power*. New York, 1942.

Sullivan, Robert. "Nobody Listens to a Prophet." *New York News*, December 28, 1941, pp. 40–41, 52.

Sun Yat-sen. Kuo fu ch'üan chi [*The Complete Works*], 5 vols., Taipei, 1973.

_____. *Memoirs of a Chinese Revolutionary*. London, 1927.

_____. "My Reminiscences." *Strand Magazine* (London) 40 (March 1912): 301–7.

T'ang Leang-li. *The Inner History of the Chinese Revolution*. London, 1930.

Tessan, François de. "Loti en Amérique." *Demain* (Paris), 1924, pp. 184–85.

_____. *Promenade au Far West*. Paris, 1912.

Thomas, Lowell. *Born to Raise Hell. The Life Story of Tex O'Reilly, Soldier of Fortune*. New York, 1936.

Time Magazine.

Times (London).

Trent, Payson J. *The Far East. A Political and Diplomatic History*. New York, 1935.

Tse Tsan Tai. *The Chinese Republic. Secret History of the Chinese Revolution*. Hong Kong, 1924.

U.S. National Archives. General Records, State Department.

_____. Records Relating to the Internal Affairs of China, 1910–29, State Department.

_____. Records of the Adjutant General's Office, War Department.

Vagts, Alfred. *A History of Militarism*. New York, 1959.

Wakeman, Jr., Frederic. *The Fall of Imperial China*. New York, 1975.

Weinberg, Albert K. *Manifest Destiny. A Study of Nationalist Expansionism in American History*. Chicago, 1963.

Who's Who in America, 1908–1909. Vol. 5, pp. 304–5.
Who's Who in America, 1910–1911. Vol. 6, p. 1129.

Wilbur, C. Martin. *Sun Yat-sen. Frustrated Patriot*. New York, 1976.

Wilhelm, Hellmut. "The Poems from the Hall of Obscured Brightness." In Jung-pang Lo, *K'ang Yu-wei. A Biography and a Symposium*. Tucson, 1967.

Willoughby, Charles A., and John Chamberlain. *MacArthur, 1941–1951*. New York, 1954.

Worden, Robert Leo. "A Chinese Reformer in Exile: The North American Phase of the Travels of K'ang Yu-wei, 1899–1909." Ph. D. dissertation, Georgetown University, 1972.

Worthy, Jr., Edmund H., "Yung Wing in America." *Pacific Historical Review* 34 (1965): 265–87.

Wright, Mary Clabaugh, ed. "Introduction" to *China in Revolution: The First Phase, 1900–1913*. New Haven, 1968.

Wright, Willard Huntington. "Homer Lea Sorely Stricken." *Los Angeles Times*, August 4, 1912, pt. 5, p. 21.

Wu, John C. H. *Sun Yat-sen. The Man and His Ideas*. Taipei, 1971.

Young, Ernest P., "The Rise of Yuan Shih-kai." In Mary Clabaugh Wright, ed., *China in Revolution: The First Phase, 1900–1913*. New Haven, 1968.

Young, Marilyn Blatt. *The Rhetoric of Empire. American China Policy, 1895–1901*. Cambridge, Mass., 1968.

Young, Robert. "The Impudence of Charlatanism." *World Peace Foundation Pamphlet Series*. Vol. 2, no. 5, 1912.

Yung Wing. *Diary for the Year 1902*. Connecticut State Library, Hartford, 1902.

_____. *My Life in China and America*. New York, 1909.

INDEX

Adams, Brooks, 183
Adams, Henry, 183
Ah Mow, 45–46
Alexander, J., 63
Allen, W. W., 96, 118; involved in Red
Dragon scheme, 121–124; involved in
other conspiracies, 126–33; his opinion
of Yung Wing, 126, 137; his opinion
of Sun Yat-sen, 135; attempts to raise
funds for Sun Yat-sen, 144–45
Alton, John, 36, 40, 44, 49
American Baptist Missionary Union,
speeches of K'ang Yu-wei and Homer
Lea before, 72
American Magazine, 101
Anderson, George Everett, 168, 169, 170,
171; on Homer Lea's influence
over Sun Yat-sen, 165; joint cable
with Sun Yat-sen and Homer Lea
to U.S. Department of State, 166
Angell, Norman, 186; *Europe's Optical
Illusion* (*The Great Illusion*), 186; on
Valor of Ignorance, 186
Anglo-Japanese Alliance, 159
Asquith, Herbert Henry, 159

Barnard College, 87
Belford, Robert J., 178
Beresford, Lord Charles William de la
Poer, 149, 156
Bernhardi, Friedrich von, 186; his milita-
rism compared to Lea's, 190
Big Sword Society, 125, 139
Bismarck, Otto von, 151
Blake, Sir Henry, on Lea's presence in
Hong Kong and Macao in 1900, 15; on
Lea's plans for a campaign, 25
Bland, J. O. P., on Sun's gift for self-pro-
motion, 17–18

Boothe, Charles Beach, xv, 86, 87, 89,
96, 149; seeks diplomatic appointment
for Lea, 115, 116, 118–19, 121; takes
part in Red Dragon, 120–124; participates in more conspiracies, 125–32;
participates in Sun's revolutionary
plans, 232–39; appointed financial
agent of Chinese Alliance, 141; attempts to raise funds for Sun, 142–48
Boothe Luce, Clare, 100
Boulger, Demetrius Charles de
Kavanagh, *History of China*, 117
Bourne, Randolph, 194–96; "The Handicapped," 194
Boxer Rebellion, 12, 13–14, 15, 19, 27,
34, 59, 60; Lea's alleged part in its
suppression, 21–22
Broad Sword Society, *see* Big Sword
Society
Brooks, Van Wyck, 195
Bryant, Agnes, 29, 150, 175, 176
Buck, Alfred E., 14
Burton, General, 177

Caesar, Julius, 3
Calhoun, William James, 168
California National Guard, 5, 35, 52, 59, 63
Calvinism in American life, 183
Carr, C. C., 38
Carr, Harry, 178
Chaffee, Adna R., 21–22; allegedly rec-
ommends O'Banion to Lea, 38–39; in-
vestigates Lea's military organization,
67–68; writes foreword to *Valor of Ignorance*, 96; first acquaintance with
Lea, 96; suggests Plan Orange, 98; declines support of Lea's diplomatic as-
signment, 119; visits Lea during fatal
illness, 177

About the Author

Eugene Anschel was born in Germany and educated at the Universities of Berlin, Munich, Bonn and Cologne. His fields of study comprised law, political science and history. He graduated with an LL.D. in 1933. That same year the political events in Germany forced him to emigrate. After living three years in Spain he came to the United States in 1937. At first he worked with the Institute for Social Research, then associated with Columbia University. Later he entered the career of foreign trade specialist and international business executive. He maintained, however, his ties to the academic community though not affiliated with any institution. Already during his years of study Anschel had done research on the historical development of legal and political concepts and institutions. That same interest led him in later life to historical and historiographical investigations, as a result of which he published in 1974 *The American Image of Russia, 1775–1917*, and in 1978 *American Appraisals of Soviet Russia, 1917–1977*. The present book is his first political biography.